HIDDEN ®
San Diego

HIDDEN®

San Diego

Including La Jolla, the Zoo, San Diego
County Beaches, and Tijuana

Ellen Clark & Ray Riegert

FIRST EDITION

Ulysses Press®
BERKELEY, CALIFORNIA

Published by: ULYSSES PRESS
             P.O. Box 3440
             Berkeley, CA 94703
             www.ulyssespress.com

ISSN 1551-2525
ISBN 1-56975-458-6

Printed in Canada by Transcontinental Printing

10 9 8 7 6 5 4 3 2 1

MANAGING EDITOR: Claire Chun
EDITOR: Lily Chou
EDITORIAL ASSOCIATES: Leona Benten, Laura Brancella, Jay Chung
TYPESETTERS: Lisa Kester, James Meetze
CARTOGRAPHY: Pease Press
COVER DESIGN: Leslie Henriques, Sarah Levin
INDEXER: Sayre Van Young
COVER PHOTOGRAPHY: Jupiterimages.com

Northern Baja material from *Hidden Baja* by Richard Harris

Distributed in the United States by Publishers Group West and
in Canada by Raincoast Books

HIDDEN is a federally registered trademark
of BookPack, Inc.

Ulysses Press 宏 is a federally registered
trademark of BookPack, Inc.

Write to us!

If in your travels you discover a spot that captures the spirit of the San Diego area, or if you live in the region and have a favorite place to share, or if you just feel like expressing your views, write to us and we'll pass your note along to the author.

We can't guarantee that the author will add your personal find to the next edition, but if the writer does use the suggestion, we'll acknowledge you in the credits and send you a free copy of the new edition.

ULYSSES PRESS
P.O. Box 3440
Berkeley, CA 94703
E-mail: readermail@ulyssespress.com

What's Hidden?

At different points throughout this book, you'll find special listings marked with this symbol:

◄ HIDDEN

This means that you have come upon a place off the beaten tourist track, a spot that will carry you a step closer to the local people and natural environment of the San Diego area.

The goal of this guide is to lead you beyond the realm of everyday tourist facilities. While we include traditional sightseeing listings and popular attractions, we also offer alternative sights and adventure activities. Instead of filling this guide with reviews of standard hotels and chain restaurants, we concentrate on one-of-a-kind places and locally owned establishments.

Our authors seek out locales that are popular with residents but usually overlooked by visitors. Some are more hidden than others (and are marked accordingly), but all the listings in this book are intended to help you discover the true nature of the San Diego area and put you on the path of adventure.

Contents

1 SAN DIEGO DREAMING   I

Where to Go   6
When to Go   8
Seasons   8
Calendar of Events   9
Before You Go   12
Visitors Centers   12
Packing   13
Lodging   13
Dining   14
Traveling with Children   14
Women Traveling Alone   15
Gay & Lesbian Travelers   16
Senior Travelers   16
Disabled Travelers   17
Foreign Travelers   17
Outdoor Adventures   19
Transportation   31

2 CENTRAL SAN DIEGO   34

Downtown San Diego   34
Balboa Park and the San Diego Zoo   51
Hillcrest & Uptown   59
Inland Neighborhoods   66
Old Town Area   71

3 SAN DIEGO'S WATERFRONT   79

Coronado   79
San Diego Harbor   86
Point Loma Area   91
Mission Bay Park Area   97

4 LA JOLLA   **105**
Sights   106
Lodging   110
Dining   112
Shopping   115
Nightlife   116
Beaches & Parks   117

5 NORTH COUNTY & INLAND SAN DIEGO   **121**
North County   121
Inland San Diego   141

6 SOUTH BAY & NORTHERN BAJA   **154**
South Bay   155
Tijuana   161
Ensenada Area   176

Index   197
Lodging Index   202
Dining Index   204
About the Authors   209

Maps

San Diego & Beyond	3
Central San Diego	37
Downtown San Diego	39
Balboa Park and the San Diego Zoo	53
Hillcrest & Uptown	61
Inland Neighborhoods	67
Old Town Area	73
San Diego's Waterfront	81
Coronado	83
San Diego Harbor	87
Point Loma Area	93
La Jolla	107
North County & Inland San Diego	123
North County	125
Inland San Diego	141
South Bay & Northern Baja	157
South Bay	159
Downtown Tijuana	167
Ensenada	177

OUTDOOR ADVENTURE SYMBOLS

The following symbols accompany national, state and regional park listings, as well as beach descriptions throughout the text.

△	Camping	🎿	Waterskiing
🚶	Hiking	🏄	Windsurfing
🚲	Biking	🛶	Canoeing/Kayaking
🐎	Horseback Riding	🚤	Boating
🏊	Swimming	🚤	Boat Ramps
🤿	Snorkeling	🐟	Fishing
🏄	Surfing		

ONE

San Diego Dreaming

San Diego County's 4261 square miles occupy a Connecticut-size chunk of real estate that forms the southwestern corner of the continental United States. Geographically, it is as varied a parcel of landscape as any in the world. Surely this spot is one of the few places on the planet where, in a matter of hours, you can journey from bluff-lined beaches up and over craggy mountain peaks and down again to sun-scorched desert sands.

Moving east, from the Pacific to the county's interior, travelers discover lush valleys and irrigated hillsides. Planted with citrus orchards, vineyards and rows of vegetables, this curving countryside eventually gives way to the Palomar and Laguna mountains—cool, pine-crested ranges that rise over 6500 feet.

But it is the coast—some 76 sparkling miles stretching from San Mateo Point near San Clemente to the Mexican border—that has always held the fascination of residents and visitors alike.

When Portuguese explorer Juan Rodríguez Cabrillo laid eyes on these shores in 1542, he discovered a prospering settlement of Kumeyaay Indians. For hundreds of years, these native peoples had been living in quiet contentment on lands overlooking the Pacific; they had harvested the rich estuaries and ventured only occasionally into the scrubby hills and canyons for firewood and game.

Sixty years passed before the next visitor, Spanish explorer Sebastian Vizcaíno, came seeking a hideout for royal galleons beset by pirates. It was Vizcaíno who named the bay for San Diego de Alcalá.

In 1769, the Spanish came to stay. The doughty Franciscan missionary Junípero Serra marched north from Mexico with a company of other priests and soldiers and built Mission San Diego de Alcalá. It was the first of a chain of 21 missions and the earliest site in California to be settled by Europeans. Father Serra's mission, relocated a few miles inland in 1774, now sits incongruously amid the shopping centers and housing developments of Mission Valley.

California's earliest civilian settlement evolved in the 1820s on a dusty mesa beneath the hilltop presidio that protected the original mission. Pueblo San Diego quickly developed into a thriving trade and cattle ranching center after the ruling Spanish colonial regime was overthrown and replaced by the Republic of Mexico.

By the end of the century, new residents, spurred partly by land speculators, had taken root and developed the harbor and downtown business district. After the rails finally reached San Diego in 1885, the city flourished. Grand Victorian buildings lined 5th Avenue all the way from the harbor to Broadway and 1400 barren acres were set aside uptown for a city park.

After its turn-of-the-20th-century spurt of activity, the city languished until World War II, when the U.S. Navy invaded the town en masse to establish the 11th Naval District headquarters and one of the world's largest Navy bases. San Diego's reputation as "Navytown USA" persisted well after the war-weary sailors went home. Despite the closure of the San Diego Naval Training Center in 1997, some 103,000 Navy and Marine personnel are still based in San Diego and at Camp Pendleton to the north. With 101,000 family members, 26,000 civilian Navy employees and 59,000 Navy retirees, the military presence remains a major influence, but this is changing as high-tech industries locate in San Diego, bringing "new economy" diversity and a spirit of renewal.

The military has not been the only force to foster San Diego's growth. In the early 1960s, construction began on an important university that was to spawn a completely new industry. Many mark the emergence of the "new" San Diego with the opening of the University of California's La Jolla campus. Not only did the influx of 15,000 students help revive a floundering economy, it tended to liberalize an otherwise insular and conservative city.

Truth is, San Diego is no longer the sleepy, semitransparent little resort city it once was. Nowhere is the fact more evident than in the downtown district, where a building boom has brought new offices, condominiums and hotels.

Text continued on page 6.

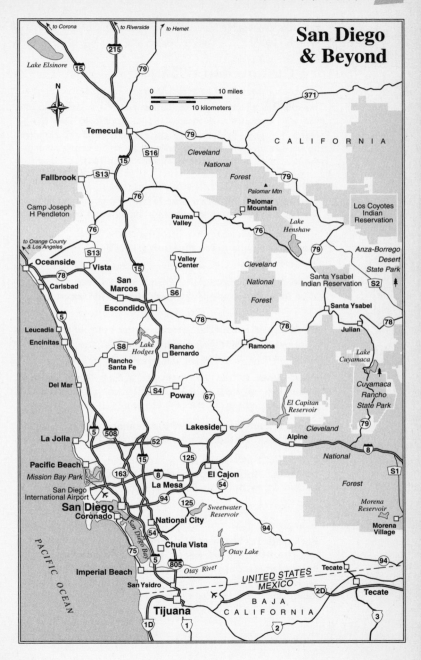

San Diego & Beyond

to Corona
to Riverside
to Hemet
Lake Elsinore
215
15
79
N
0   10 miles
0   10 kilometers
371
Temecula
79
CALIFORNIA
S16
Cleveland
National
Fallbrook
S13
Forest
15
Palomar Mtn
79
Camp Joseph
H Pendleton
76
Palomar
Mountain
Los Coyotes
Indian
Reservation
Pauma
Valley
Lake
Henshaw
76
to Orange County
& Los Angeles
76
Anza-Borrego
Desert
State Park
S13
Valley
Center
Cleveland
Santa Ysabel
Indian Reservation
S2
Oceanside
Vista
San
Marcos
15
National
Carlsbad
S6
Santa Ysabel
Escondido
Forest
78
78
Julian
Leucadia
5
78
Encinitas
S8
Lake
Hodges
Rancho
Bernardo
Lake
Cuyamaca
Ramona
Del Mar
Rancho
Santa Fe
Cuyamaca
Rancho
State Park
S4
Poway
67
El Capitan
Reservoir
79
La Jolla
5
508
Lakeside
Cleveland
52
Alpine
Pacific Beach
15
125
National
8
Mission Bay Park
163
8
El Cajon
S1
San Diego
International Airport
La Mesa
54
Forest
San Diego
94
125
Morena
Reservoir
Coronado
National City
Sweetwater
Reservoir
54
94
Morena
Village
75
Chula Vista
Otay Lake
PACIFIC
Imperial Beach
5
805
Otay River
UNITED STATES
MEXICO
Tecate
94
San Ysidro
2D
Tecate
OCEAN
BAJA
3
Tijuana
1D
1
CALIFORNIA
2

Three-day Weekend

History, Culture and Wildlife

This tour will introduce you to the many facets of San Diego in a brief visit. Conspicuously absent here is **SeaWorld San Diego** (page 97), a sprawling theme park that's a must-see if you have kids and will take up most of the day. Another all-day adventure for those who have extra time is a visit to **Tijuana** (page 161).

DAY 1
- Start your day in **Old Town** (page 71) with a tour on the Old Town Trolley, then stroll through the lively **Bazaar del Mundo** (page 72) marketplace.

- Visit the **Junipero Serra Museum** (page 73) for an account of San Diego's birth.

- In the mood for Mexican food? Enjoy a leisurely lunch at **Casa de Pico** (page 75) or one of the many other good Mexican restaurants in Old Town.

- If you wish, round out the historical segment of your tour with a drive out to **Mission San Diego de Alcalá** (page 73), the first California mission church, now surrounded by suburban sprawl.

- Head down to the waterfront for a **San Diego Harbor Excursion** (page 86) to see the commercial shipping and U.S. Navy activity that drives the city's economy.

- Enjoy a seafood feast at **Star of the Sea** (page 89) or the adjoining, less pricey **Anthony's Fish Grotto** (page 89).

- If you're still bursting with energy after this busy day, why not drive out to the near-island of Coronado for cocktails at the classy **Babcock & Story Bar** (page 85) in the Hotel del Coronado?

DAY 2
- Pack a picnic lunch and plan your day around a visit to **Balboa Park** (page 52), where you can choose among world-class museums devoted to fine art, folk art, photography, astronomy, natural history, aerospace technology, anthropology, sports and model railroads. Between museums, take plenty of time to stroll this magnificently landscaped 1400-acre park with its Spanish Colonial revival architecture.

- Dine in downtown San Diego's Gaslamp Quarter at **Ida Bailey's Restaurant** (page 45), an elegant Victorian-style restaurant named for the madam who used to run a house of ill repute there. Later, stick around the Quarter and hop your way among the many nightclubs of San Diego's premier entertainment zone.

DAY 3
- Drive up north to the **San Diego Zoo's Wild Animal Park** (page 144) to spend the morning watching the free-roaming wildlife from the monorail and walkways.

- Returning from the animal park, stop for lunch in Del Mar at **The Fish Market** (page 132).

- Follow the coast highway down to La Jolla. Round out your wildlife-watching day with a stop at the **Birch Aquarium at Scripps** (page 108).

- Head up to the top of the bluffs in **Torrey Pines State Reserve and Beach** (page 109) for a great sunset view.

- Return to La Jolla for dinner at one of The Village's many great restaurants, such as **George's at the Cove** (page 112).

But for all the city's manmade appeal, it is nature's handi-
work and an ideal Mediterranean climate that most delight San
Diego visitors. With bays and beaches bathed in sunshine 75 percent of the time, less than ten inches of rainfall per year and average temperatures that mirror a proverbial day in June, San
Diego offers the casual outdoor lifestyle that fulfills vacationers'
dreams.

Where to Go

Situated a smug 120 miles south of Los Angeles on
Route 5, San Diego is not so much a city as a collection
of communities hiding in canyons and gathered on
small shoulders of land that shrug down to the sea. As a result,
it hardly seems big enough (a bit over 1.25 million) to rank as
America's seventh largest city. Total county population is 2.8 million, and nine of ten residents live within 30 miles of the coast.

The city of San Diego is divided into several geographic sections. To the south lies Coronado, nestled on a peninsula jutting
into San Diego Bay and connected to the mainland by a narrow
sandbar known as the Silver Strand.

Although they are within the boundaries of the city of San
Diego, the seaside communities of Ocean Beach, Mission Beach,
Pacific Beach and La Jolla have developed their
own identities, moods and styles.

The San Diego area has a
beach for every taste, ranging from broad sweeps of
white sand to slender
scimitars beneath
eroded sandstone
bluffs.

"OB," as the first of these is known, along with
Mission and Pacific beaches, exults in the sunny,
sporty Southern California lifestyle fostered by
nearby Mission Bay Park. These neighboring communities are fronted by broad beaches and an almost con-
tinuous boardwalk that is jammed with joggers, skaters
and cyclists. The beaches are saturated in the summer with
local sun-seekers, but they have much to offer visitors.

Like a beautiful but slightly spoiled child, La Jolla is an enclave of wealth and stubborn independence that calls itself "The
Village" and insists on having its own post office, although it's
actually just another part of the extended San Diego family.
Mediterranean-style mansions and small cottages shrouded by
jasmine and hibiscus share million-dollar views of beaches, coves
and wild, eroded sea cliffs. Swank shops and galleries, trendy
restaurants and classy little hotels combine in a Riviera-like setting that rivals even Carmel for chicness.

North County is a string of beach towns stretching from Oceanside south to Del Mar, where outdoor enthusiasts can find their fill of white-sand beaches, world-class golf courses and state parks. Shops and restaurants dot Route 101, the coastal highway that threads through the towns of Oceanside, Carlsbad, Leucadia, Encinitas, Cardiff-by-the-Sea and Del Mar. These North County towns boast residents from every walk of life—from the ultra-wealthy (found in La Costa and Del Mar), to the artisans (found in Leucadia), to the short-haired Marines of Oceanside.

Just south of the Mexican border, Tijuana is a popular destination that attracts many daytrippers with its duty-free shopping, raunchy nightlife and bullfights. An hour's drive south of Tijuana on the Baja Highway, Ensenada offers shopping and sightseeing possibilities along with plenty of traditional Mexican seaport charm. The coastline and mild, sometimes misty climate resemble San Diego's.

While there are plenty of attractions in San Diego for every age and interest, there are some that shouldn't be missed, with the waterfront, Balboa Park and the San Diego Zoo and Old Town San Diego Historic Park topping the list.

Early explorers were first attracted to San Diego because of its miles of waterfront property, and it remains today one of the city's most appealing attractions. Covering 76 miles to the Mexican border, there are beaches for surfing, swimming, and sunning, an excellent maritime museum, and a downtown harbor filled with boats of every type and size. A ferry ride to Coronado or a harbor cruise are excellent ways to get a from-the-water view of the harbor and the city skyline.

Balboa Park is not only one of the country's largest urban parks, but full of more and varied things to see and do than maybe any park anywhere. Museum lovers can view everything from fine art to model trains, theater goers options range from organ recitals to Shakespeare performed in a Tony award winning theater, and no trip to San Diego would be complete without a trip to the world's top rated zoo.

With plenty of historic buildings, Old Town San Diego State Historic Park provides a feel for what the city was like in its infancy, while the influence of the city's neighbors to the south is celebrated in the shops and restaurants that are filled with Mexican made souvenirs and South of the Border delicacies.

It is safe to say that the San Diego area is not as eccentric and sophisticated as San Francisco, nor as glamorous and fast-paced as Los Angeles. But those who still perceive it as a laid-back mecca for beach bums—or as a lunch stop en route to Mexico—are in for a huge surprise.

When to Go

SEASONS

It could be said that one of the most boring jobs imaginable is being a weather forecaster in San Diego. San Diegans claim that the United States Weather Bureau has declared their lovely year-round weather to be as close to perfect as it is anywhere in the country.

Throughout most of San Diego County, temperatures average about 70.5°F (21.4°C); there are, of course, variations between the coast, mountain and desert environments, with temperatures in the desert soaring into the triple digits in the summer and the mountains dipping into the teens in the winter.

Along the Pacific and on the coastal plain, where most visitors concentrate, the climate is Mediterranean, with mild temperatures year-round. Because the coastal fog creates natural air conditioning and insulation, the mercury rarely drops below 50 or rises above 77. August and September are the hottest months, December and January the coolest.

Spring and particularly autumn are ideal times to visit. Winter is the rainy season, which extends from November to April, with the heaviest showers from January through March. During the rest of the year there is almost no rain. Summer is the peak tourist season, when large crowds can present problems. Like spring, it's also a period of frequent fog; during the morning and evening, fog banks from offshore blanket the coast, burning off around midday.

In California, most winter storms sweep in from the north, so the average annual rainfall and the length of the rainy season diminish as you go south, with San Diego getting only ten inches of rain annually. However, the area in and around the small inland community of Julian can experience more than 25 inches of rainfall a year. The ocean air also creates significant moisture, keeping the average humidity around 68 percent and making some areas seem colder than the thermometer would indicate.

Though San Diego County can't claim to be smog free, the air is considerably better than in the surrounding counties to the north and east. Smog is heaviest during August and September. Also, in the autumn the Santa Ana winds kick up out of the desert. Hot, dry gusts from the northeast, they sometimes reach velocities of 35 to 50 miles per hour, blowing sand, fanning forest fires and making people edgy.

It's no secret that the desert is hot in the summer, with temperatures often rising well above 100°F. Spring is a particularly pretty time to visit, when the weather is cooler and the wildflowers, particularly in Anza-Borrego State Park, cover the desert floor. Autumn and winter are also quite pleasant.

The mountains are cold in winter and cool during spring and autumn. Surprisingly, they are hotter than the coastal regions in summer, due to a temperature inversion layer and the fact that they are too far from the coast to experience significant ocean cooling. You can expect more precipitation than there is along the coast.

CALENDAR OF EVENTS

JANUARY

Central San Diego San Diego Boat Show at the San Diego Convention Center and Marriott Hotel and Marina showcases the latest in marine gear, from the smallest accessories to the boats themselves.

La Jolla Annual Nations of San Diego International Dance Festival at UCSD's Mandeville Auditorium is Southern California's largest ethnic dance festival, with over 250 dancers.

South Bay & Northern Baja Not many events take place in January, though the snowbird season is at its peak. El Día de los Santos Reyes, January 6, marks the end of the Christmas holiday season. It is on this day, not Christmas Day, that Mexicans feast and exchange gifts.

FEBRUARY

Central San Diego Mardi Gras festivities take to the streets in San Diego's historic Gaslamp Quarter. The annual Kumba Fest celebrates Black History Month and our African-American heritage through drama, song and poetry at the Lyceum Theatre, Horton Plaza.

South Bay & Northern Baja In Ensenada, Carnaval (the Latin Mardi Gras) is celebrated with five days of parades, fireworks, costumes and dancing in the streets. Monday of Carnaval week is "henpecked husbands' day," when men are allowed 23 hours to indulge every desire—at their own risk.

MARCH   **Central San Diego**   The Gaslamp Quarter block party celebrates St. Patrick's Day with music and entertainment. **San Diego Latino Film Festival** in Mission Valley showcases films of varying lengths that are by Latinos and/or about the Latino experience.

APRIL   **San Diego's Waterfront**   **Motorcars on Main Street** in Coronado features 150 pre-1972 automobiles. **Coronado Flower Show Weekend** bills itself as the largest flower show under a tent in the Western United States.

South Bay & Northern Baja   Holy Week (**Semana Santa**), the week before Easter, is not as crowded in Baja as elsewhere in Mexico. But many people visit relatives on the "mainland," and many businesses shut down from Wednesday through Sunday. Around the same time, 10,000 cyclists participate in the semiannual **Rosarito to Ensenada Bicycle Race,** and the **Newport-Ensenada Yacht Race** draws so many boaters that it claims to be the world's largest regatta. In late April, what better place to recover from the month's fitness events than at the **Tijuana Pizza Festival?**

MAY   **Central San Diego**   Old Town celebrates **Cinco de Mayo** with mariachis, traditional Mexican folk dancers, food and displays.

North County & Inland San Diego   Carlsbad hosts its first **Village Faire** of the year (the other one is in November), with hundreds of arts-and-crafts booths, lots of rides and countless foodstands.

IN THE KNOW

Visitors can find out about the very latest happenings around town from San Diego's free publications. The weekly **San Diego Reader** is an oversize magazine just jammed with information on everything that's going on around town during the week, from Shakespeare to dive bars. **What'sPlaying** is a bimonthly guide to San Diego's performing arts, be it dance or drama. **San Diego This Week** covers the area from Baja to Orange County, with daily events listings and tips on what's hot around the county. While it's not exactly free, unless you can find an abandoned copy at a local coffee emporium, the San Diego Union-Tribune's Thursday entertainment guide, **Night & Day**, gives the lowdown on what's happening around town for the next week.

South Bay & Northern Baja   Cinco de Mayo, a major holiday all over Mexico, is observed in most Baja communities.

Central San Diego   Balboa Park hosts the **The Old Globe Shakespeare Festival,** a series of five plays performed at three theaters in the park. **Suzuki Rock 'n' Roll Marathon** is a 26.2-mile run that begins in Balboa Park and ends at the Marine Corps Recruit Depot, with 26 bands playing live music along the way.

JUNE

Central San Diego   **San Diego Lesbian and Gay Pride Parade, Rally and Festival** offers a weekend of festivities in the Hillcrest and Balboa Park areas to celebrate San Diego's gay and lesbian community.

JULY

South Bay & Northern Baja   The annual **U.S. Open Sandcastle Competition** at the Imperial Beach Pier includes a parade, sandcastle contests for adults and children, and fireworks. July 11 marks the **Anniversary of Tijuana,** founded in 1899. The fiesta lasts all month; it's sure to be especially crazy in 1999. Baja's economic development, from factories to farming cooperatives, is the focus of **Expo Ensenada.**

La Jolla   Crowds in costume liven up San Diego's 20 miles of coastline during the **Midnight Madness Fun Bicycle Run.** Chamber music concerts, lectures and workshops are all part of the three-week **SummerFest La Jolla.**

AUGUST

North County & Inland San Diego   National and international body surfers compete at the annual **World Body Surfing Championships** at the Oceanside Pier and beach.

South Bay & Northern Baja   The **Feria de Tijuana** features entertainment, carnival rides and livestock shows at Agua Caliente racetrack from mid-August to mid-September.

Central San Diego   **Old Town Fiestas Patrias** celebrates the Hispanic heritage with food, crafts, music and dance.

SEPTEMBER

San Diego's Waterfront   **Pacific Islander Festival** on Mission Bay showcases the cultures, crafts, customs and cuisines of Melanesia, Micronesia and Polynesia.

Central San Diego   **Little Italy Annual Festa** not only highlights its heritage with music and food, but includes "Chalk La

OCTOBER

Strada," a traditional event where artists do chalk drawings on the pavement.

North County & Inland San Diego   In the San Diego area, **La Mesa Oktoberfest** features Bavarian bands, beer gardens and arts and crafts.

South Bay & Northern Baja   In late October, the 50-mile **Rosarito-Ensenada Bicycle Race** draws even more participants than the same race held in the springtime; cyclists have numbered around 16,000 in recent years.

NOVEMBER   **North County & Inland San Diego**   Carlsbad hosts the year's second **Village Faire** (see May listing).

South Bay & Northern Baja   **El Día de los Muertos**, or Day of the Dead—actually two days, November 1 and 2—is generally a quiet, stay-at-home time in Baja; most businesses close.

DECEMBER   **Throughout San Diego**   Several coastal communities mark the season with **Christmas Boat Parades.** San Diego also celebrates the Mexican yuletide with **Las Posadas.**

▼▼▼▼▼▼▼▼▼▼▼▼
Before You Go

VISITORS CENTERS

Several agencies provide free information for travelers. The **California Office of Tourism** will help guide you to areas throughout the state. ~ 801 K Street, Suite 1600, Sacramento, CA 95814; 800-862-2543; www.visitcalifornia.com. In San Diego, the **San Diego Convention and Visitors Bureau** is a good source of information. ~ 401 B Street, Suite 1400, San Diego, CA 92101; 619-236-1212; www.sandiego.org. For information about La Jolla, contact the **La Jolla Visitor Center.** ~ 7966 Herschel Avenue, Suite A, La Jolla, CA 92037; 619-236-1212, fax 619-230-7084; www.sandiego.org. For Carlsbad information, check with the **Carlsbad Convention & Visitors Bureau.** ~ 400 Carlsbad Village Drive, Carlsbad, CA 92008; 760-434-6093, 800-227-5722, fax 760-434-6056; www.visitcarlsbad.org. To find out about Chula Vista, contact the **Chula Vista Convention & Visitors Bureau.** ~ 750 E Street, Chula Vista, CA 91910; 619-425-4444, fax 619-425-4860; www.chulavistaconvis.com. For information about northern San Diego County contact, **San Diego North Convention & Visitors Bureau.** ~ 360 North Escondido Boulevard, Escondido, CA 92025; 760-745-4741, 800-848-3336, fax 760-745-4796; www.sandiegonorth.com. For information about crossing the border into Baja, contact **Border Station Parking & Tourist Information**. ~ 4570 Camino de la Plaza, San Ysidro, CA 92173; 619-428-6200, fax 858-451-9568; www.gototijuana.com/bsp.

Two important guidelines should determine what you take on a trip. The first is as true for San Diego as for anywhere in the world—pack light. Also, dress styles here are relatively informal, so try to keep it casual. The airlines usually allow you two pieces of checked baggage and a carry-on.

    The second rule is to prepare for temperature variations. A warm sweater and a jacket are absolute necessities year-round, in addition to shorts and T-shirts. Pack a raincoat if you're planning to visit from December to February.

PACKING

Overnight accommodations in the San Diego area are as varied as the region itself. They range from high-rise hotels and neon motels to hostels and bed-and-breakfast inns. Check through the various regional chapters and you're bound to find something to fit your budget and taste.

LODGING

San Diego has been the backdrop for a number of Hollywood films, including *Charlie's Angels: Full Throttle*, *Bruce Almighty*, *Traffic* and *The Scorpion King*.

    The neon motels offer bland facilities at low prices and are excellent if you're economizing or don't plan to spend much time in the room. Larger hotels often lack intimacy, but provide such conveniences as restaurants and shops in the lobby. My personal preference is for historic hotels, those slightly faded classics that offer charm and tradition at moderate cost. Bed-and-breakfast inns present an opportunity to stay in a homelike setting. Like hostels, they provide an excellent way to meet fellow travelers; but unlike hostels, some of San Diego's B&Bs can be quite expensive.

    To help you decide on a place to stay, I've organized the accommodations not only by area but also according to price (prices listed are for double occupancy during the high season; prices may decrease in the low season). *Budget* hotels generally are less than $60 per night for two people; the rooms are clean and comfortable, but not luxurious. The *moderately* priced hotels run $60 to $120 and provide larger rooms, plusher furniture and more attractive surroundings. At a *deluxe* hotel you can expect to spend between $120 and $175 for two people. You'll check into a spacious, well-appointed room with all modern facilities; downstairs, the lobby will be a fashionable affair, usually with a restaurant, lounge and cluster of shops. If you want to spend your time (and money) in the city's very finest hotels, try an *ultra-deluxe* facility, which will include all the amenities and cost more than $175.

DINING

I've organized San Diego's veritable parade of dining places according to location and cost. Restaurants listed in this book offer lunch and dinner, unless otherwise noted.

Within a particular chapter, the restaurants are presented geographically and characterized as budget, moderate, deluxe or ultra-deluxe in price. Dinner entrées at *budget* restaurants usually cost $9 or less. The ambience is informal—café-style—and the crowd is often a local one. *Moderately* priced restaurants range between $9 and $18 at dinner and offer pleasant surroundings, a more varied menu and a slower pace. *Deluxe* establishments tab their entrées above $18, and feature sophisticated cuisines, plush decor and more personalized service. *Ultra-deluxe* dining rooms, where $25 will only get you started, are gourmet gathering places in which cooking (one hopes) is a fine art and service a way of life.

Breakfast and lunch menus vary less in price from restaurant to restaurant. Even deluxe kitchens usually offer light breakfasts and lunch sandwiches, which place them within a few dollars of their budget-minded competitors. These early meals can be a good time to try out expensive restaurants.

TRAVELING WITH CHILDREN

Visiting San Diego with kids can be a real adventure, and if properly planned, a truly enjoyable one. To ensure that your trip will feature the joy, rather than the strain, of parenthood, remember a few important guidelines.

Use a travel agent to help with arrangements; they can reserve spacious bulkhead seats on airlines and determine which flights are the least crowded. Also, plan to bring everything you need on-board: diapers, food, toys—and extra clothes for kids and parents alike. If the trip to San Diego involves a long journey, plan to relax and do very little during the first few days after you arrive.

Always allow extra time for getting places. Book reservations well in advance and make sure the hotel has the extra crib, cot or bed you require. It's smart to ask for a room at the end of the hall, to cut down on noise. Be aware that many bed-and-breakfast inns do not allow children.

Most neighborhood communities have stores that carry diapers, food and other essentials; 7-11 stores are sometimes open all night (check the Yellow Pages for addresses). Hotels often provide access to babysitters, or check the Yellow Pages for state licensed and bonded babysitting agencies. A first-aid kit is always a good idea. Consult with your pediatrician for special medicines and dosages for colds and diarrhea.

Traveling solo grants you an independence and a freedom you don't have when you travel with a partner, but single travelers are more vulnerable to crime and should take additional precautions.

WOMEN TRAVELING ALONE

It is better not to let strangers know that you are traveling alone or where you are staying or planning to travel. It's unwise to hitchhike and probably best to avoid inexpensive accommodations on the outskirts of town; the money saved does not outweigh the risk. Bed and breakfasts, youth hostels and YWCAs are generally your safest bets for lodging, and they also foster an environment ideal for bonding with fellow travelers.

Finding activities to interest children in San Diego couldn't be easier. Especially helpful in deciding on the day's outing is the "Family" section of the Saturday *San Diego Union-Tribune* and the "Calendar" section of the *San Diego Reader*.

It's best to avoid accommodations at motels in industrial areas or other places where there is no real neighborhood after dark. When requesting reservations at hotels and motels, ask for a room near the elevator or facing a central courtyard rather than find yourself in a remote location. For more hints, get a copy of *Safety and Security for Women Who Travel* (Travelers Tales).

Keep all valuables well hidden and keep a good hold on your camera and purse. Avoid late-night treks or strolls through undesirable parts of town, but if you find yourself in this situation, continue walking with a confident air until you reach a safe haven. A fierce scowl never hurts.

These hints should by no means deter you from seeking out adventure. Wherever you go, stay alert, use your common sense and trust your instincts. If you are hassled or threatened in some way, never be afraid to call for assistance. It's also a good idea to carry change for a phone call and to know a number to call in case of emergency. San Diego's crime victims hotline is 619-688-9200; the rape hotline is 858-272-1767. Feminist bookstores are also good sources of information about women's resource centers.

**GAY &
LESBIAN
TRAVELERS**

San Diego's Hillcrest district is the focus of the city's gay scene, with guesthouses, stores and cafés. (See "Hillcrest & San Diego Gay Scene" in Chapter Two.)

Look for the biweekly *Frontiers Newsmagazine*; it's full of movie, theater and nightclub reviews that cover the region between San Francisco and San Diego. ~ 5657 Wilshire Boulevard, Los Angeles, CA 90036; 323-848-2222; www.frontiersnews magazine.com.

In San Diego, get a copy of *Gay & Lesbian Times*, a weekly publication with local and world news, sports, features and commentary, a dining guide and an arts section. It also contains a calendar of events and a directory of gay-friendly businesses and establishments. ~ 1730 Monroe Avenue, San Diego; 619-299-6397; www.gaylesbiantimes.com. **The Lesbian Gay Bisexual and Transgender Community Center** offers referrals for those seeking drop-in counseling, mental health services or support groups—or stop by on Tuesday nights for bingo. Closed Sunday. ~ 3909 Centre Street, San Diego; 619-692-2077; www.thecentersd.org.

For information on services aimed at gay travelers, see "Gay-friendly travel" in the index.

sdPride.com is a free website that lists San Diego's gay-friendly businesses and provides other information about services for gays and lesbians in the San Diego area.

**SENIOR
TRAVELERS**

San Diego is ideal for older vacationers. The mild climate makes touring in the off-season possible, helping to cut down on expenses. Many museums, theaters, restaurants and hotels have senior discounts (available when you show a driver's license, Medicare card or other age-identifying card). Ask your travel agent when you book reservations.

The **AARP** offers members travel discounts and provides referrals for escorted tours. ~ 601 E Street Northwest, Washington, DC 20049; 800-424-3410; www.aarp.org. For those 55 or over, **Elderhostel** provides educational programs throughout California. ~ 11 Avenue de Lafayette, Boston, MA 02111; 877-426-8056; www.elderhostel.org.

Be extra careful about health matters. Bring along any medications you ordinarily use, together with the prescriptions for obtaining more. Consider carrying a medical record with you—including your medical history and current medical status as well as your doctor's name, phone number and address. Also be sure to confirm that your insurance covers you when you're away from home.

California stands at the forefront of social reform for travelers with disabilities. During the past decade, the state has responded to the needs of the blind, the wheelchair-bound and others with a series of progressive legislative measures.

DISABLED TRAVELERS

An agency called the **Access Center** assists persons with disabilities in the San Diego area. ~ 1295 University Avenue, Suite 10, San Diego; 619-293-3500; www.accesscentersd.org.

There are numerous national organizations offering general information. Among these are:

The **Society for Accessible Travel & Hospitality (SATH)**. ~ 347 5th Avenue #610, New York, NY 10016; 212-447-7284; www.sath.org.

Flying Wheels Travel. ~ 143 West Bridge Street, P.O. Box 382, Owatonna, MN 55060; 507-451-5005; www.flyingwheels travel.com.

Travelin' Talk, a network of people and organizations, also provides assistance. ~ P.O. Box 1796, Wheat Ridge, CO 80034; 303-232-2979; www.travelintalk.net.

Access-Able Travel Source has worldwide information on-line. ~ 303-232-2979; www.access-able.com.

Or consult the comprehensive guidebook, *Access to the World—A Travel Guide for the Handicapped*, by Louise Weiss (Henry Holt & Company, Inc., 1983).

Be sure to check in advance, when making room reservations, that your hotel has the kind of accommodations you want. For example, many hotels and motels have facilities for travelers in wheelchairs.

The Department of Motor Vehicles provides special parking permits for the disabled (check the phone book for the nearest location). Many local bus lines and other public transit facilities are wheelchair accessible.

Passports and Visas   Most foreign visitors need a passport and tourist visa to enter the United States. Contact your nearest U.S. Embassy or Consulate well in advance to obtain a visa and to check on any other entry requirements.

FOREIGN TRAVELERS

Customs Requirements   Foreign travelers are allowed to carry in the following items: 200 cigarettes (1 carton), 50 cigars or 2 kilograms (4.4 pounds) of smoking tobacco; one liter of alcohol for personal use only (you must be 21 years of age to bring in alcohol); and US$100 worth of duty-free gifts that can include an additional quantity of 100 cigars (except Cuban cigars). You may bring in any amount of currency, but you must fill out a form if you bring in over US$10,000. Carry any prescription drugs in clearly marked containers. (You may have to produce a written prescription or doctor's statement for the customs officer.) Meat or meat products, seeds, plants, fruits and narcotics cannot be brought into the United States. Contact the **United States Customs and Border Protection** for further information. ~ 1300 Pennsylvania Avenue NW, Washington, DC 20229; 202-927-1770; www.cbp.gov.

Driving   If you plan to rent a car, you should get an international driver's license before you arrive in the United States. Some car rental agencies require both a foreign license and an international driver's license. Many also require the lessee to be at least 25 years of age; all require a major credit card. Remember: Seat belts are mandatory for the driver and all passengers. Children under age six or 60 pounds should be in the back seat in approved child safety restraints.

Currency   United States money is based on the dollar. Bills generally come in denominations of $1, $5, $10, $20, $50 and $100. A dollar ($1) is divided into 100 cents. Coins are the penny (1 cent), nickel (5 cents), dime (10 cents) and quarter (25 cents). Half-dollar and dollar coins are rarely used, as are $2 bills. You may not use foreign currency to purchase goods and services in the United States. Consider buying traveler's checks in dollar amounts. You may also use credit cards affiliated with an American company, such as Interbank, Visa and American Express.

Electricity and Electronics   Electric outlets use currents of 110 volts, 60 cycles. For appliances made for other electrical systems, you need a transformer or other adapter. Travelers who use laptop computers for telecommunications should be aware that modem configurations for U.S. telephone systems may be different from their European counterparts. Similarly, the U.S. format for videotapes is different from that in Europe; National Park

Service visitors centers and other stores that sell souvenir videos often have them available in European format on request.

Weights and Measurements   The United States uses the English system of weights and measures. American units and their metric equivalents are: 1 inch = 2.5 centimeters; 1 foot (12 inches) = 0.3 meter; 1 yard (3 feet) = 0.9 meter; 1 mile (5280 feet) = 1.6 kilometers; 1 ounce = 28 grams; 1 pound (16 ounces) = 0.45 kilogram; 1 quart (liquid) = 0.9 liter.

Outdoor Adventures

CAMPING

The California State Park System oversees 277 camping facilities. Amenities at each campground vary, but there is a day-use fee of $2 to $14 per vehicle. Campsites range from about $9 to $25 (a little less in the off-season). For a complete listing of all state-run campgrounds, send for *California Escapes*, published by the **California Department of Parks and Recreation**. ~ P.O. Box 942896, Sacramento, CA 94296; 916-653-6995; www.parks. ca.gov. For campground reservations call 800-444-7275.

For general information on National Park campgrounds, contact the **National Park Service**. ~ Western Information Center, Fort Mason, Building 201, San Francisco, CA 94123; 415-561-4700; www.nps.gov or www.nps. gov/goga. To reserve a National Park campsite, call the individual park directly or call 800-365-2267. In addition, the National Park Service offers a **National Parks Pass**, which costs $50 and admits you and your family to all national parks for a year from the date of issue. Just keep in mind that other fees, such as boating and camping, may not be waived.

In San Diego, flowers bloom throughout the winter and most trees don't lose their leaves.

Reservations for **U.S. Forest Service** campsites must be made by calling the National Forest Reservation System at 800-280-2267. A fee is charged at these facilities and the length of stay varies from forest to forest. It's best to reserve in advance, though many forests keep some sites open to be filled daily on a first-come, first-served basis. For more information contact the National Forest Service's Pacific Southwest regional office. ~ 1323 Club Drive, Vallejo, CA 94592; 707-562-8737; www.fs.fed.us/r5.

San Diego also offers municipal, county and private facilities. See the "Beaches & Parks" sections in the area chapters for the locations of these.

PERMITS   **Wilderness Permits**   For camping and hiking in the wilderness and primitive areas of national forests, a wilderness permit is required. Permits are largely free and are issued for a specific period of time, which varies according to the wilderness area. Information is available through the **U.S. Forest Service.** ~ 1323 Club Drive, Vallejo, CA 94592; 707-562-8737; www.fs.fed. us/r5. You can obtain permits from ranger stations and regional information centers, as described in the "Beaches & Parks" sections in the area chapters.

Boating Permits   Permits, which cost from $2 to $15 and can usually be applied for up to 60 days in advance, are required for independent rafting or kayaking on most popular whitewater rivers. There is no central agency to process permit applications. Different rivers, and sometimes different stretches of the same river, are administered by various forest service or state park ranger stations or river conservancy groups. For information, contact American Whitewater. ~ 1424 Fenwick Lane, Silver Spring, MD 20910; 866-262-8429; www.americanwhite water.org, e-mail info@amwhitewater.org.

FISHING & SPORT-FISHING   The lure of sportfishing attracts thousands of enthusiasts to San Diego every year. Yellowtail, sea bass, bonito and barracuda are the local favorites, with marlin and tuna the prime objectives for multiday charters. Most outfitters provide bait and rent tackle.

For current information on the fishing season and state license fees, contact the **California Department of Fish and Game.** ~ 1416 9th Street, Sacramento, CA 95814; 916-653-7664; www. dfg.ca.gov.

UP, UP AND AWAY

Hot-air ballooning is a romantic pursuit that has soared in popularity in the Del Mar area. A number of companies provide spectacular dawn and sunset flights, most concluding with a traditional champagne toast. Contact **A Skysurfer Balloon Company** for daily sunset flights over the coastal valley area. The 45-minute to one-hour affair includes on-board champagne and soft drinks, and concludes with a first-flight certificate. ~ 2658 Del Mar Heights Road, Del Mar; 858-481-6800, 800-660-6809; www.sandiegohotairballoons.com.

Call **Fish 'N Cruise** for custom-designed charters. ~ 1551 Shelter Island Drive, San Diego; 619-224-2464; www.sandiego yachts.com.

Point Loma Sportfishing operates a fleet of ten boats. Their daytrip goes down to Mexico for tuna. ~ 1403 Scott Street, Point Loma; 619-223-1627; www.pointlomasportfishing.com. Also in Point Loma is **Fisherman's Landing**, which takes groups of 6 to 35 on fishing excursions. The 23-day charter winds up in Cabo San Lucas. ~ 2838 Garrison Street, Point Loma; 619-222-0391; www.fishermanslanding.com. **H & M Landing** arranges half-day jaunts to local kelp beds or 18-day expeditions past the tip of Baja for giant yellowfin tuna. ~ 2803 Emerson Street, Point Loma; 619-222-1144; www.hmlanding.com. **Seaforth Sportfishing** uses 36- to 85-foot boats for their runs. Longer trips in summer head out to Mexican waters for albacore. ~ 1717 Quivira Road, Mission Bay, plus locations downtown and in Coronado; 619-224-3383; www.seaforth.com. **Islandia Sportfishing** offers trips for albacore, mackerel and skipjack. ~ 1551 West Mission Bay Drive, Mission Bay; 619-222-1164; www.is landiasportfishing.com.

For deep-sea and local sportfishing, contact **Helgren's Sportfishing**; five-day excursions lead down into Mexico. ~ 315 Harbor Drive South, Oceanside; 760-722-2133; www.helgrens sportfishing.com.

Spearfishing is very popular off La Jolla beaches, especially south of La Jolla Cove. Contact **San Diego Divers Supply** for supplies, tours and information. ~ 4004 Sports Arena Boulevard, San Diego; 619-224-3439. *Note:* Spearfishing is not allowed in protected reserves from La Jolla Cove north.

Near Tijuana, **Islas los Coronados** is a favorite area for yellowtail, sea bass, halibut and barracuda. Charters can be arranged informally at San Antonio del Mar. Most fishing charters that operate in this area are based in San Diego. Contact **H&M Landing**. ~ 2803 Emerson Street, San Diego; 619-222-1144; www.hmlanding.com. You can also book a charter at **Fisherman's Landing**. ~ 2838 Emerson Street, San Diego; 619-221-8500; www.fishermanslanding.com.

The waters around Ensenada are famed for California yellowtail. Other game fish include white sea bass, albacore, bonito and barracuda. Fishing charter offices are located near the fish market, and you can save money by joining a group charter with any of several outfitters, such as **Gordo's Sport Fishing** (Paseo Costero at Avenida Gastelum; 646-178-3515) and the **Ensenada Clipper Fleet** (Paseo Costero at Avenida Gastelum; 646-178-2185).

KAYAKING   The **Islas de Todos Santos**, at the mouth of the Bahía de Todos Santos, are a six-and-a-half-mile paddle from Punta Banda. Visitors to the islands will find soaring cliffs and sun-soaked beaches, harbor seals sea lions and abundant bird life. Kayak trips to the area, including transportation and kayaks, can be arranged through **Southwest Sea Kayaking** in San Diego. ~ 619-222-3616 in the U.S.

WHALE WATCHING   The stately progress of our fellow mammalians in migration is a wonderful sight to behold. To get an even closer look at these mammoth cetaceans, book a charter with one of the many whale-watching companies; most outfitters guarantee marine sightings. The season generally runs from late December through late February (mid-January is the best time).

San Diego Harbor Excursion provides three-hour whale-watching tours during winter. ~ 1050 North Harbor Drive; 619-234-4111, 800-442-7847; www.sdhe.com.

In Point Loma, **H & M Landing** takes you out on 65- to 85-foot boats in search of whales. ~ 2803 Emerson Street, Point Loma; 619-222-1144; www.hm landing.com. **Point Loma Sportfishing** offers three-hour trips through local waters. ~ 1403 Scott Street, Point Loma; 619-223-1627; www.pointlomasportfishing.com.

A free whale-watching station at Cabrillo National Monument on Point Loma features a glassed-in observatory.

Islandia Sportfishing serves the Mission Bay area, accommodating up to 150 guests. ~ 1551 West Mission Bay Drive, Mission Bay; 619-222-1164; www.islandiasportfishing.com.

Helgren's Sportfishing sets sail from mid-December to mid-April—that's when you'll see California gray whales. ~ 315 Harbor Drive South, Oceanside; 760-722-2133; www.helgrensport fishing.com.

During winter, whale-watching excursions to the Islas de Todos Santos can be arranged through the **Caracol Museo de Ciencias**. ~ Avenida Obregón 1463; 646-178-7192.

DIVING   San Diego offers countless spots for diving. The rocky La Jolla coves boast the clearest waters on the California coast. Bird

Rock, La Jolla Underwater Park and the underwater Scripps Canyon are ideal havens for divers. In Point Loma try the colorful tidepools at Cabrillo Underwater Reserve; at No Surf Beach (located on Sunset Cliffs Boulevard), pools and reefs are for experienced divers only.

San Diego Shark Diving Expeditions offers one-day trips off the coast of San Diego to dive within the safety of a shark cage and observe (or photograph) free-swimming blue, white and mako sharks. For the less adventurous, there are two-tank trips to kelp beds or Wreck Alley and three-tank trips to the Coronado Islands off Baja, Mexico. Reservations are a must. ~ 6747 Friar's Road #112, San Diego; 619-299-8560; www.sdsharkdiving. com. **Ocean Enterprises** teaches a variety of diving classes. They also rent and sell gear. ~ 7710 Balboa Avenue, San Diego; 858-565-6054; www.oceanenterprises.com. You can also arrange dives with **San Diego Divers Supply**. They provide instruction, sell gear and do repairs. ~ 4004 Sports Arena Boulevard, San Diego, 619-224-3439.

In Pacific Beach, the **Diving Locker** offers open-water certification. They also rent and sell gear. ~ 1020 Grand Avenue, Pacific Beach; 858-272-1120; www.divinglocker.com.

For diving rentals, sales, instruction and tips, contact **Underwater Schools of America**. ~ 225 Brooks Street, Oceanside; 760-722-7826; www.usascuba.com.

Islas los Coronados is an enormously popular area for scuba diving. Although the islands may not look like much from the surface, they are the summits of a cluster of steep underwater mountains whose rock faces, like coral reefs, teem with sea life. The best dive areas lie 60 to 90 feet below the surface and can be hazardous for inexperienced divers. A popular spot for easy diving is the kelp forest off the southern tip of the southernmost island. There are no regularly scheduled commercial dive trips, and most scuba enthusiasts come in their own boats.

Scuba diving adventures off the rocky coast of Bahía Bufadora can be arranged at **Dale's La Bufadora Dive Shop**. ~ La Bufadora turnoff from the Transpeninsular Highway; 661-175-0000.

The surf's up in the San Diego area. Pacific, Mission and Ocean beaches, Tourmaline Surfing Park and Windansea, La Jolla Shores, Swami and Moonlight beaches are well-known hangouts for surfers. Sailboarding is concentrated within Mission Bay. Ocean-

SURFING & WIND- SURFING

side is home to annual world-class boogieboarding and surfing competitions.

C. P. Water Sports has windsurfing rentals and lessons. ~ 1775 East Mission Bay Drive, Mission Bay; 619-275-8945. Surfboards, boogieboards, and sailboards are available at **Mission Bay Sportcenter**. They have wetsuits and surfing instruction as well. ~ 1010 Santa Clara Place, Mission Bay; 858-488-1004; www.missionbaysportcenter.com.

For surfboard, bodyboard, wetsuit and snorkel rentals and sales, try **Mitch's**. ~ 631 Pearl Street, La Jolla; 858-459-5933.

Surfride rents and sells surfboards, boogieboards, bodyboards, fins and wetsuits. ~ 1909 South Coast Highway, Oceanside; 760-433-4020; www.surfride.com. **Hansen Surfboards** rents recreational gear such as snorkel equipment, surfboards and bodyboards, as well as wetsuits. ~ 1105 South Coast Highway, Encinitas; 760-753-6595; www.hansensurf.com.

The beaches around **Rosarito** have been attracting hordes of surfers since the Beach Boys were kids. But the pros say the greatest surfing in the Ensenada area is to be found at **Islas de Todos Santos**, a pair of islands six and a half miles offshore at the mouth of Bahía de Todos Santos. Waves here can reach a height of 30 feet. The beach on the ocean side of the south island catches the waves in a long, rolling break that is a surfer's dream, and the accelerated swells that speed through the narrow passage between the south and north islands are a superthrill. You'll find current surf information and boards for sale (but not for rent) at **Tony's Surf Shop**. ~ Boulevard Juárez 312; 646-172-1192.

BOATING & SAILING

Fabulous weather allows plenty of opportunities to sail under the Coronado Bridge, skirt the gorgeous downtown skyline and even get a taste of open ocean in this sailing mecca.

Several sailing companies operate out of Harbor Island West in San Diego, including **Harbor Sailboats**. They offer instruction as well as sailboat rentals. ~ 2040 Harbor Island Drive, Suite 104, San Diego; 619-291-9568; www.harborsailboats.com. For sailboat rentals and party yacht charters, try **San Diego Yacht Charters**. ~ 1880 Harbor Island Drive, San Diego; 619-297-4555; www.sdyc.com. Charter a yacht through **Hornblower Dining Yachts**. ~ 1066 North Harbor Drive, San Diego; 619-234-8687; www.hornblower.com.

The **Coronado Boat Rentals** has motorboats and sailboats. ~ 1715 Strand Way, Coronado; 619-437-1514.

Motorboat, sailboat and kayak rentals can be found at **C. P. Water Sports.** ~ 1775 East Mission Bay Drive, Mission Bay; 619-275-8945. Powerboat, sailboat, catamaran and kayak rentals are also available from **Mission Bay Sportcenter.** In addition, they can teach you how to sail and waterski. ~ 1010 Santa Clara Place, Mission Bay; 858-488-1004; www.missionbaysportcenter.com. **Seaforth Mission Bay Boat Rental** rents motorboats, sailboats, paddleboats, canoes and kayaks. Sailing lessons are available. ~ 1641 Quivira Road, Mission Bay; 619-223-1681; www.seaforthboatrental.com. Seaforth has two other locations, downtown and in Coronado.

The place to arrange for a bird's-eye view of Ensenada is Baja Para-Sail, located near the tourist office on the waterfront. ~ Paseo Costero 609; 646-178-1641.

HANG GLIDING

Torrey Pines Glider Port is an expert-rated hang-gliding and paragliding site, located atop a towering sandstone bluff overlooking Black's Beach. Lesson packages and half-hour tandem flights are available. If you're not yet an expert, it's a great vantage point to watch from. ~ 2800 Torrey Pines Scenic Drive, La Jolla; 858-452-9858; www.flytorrey.com, e-mail info@flytorrey.com.

GOLF

You don't have to look far for a green to practice your swing. Most courses in San Diego rent clubs and carts, so you're in luck even if you didn't plan ahead.

CENTRAL SAN DIEGO A duffer's delight, the 18-hole **Balboa Park Municipal Golf Course** is a par-72 championship course. It also features a nine-hole executive course. ~ Golf Course Drive, Balboa Park; 619-570-1234.

SAN DIEGO'S WATERFRONT The **Coronado Municipal Golf Course,** an 18-hole green, runs along Glorietta Bay. ~ 2000 Visalia Row, Coronado; 619-435-3121. **Mission Bay Golf Resort** is a public 18-hole course. It's San Diego's only lighted course. ~ 2702 North Mission Bay Drive, Mission Bay; 858-581-7880.

LA JOLLA Beautiful **Torrey Pines Municipal Golf Course** is famous for its two 18-hole, par-72 championship courses. ~ 11480 North Torrey Pines Road, La Jolla; 619-570-1234.

NORTH COUNTY & INLAND SAN DIEGO The 18-hole **Emerald Isle Golf Course** is a public, executive course. ~ 660 South El Camino Real, Oceanside; 760-721-4700; www.emeraldislegolf.net.

Tee off at **Oceanside Golf Course,** a public 18-hole course. At the 13th hole, take a minute to admire the view of rolling hills and majestic mountains. ~ 825 Douglas Drive, Oceanside; 760-433-1360. You'll have to caddy your clubs by pull cart at the executive, public **Rancho Carlsbad Golf Course,** a par-56, 18-hole facility. ~ 5200 El Camino Real, Carlsbad; 760-438-1772. The par-58 **Lake San Marcos Executive Course** is open to the public. ~ 1556 Camino del Arroyo, San Marcos; 760-744-9092. Tee off at the **Welk Resort Village Golf Courses,** which has two public, 18-hole courses: the executive Fountain and the smaller par-3 Oaks. Both are dotted with lakes and ponds. ~ 8860 Lawrence Welk Drive, Escondido; 760-749-3000. The public, 18-hole, championship **Rancho Bernardo Inn Golf Course** includes a cart with the greens fee. ~ 17550 Bernardo Oaks Drive, Rancho Bernardo; 858-487-0700.

For the Inland San Diego County area, consider the public, 18-hole **Fallbrook Golf Club,** which rents only carts. ~ 2757 Gird Road, Fallbrook; 760-728-8334. The 18-hole **San Luis Rey Downs Golf Resort & Country Club** is a public facility. ~ 31474 Golf Club Drive, Bonsall; 760-758-9699, 800-783-6967; www.slrd.com. In El Cajon, the semiprivate **Singing Hills Golf Courses** feature three 18-hole courses: two championship and one par-3. The 12th hole on the Willow Glen championship course is over a fountain. There's also a driving range. ~ 3007 Dehesa Road, El Cajon; 619-442-3425; www.singinghills.com.

SOUTH BAY & NORTHERN BAJA The semiprivate **Tijuana Country Club** (also called the Club Social y Deportivo Campestre) has a long 18-hole course that sometimes hosts the Mexican Open Golf Tournament. ~ Boulevard Agua Caliente; 664-681-7851.

South of Tijuana on the way to Rosarito, the 18-hole course at the **Real del Mar Golf Resort** is open to the public and has club and cart rentals and a complete pro shop. ~ Route 1-D Km. 18; 664-613-3401; www.realdemar.com.

The only game in town—or anywhere in the region—is the 18-hole course at the **Hacienda Don Juan Resort.** Club and cart rentals are available. ~ Playa Faro; 646-177-4094.

TENNIS   **SAN DIEGO WATERFRONT** San Diego has many private and public hard courts and even a few public clay courts. The

Coronado Tennis Center has eight outdoor courts, three of which are lighted. ~ 1501 Glorietta Boulevard; 619-435-1616. The **Barnes Tennis Center** has 25 public outdoor courts; 4 are clay; 24 are lighted. ~ 4490 West Point Loma Boulevard, San Diego; 619-221-9000; www.barnestenniscenter.com. You'll find two unlighted courts at the **Cabrillo Recreation Center.** ~ 3051 Canon Street, Point Loma; 619-531-1534. If you're in Ocean Beach, try the 12 public courts at **Peninsula Tennis Club,** which are outdoor and lighted. Fee. ~ 2525 Bacon Street, Ocean Beach; 619-226-3407.

Riding horses on the beach is a popular activity in Rosarito. Every day, cowboys bring strings of rental horses to the beach to wait for customers, especially in the area of the Rosarito Beach Hotel.

LA JOLLA Five of the nine outdoor courts at the **La Jolla Recreation Center** are lighted. Fee. ~ 7632 Draper Avenue, La Jolla; 858-454-4434.

NORTH COUNTY & INLAND SAN DIEGO North County suffers from a lack of public tennis courts; however, Del Mar has free courts located off 22nd Street between Camino del Mar and Jimmy Durante Boulevard. **Kit Carson Park** in Escondido has ten courts available, four of which are lighted. ~ 3333 Bear Valley Parkway, Escondido; 760-839-4691.

In Bonsall, try the six outdoor lighted courts at **San Luis Rey Downs Tennis Club.** Fee. ~ 31474 Golf Club Drive, Bonsall; 760-758-1318, 800-783-6967; www.slrd.com. The **Parkway Sports Center** in El Cajon has four lighted courts. Instruction is available. Fee. ~ 1055 Ballantyne Street, El Cajon; 619-442-9623.

SOUTH BAY & NORTHERN BAJA Tennis courts are hard to find in Tijuana; most visitors who are inclined toward gringo sports head for the resorts at nearby Rosarito. The best bet for Tijuana tennis is the **Gran Hotel Tijuana,** which has two hard-surfaced courts for guest use. ~ Boulevard Agua Caliente 4500; 664-681-7000.

A number of resorts in the Rosarito and Ensenada area have tennis courts for guest use, but only the **Baja Beach and Tennis Club** is open to the general public. Court fees are expensive. ~ Isla San Benito 123, south of Ensenada; 646-176-2113.

San Diego's backcountry boasts hundreds of miles of riding trails. Cleveland National Forest, Palomar Mountain Park, William Heise County Park and Cuyamaca Rancho State Park

RIDING STABLES

all feature fine mountain riding. **Julian Stables** offers hour-long trail rides throughout a 30-acre ranch. Riders are rewarded with views of the Volcan Mountain Preserve and the peaks of Cuyamaca Rancho State Park. Reservations are required. ~ P.O. Box 881, Julian, CA 92036; 760-765-1598; www.julianactive.com, e-mail info@julianactive.com. For treks through the Anza-Borrego Desert State Park, **Smoketree Institute and Ranch**, and its Equine Encounters Program, leads guided tours year-round. Lessons and pony rides are offered daily. Reservations required. ~ 302 Palm Canyon Drive, Borrego Springs; 760-767-5850; www.smoketree.arabianranch.com, e-mail sthorpe@uia.net.

BIKING   Cycling has skyrocketed in popularity throughout San Diego County, especially in coastal areas. The **Mission Bay Bike Path** (18 miles) starts at the San Diego Convention Center, winds along the harbor, crosses Mission Bay and heads up the coast to La Jolla. **Balboa Park** and **Mission Bay Park** both have excellent bike routes (see the "Balboa Park and the San Diego Zoo" and "Mission Bay Park Area" sections of this chapter). Check with Ridelink about their special bike-path maps of the San Diego area. ~ 619-231-2453; www.ridelink.org.

North County's **Old Route 101** provides almost 40 miles of scintillating cycling along the coast from Oceanside to La Jolla. Traffic is heavy but bikes are almost as numerous as autos along this stretch. Bike lanes are designated along most of the route.

Inland, **Julian** makes a good base for bicycling the hilly country roads such as the nine-mile loop to Wynola.

It's hard to imagine vacationers visiting Tijuana by bike. The risk of theft is tremendous, and most places of interest to tourists are within walking distance of the border crossing. But if you choose to bike to Tijuana, you'll be pleased to learn that a newly opened bike lane, designed to accommodate the thousands of Mexican workers who commute daily to San Diego, makes cycling the fastest way to get through U.S. Customs and Immigration. In fact, Mexican entrepreneurs have started renting bicycles there in five-minute increments. When you get across the border, you drop the bike off at a stand on the U.S. side, and a youngster pedals it back to Mexico for the next customer.

Bike Rentals and Tours   To rent a bicycle (mountain, road, or kid's) in downtown San Diego, contact **Pennyfarthings Bicycle**

Store. ~ 630 C Street; 619-233-7696. **Holland's Bicycles** sells, rents and repairs cruisers, mountain bikes and tandems. Rentals come with helmets and locks. ~ 977 Orange Avenue at 10th Street, Coronado; 619-435-3153; www.hollandsbicycles.com.

Most of the San Diego County coastline is developed for either residential or commercial purposes, limiting the hiking possibilities. There are some protected areas set aside to preserve remnants of the county's unique coastal chaparral communities and tidelands. These reserves offer short hiking trails. Inland San Diego County, particularly in the Palomar and Laguna mountains, also provides backpacking opportunities. A trail map packet is available from the San Diego County Department of Public Works. ~ 858-694-3215.

HIKING

Serious hikers might consider taking on the San Diego section of the **California Coastal Trail**. It follows the shoreline from the Mexican border to San Onofre State Beach.

All distances listed for hiking trails are one way, unless otherwise noted.

SAN DIEGO'S WATERFRONT   **Cabrillo National Monument** offers the moderate **Bayside Trail** (1 mile). It begins at the Old Point Loma Lighthouse, beautifully restored to its original 1855 condition, and meanders through the heart of a scenic coastal chaparral community. A wide variety of native plants, including prickly pear cactus, yucca, buckwheat and Indian paintbrush, grow along the path. In addition to stunning views of San Diego, there are remnants of the coastal defense system built here during World Wars I and II. ~ 619-557-5450; www.nps.gov/cabr.

LA JOLLA   Without a doubt, the 1750-acre **Torrey Pines State Park and Reserve** offers the county's best hiking. It was named for the world's rarest pine tree *(Pinus torreyana)*, which the re-

AUTHOR FAVORITE

The one-mile **La Jolla Coastal Walk**, a dirt path atop La Jolla Bluffs, affords some of the most spectacular views anywhere on the San Diego County coastline. It begins on Coast Boulevard just up the hill from La Jolla Cove and continues past a sea cave accessible from the trail.

serve was established to protect. An estimated 6000 of the gnarled and twisted trees cling to rugged cliffs and ravines, some growing as tall as 60 feet.

Several major trails offer hikers a variety of challenges and natural attractions. Most are easily walked loops through groves of pines, such as **Guy Fleming Trail** (.6-mile loop), which scans the coast at South and North overlooks. There are more strenuous treks, such as the **Razor Point Trail** (.6 mile), which follows the Canyon of the Swifts, then links up with the **Beach Trail** (.8 mile); and the south fork of **Broken Hill Trail** (1.3 miles), which zigzags to the coast past chamiso and scrub oak (the north fork is 1.2 miles).

Torrey Pines State Park and Reserve's Parry Grove Trail (.5-mile loop) passes stands of manzanita, yucca and other shrubs.

NORTH COUNTY & INLAND SAN DIEGO   Three Lagoons Trail (5 miles) originates on the beach in Leucadia and heads north along the sand past three saltwater lagoons, ending in Carlsbad. The best place to begin is at the beach parking lot at Grandview Street in Leucadia.

Rising along San Diego County's northern border, the **Palomar Mountain Range** provides a number of demanding trails. Well-protected and well-maintained within Cleveland National Forest, they offer hikers a prime wilderness experience. ~ 858-673-6180, 760-788-9250.

Observatory Trail (1 mile) is one of the area's easiest treks and rewards the hiker with a view of that famous silver hemisphere, the Palomar Observatory.

The **Agua Tibia Wilderness Area** in the northwest corner of Cleveland National Forest is the setting for rugged **Dripping Springs Trail** (6.8 miles). Ascending the side of Agua Tibia Mountain, the trail leads through precipitous canyons to vista points with views of the Pacific, more than 40 miles away.

Scott's Cabin Trail (1 mile) wends through varied terrain in **Palomar Mountain State Park**. This moderate trail passes the remains of a homesteader's cabin, descends into a fir forest and climbs to a lookout tower.

The challenging **Stonewall Peak Trail** (2 miles) zigzags to the summit of 5730-foot Stonewall Peak, with views of an 1870s-era mine site along the way. Nearby, the moderate **Azalea Glen Trail** (4 mile loop) passes through open meadows as well as forests of oak and pine. **Paso Nature Trail** (.8 mile) is an easy, self-guided loop designed to introduce visitors to the local flora.

SOUTH BAY & NORTHERN BAJA Four miles of hiking trails crisscross the dunes and marshes of the largely undeveloped **Tijuana River National Estuarine Research Reserve**, which forms the coastal border between the United States and Mexico. Trails lead through dunes anchored by salt grass, pickleweed and sand verbena. The marshy areas, especially those in the wildlife refuge around the Tijuana River estuary, provide feeding and nesting grounds for several hundred species of native and migratory birds, including hawks, pelicans, plovers, terns and ducks.

Border Field to Tijuana River Trail (1.5 miles) is a level beach walk past sand dunes and the Tijuana River Estuary.

Transportation

CAR

Even though it is located in California's extreme southwest corner, San Diego is the hub of an elaborate highway network. The city is easily reached from north or south via **Route 5**; **Route 8** serves drivers from the east; and **Route 15** is the major inland freeway for travelers arriving from the mountain west. **Route 76** runs inland from Oceanside to the Palomar Mountains, then becomes **Route 79**, which leads to Julian. From Carlsbad, **Route 78** connects the coast with inland communities like Escondido.

AIR

San Diego International Airport (Lindbergh Field) lies just three miles northwest of downtown San Diego and is easily accessible from either Route 5 or Route 8. The airport is served by most major airlines, including Alaska Airlines, America West Airlines, American Airlines, Continental Airlines, Delta Air Lines, Frontier Airlines, JetBlue Airways, Northwest Air Lines, Southwest Airlines, United Airlines and USAirways. ~ www.san.org.

Taxis, limousines and buses provide service from the airport. **San Diego Transit System** bus #992 carries passengers to downtown. ~ 619-233-3004. Or try the **Southwest Shuttle**, which travels to major points in the city as well as to Orange County and Los Angeles. ~ 619-231-1123.

BUS

Greyhound Bus Lines (800-231-222; www.greyhound.com) services San Diego from around the country. The terminal is downtown at 120 West Broadway and 1st Avenue; 619-239-3266. Greyhound also carries passengers inland from San Diego to Escondido at 700 West Valley Parkway, 760-745-6522; and El Cajon at 250 South Marshall Avenue, 619-444-2591. There's also an Oceanside station at 205 South Tremont Street; 760-722-1587.

TRAIN

Chugging to a stop at historic Santa Fe Depot, at 1050 Kettner Boulevard and Broadway downtown, is a nice and convenient way to arrive in San Diego. **Amtrak** offers several coast-hugging roundtrips daily between Los Angeles and San Diego, with stops at Oceanside and Solano Beach. ~ 800-872-7245; www.amtrak.com.

CAR RENTALS

San Diego is spread out over a wide area and is best seen by car. Car rental companies abound. Most major rental agencies have franchises at the airport. These include **Avis Rent A Car** (800-831-2847), **Dollar Rent A Car** (800-800-4000), **Hertz Rent A Car** (800-654-3131) and **National Car Rental** (800-227-7368).

For better rates (but less convenient service) try agencies located near the airport that provide pick-up service: **Thrifty Car Rental** (800-367-2277), **Rent A Wreck** (800-535-1391) and **Budget Car & Truck Rental** (800-527-0700).

PUBLIC TRANSIT

Several modern and efficient public transportation systems operate throughout San Diego. Information and schedules are available for all systems by calling **Regional Transit**. ~ 619-233-3004, 800-266-6883 (San Diego County only).

The Regional Transit bus system is the city's largest public transportation network, with lines linking all major points. All Regional Transit stops are marked with a blue rectangle.

San Diego Transit Corporation, the largest operator in the Metropolitan Transit System (MTS), operates 31 bus routes. ~ 619-238-0100, fax 619-696-8159; www.sdcommute.com.

The city's most venturesome mode of public transportation is the **San Diego Trolley**. The light rail system's line operates daily. Understandably, the line running between Mission San Diego and the Mexican border is known as the "Tijuana Trolley," or the Blue Line. It also serves Old Town and the South Bay cities of National City, Chula Vista and Imperial Beach. The Orange

Line travels between Santee and downtown, including Seaport Village and the Gaslamp Quarter. ~ 619-233-3004.

North County Transit District, or NCTD, covers the general area from Camp Pendleton to Del Mar along the coast. NCTD operates numerous North County bus routes that service the communities of Oceanside, Carlsbad, Encinitas, Leucadia, Cardiff, Solana Beach, Del Mar and Rancho Santa Fe. ~ 760-966-6500, 800-266-6883; www.gonctd.com.

For Inland San Diego, NCTD provides bus service from Escondido to Ramona. **Northeast Rural Bus System** takes passengers from El Cajon to Julian, Santa Ysabel and Cuyamaca Rancho. ~ 760-767-4287.

National City Transit serves National City. ~ 619-233-3004. **Chula Vista Transit** serves Bonita and the city of Chula Vista. ~ 619-233-3004. ATC/Vancom runs from downtown San Diego to National City and Chula Vista and on to the San Ysidro international Otay Mesa borders. In addition, ATC/Vancom runs from Coronado along the Silver Strand to Imperial Beach. ~ 800-858-0291.

San Diego is not a taxi town in the usual big-city sense, but there's a cab—if you need it—just a telephone call away. Leading companies include **Silver Cab** (619-280-5555), **Yellow Cab** (619-234-6161), **Orange Cab** (619-291-3333) and **USA Cab** (619-231-1144).

In North County (Del Mar to Carlsbad), you can call **Yellow Cab** (760-753-6044) or **Oceanside Yellow Cab** (760-722-4217).

TAXIS

Several San Diego organizations and tour operators offer organized walks: **Gaslamp Quarter Historical Foundation** conducts two-hour, docent-led walking tours of the restored downtown historic district on Saturday at 11 a.m. Fee. ~ 410 Island Avenue; 619-233-4692.

Walking tours of **Old Town State Historic Park** are offered weekdays at 11 a.m. and weekends at 11 a.m. and 2 p.m. through park headquarters. ~ 4002 Wallace Street; 619-220-5422.

Join **Coronado Touring** for a leisurely 1.5-hour guided stroll through quaint Coronado. Tours leave from the Glorietta Bay Inn (1630 Glorietta Boulevard) at 11 a.m. on Tuesday, Thursday and Saturday. Fee. ~ 619-435-5993.

WALKING TOURS

TWO

Central San Diego

San Diego's first settlement sprang up in what is now Old Town in the 18th century, but by the mid-1800s the city's center had moved a few miles farther to the south, to where it is today. As the city grew, communities popped up around the main commercial area, turning San Diego into a city of neighborhoods, each with its own character. Some of the more affluent neighborhoods, such as Mission Hills and Kensington, continued to flourish, while others declined. After bleak periods, both Little Italy and the Gaslamp Quarter have been restored to their former glory, while Golden Hill and East Village are just starting to re-emerge. Hillcrest is a happening neighborhood with a thriving gay community, Balboa Park and Banker's Hill are quietly urban and Midtown is popular with young parents and professionals. With its potpourri of lifestyles and eclectic ethnic and its cultural mix, San Diego is a city of infinite variety.

▼▼▼▼▼▼▼▼▼▼▼▼▼▼
Downtown San Diego
At one time, downtown San Diego was a collection of porn shops, tattoo parlors and striptease bars. The investment of billions of dollars, to create a stunning array of new buildings and to restore many old ones, has changed all that. Within the compact city center there's Horton Plaza, an exciting example of avant-garde urban architecture, and the adjacent Gaslamp Quarter, which reveals how San Diego looked at the peak of its Victorian-era boom in the 1880s.

SIGHTS
Horton Plaza is totally unlike any other shopping center or urban redevelopment project. It has transcended its genre, with whimsical, rambling paths, bridges, towers, piazzas, sculptures,

fountains and live greenery. Fourteen different styles, ranging from Renaissance to postmodern, are employed in its design. Mimes, minstrels and fortune tellers meander about the six-block complex performing for patrons. The success of this structure sparked downtown's renewal by revamping local businesses and attracting more tourists.

Horton Plaza was inspired by European shopping streets and business districts such as the Plaka in Athens, the Ramblas in Barcelona and Portobello Road in London. ~ Horton Plaza is bounded by Broadway and G Street and 1st and 4th avenues.

The **Gaslamp Quarter** is one of America's largest national historic districts, covering a 16-block strip along 4th, 5th and 6th avenues from Broadway to the waterfront. Architecturally, the Quarter reveals some of the finest Victorian-style commercial buildings constructed in San Diego during the 50 years between the Civil War and World War I. This area, along 5th Avenue, became San Diego's first main street. The city's core began on the bay, where Alonzo Horton first built a wharf in 1869.

It was this same area that later fell into disrepute as the heart of the business district moved north, beyond Broadway. By the 1890s, prostitution and gambling were rampant. Offices above street level were converted into bordellos and opium dens. The area south of Market Street became known as the Stingaree, an unflattering epithet coined by the many who were stung by card sharks, con men and, of course, con ladies.

Rescued by the city and a dedicated group of preservationists, the area not only survived but played a major role in the massive redevelopment of downtown San Diego. The city added wide brick sidewalks, period street lamps, trees and benches. In all, more than 100 grand old Victorian buildings were restored to their original splendor. See "Walking Tour" in this chapter for more details.

Founded in 1996 by the San Diego Chinese Historical Society, the **San Diego Chinese Historical Museum** is dedicated to preserving and sharing the Chinese-American experience. Housed in what was formerly a Chinese mission, exhibits run the gamut—from one that reveals the complete history of Chinese tea to one that demystifies Chinese opera. ~ 404 3rd Avenue; 619-338-9888, fax 619-338-9889; www.sdchm.org.

Covering 130 blocks east of the Gaslamp, **East Village** is the largest of San Diego's neighborhoods, and, up until a plan to build PETCO Park here was announced, it was also its most run-down. Now, with the state-of-the-art ballpark in full operation, development is booming. Former warehouses and other old buildings have been transformed into residential lofts appealing to artists and professionals seeking an urban living experience, while the New School of Architecture and San Diego City College attract a young and lively crowd. Big plans are afoot for this neighborhood, with a five-year plan that includes an enter-tainment district and more than 4000 dwellings.

Make a point to visit the **Villa Montezuma–Jesse Shepard House**. This ornate, Queen Anne–style Victorian mansion, mag-nificently restored, was constructed by a wealthy group of San Diegans in 1887 as a gift to a visiting musician. Culture-hungry civic leaders actually "imported" world-famous troubadour Jesse Shepard to live in the opulent dwelling as something of a court musician to the city's upper crust. Shepard stayed only two years but decorated his villa to the hilt with dozens of stained-glass windows and elaborate, hand-carved wood trim and deco-rations. Open Friday through Sunday. Admission. ~ 1925 K Street; 619-239-2211, fax 619-232-6297; www.sandiegohistory.org, e-mail admissions@sandiegohistory.org.

Instead of building its new baseball park in the hinterlands, San Diego decided to plunk **PETCO Park** down in East Village, right in the heart of things, practically spitting distance from the historic Gaslamp Quarter and the harbor. Home to San Diego's beloved Padres baseball team, this is a ballpark with a view, where fans sitting in towers and terraces have panoramic vistas of the bay, the downtown skyline, Balboa Park and the moun-tains. The ballpark prides itself on its comfortable seats, with cup holders and extra leg room. Every one of the 42,000 seats has out-standing sight lines and unobstructed views. ~ 100 Park Boule-vard; 619-795-5012, 877-374-2784 (tickets); www.sandiego.pad res.mlb.com.

Heading back towards the harbor, you'll come across the **Museum of Contemporary Art**'s downtown space, adjacent to the American Plaza Trolley Transfer Station. Two floors and four galleries provide contrast to San Diego's preserved history, and showcase an internationally renowned collection and temporary exhibits featuring cutting-edge contemporary art. Educational tours and a well-stocked bookstore complement the exhibits.

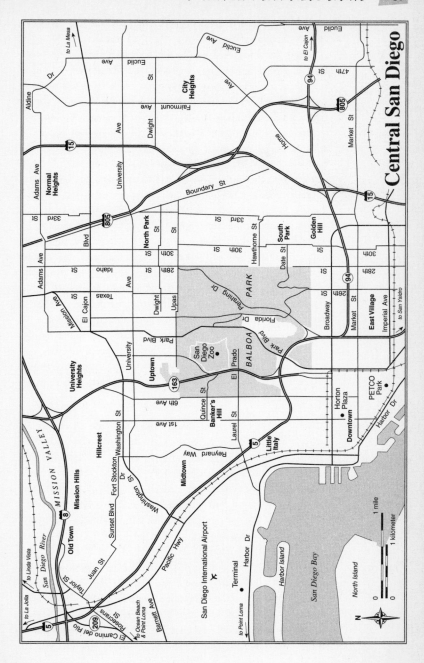

Central San Diego

Closed Wednesday. ~ 1001 Kettner Boulevard at Broadway; 619-234-1001, fax 619-232-4875; www.mcasd.org.

Don't be fooled by its historic 1915 Spanish Mission–Colonial Revival architecture—San Diego's **Santa Fe Depot** is very much a working railway station. A terminus of the nation's second-busiest Amtrak rail corridor, it's used by the San Diego Northern's Coaster commuter trains, and the Mexicoach bus routes, and is also a hub of the San Diego Trolley light rail system. ~ 1050 Kettner Boulevard; 619-239-9021.

In its heyday in the 1920s, San Diego's **Little Italy**, located just north of downtown, was home to thousands of Italian immigrants, many of whom worked in the city's thriving tuna industry. With the waning of the tuna business and the construction of Route 5, the area slipped into decline until the 1990s, when residents and business owners took matters into their own hands. With the help of the Little Italy Association, they began to improve the neighborhood with new and architecturally interesting structures, public art displays and facelifts for some commercial establishments. Today, it's once again a thriving neighborhood full of unique cafés, shops and coffeehouses.

Next door, **Midtown** is one of the city's older neighborhoods. Picture-perfect Victorians serve as both private residences and businesses in an area that appeals to young professionals, empty nesters and anyone looking for a small-town atmosphere in an urban neighborhood.

LODGING   Way before the highrises that surround and shade it were even a twinkle in a developer's eye, the **Cabrillo Garden Inn** was welcoming visitors. Though it's now owned by the Best Western hotel chain, this renovated, two-story, 1950s Spanish-style hotel is a unique property boasting garden surroundings, a convenient downtown location and reasonable prices. Special touches include imported hand-painted Spanish bathroom tiles and hypoallergenic down comforters. ~ 840 A Street; 619-234-8477, fax 619-615-0422. MODERATE.

Among the few budget-priced-but-decent downtown lodgings, **Hotel Churchill** is about the cleanest and most livable. Billed as "small, quaint and unique," this venerable, seven-story, 92-room hotel is mostly quaint. Built in 1915, it was somewhat tastelessly remodeled to "depict an authentic medieval English castle." To really save money during a downtown stay, ask for one of the rooms with a shared bathroom. ~ 827 C Street; 619-234-5186, fax 619-231-9012. BUDGET.

A prime location and bargain prices make the **USA Hostels San Diego** a favorite with younger international travelers. Advertising itself as a place run by backpackers for backpackers, the joint is always jumping, with visitors from all over the world buzzing in and out of this Gaslamp location 24 hours a day (there's no curfew). It has both dorm beds and private rooms, a cable TV room and communal kitchen, and offers a free all-you-

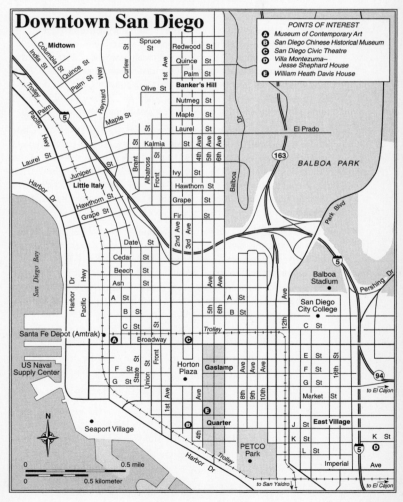

Downtown San Diego

POINTS OF INTEREST
Ⓐ Museum of Contemporary Art
Ⓑ San Diego Chinese Historical Museum
Ⓒ San Diego Civic Theatre
Ⓓ Villa Montezuma–
   Jesse Shephard House
Ⓔ William Heath Davis House

The Gaslamp Quarter

History buffs and lovers of antique buildings should don their walking shoes for a tour of the Gaslamp Quarter, accompanied by a map available at the William Heath Davis House Museum. These 16 blocks contain over 90 historic buildings, most of which now house galleries, shops, restaurants and upscale hotels. Here are a few of the highlights.

WILLIAM HEATH DAVIS HOUSE   Start your tour at the William Heath Davis House. The oldest surviving wooden structure in the downtown area, this 1850 "saltbox" prefabricated family home was framed on the East Coast and shipped around Cape Horn to San Diego. It is now filled with museum exhibits recounting the house's history. Call for museum hours. ~ 410 Island Avenue; 619-233-4692, fax 619-233-4148; www.gaslampquarter.org, e-mail tracey@gaslampquarter.org.

ROYAL PIE BAKERY   Just down the street from the William Heath Davis House is what was once the Royal Pie Bakery. Almost unbelievably, a bakery was on this site from 1871 until 1996. Around the turn of the 20th century, the bakery found itself in the middle of a red-light district, but it didn't stop turning out cakes and pies even though a notorious bordello operated on the second floor. It's now a restaurant. ~ 554 4th Street.

FIFTH AVENUE   Go back down Island Avenue to 5th Avenue and turn left. Not only was this block part of the Stingaree, but it was the heart of San Diego's Chinatown. The **Nanking Café** (now Royal Thai) was the only restaurant on the street when it was built in 1912; today there are 95 restaurants in the Gaslamp. ~ 467 5th Avenue. The nearby **Timken Building**, notable for its fancy arched-brick facade, was erected in 1894. ~ 5th Avenue and Market Street. Across the street is the **Backesto**

can-eat pancake breakfast but, make no mistake, this is a bare-bones facility that provides just the basics for flexible, budget-minded travelers. ~ 726 5th Avenue; 800-438-8622; www.usa hostels.com/sandiego. BUDGET.

Treat yourself to a nice dinner with the money you save staying at **Hostelling International—San Diego Downtown**, also centrally located in the Gaslamp Quarter. Featuring a blue-and-yellow trompe l'oeil mural on the outside, this Mediterranean-style hostelry has 25 sex-segregated dorm facilities and 17 private

Building, a beautifully restored late-19th-century structure. The tall, Romanesque Revival **Keating Building** was one of the most prestigious office buildings in San Diego during the 1890s, complete with such modern conveniences as steam heat and a wire-cage elevator. ~ 5th Avenue and F Street. Next door is the **Ingersoll Tutton Building**. When this 90-foot-long structure was built in 1894 for $20,000 it was the most expensive building on the block! ~ 832 5th Avenue.

COMMERCE ROW   Most of the block on the other side of 5th Avenue, from F up to E streets, represents the most architecturally significant row in the Gaslamp Quarter. From south to north, there's the **Marston Building** on the corner of F Street. Built in 1881, it was downtown San Diego's leading department store. Next is the 1887 **Hubbell Building**, originally a dry goods establishment. The **Nesmith-Greeley Building** next door is another example of the then-fashionable Romanesque Revival style, with its ornamental brick coursing. Featuring twin towers and intricate Baroque Revival architecture, the 1888 **Louis Bank of Commerce** is probably the most beautiful building in the quarter. It originally housed a ground-floor oyster bar that was a favorite haunt of Wyatt Earp. The famous Western lawman-turned-real-estate-speculator resided in San Diego from 1886 to 1893 and operated three Gaslamp Quarter drinking establishments. Be sure to go to the fourth floor to see the beautiful skylight.

CHINESE BENEVOLENT SOCIETY   As you return south through the Gaslamp Quarter, take a short detour west (right) along G Street, then south (left) on 3rd Avenue, to see the Chinese Benevolent Society, established in 1920, when police had shut down the bordellos and the Gaslamp Quarter had became completely Chinese. Today, Chinese holidays are still celebrated in the street in front of the Benevolent Society. ~ 428 3rd Avenue. Continue south to Island Avenue and turn east (left) to return to your starting point.

rooms, as well as a fully equipped kitchen and a common area. There is no curfew. Reservations recommended. ~ 521 Market Street, 619-525-1531, 800-909-4776, fax 619-338-0129; www. sandiegohostels.org, e-mail downtown@sandiegohostels.org. BUDGET.

Chain hotels are normally not included in these listings, but because of the lack of good, low-cost lodgings downtown, I'm compelled to tell you about **Super 8 Bayview**. This 98-room property offers pleasant, affordable rooms downtown. Queen-size beds complement a bright, functional and contemporary environment; you'll also find a pool and jacuzzi here. ~ 1835 Columbia Street; 619-544-0164, 800-537-9902, fax 619-237-9940. MODERATE.

Located in the heart of the Gaslamp Quarter, the **Bristol Hotel** is an elegant boutique hotel that leaves a lasting impression. Its ultra-modern decor creates clean, minimalist lines that are boldly accented with vivid splashes of color. The 102 rooms offer one king-size or two queen beds, and art lovers will revel in the hotel's art collection, which includes works by Peter Max, Andy Warhol, Roy Lichtenstein and other Pop Art greats. ~ 1055 1st Avenue; 619-232-6141, 800-662-4477, fax 619-232-1948; www.thebristolsandiego.com. DELUXE TO ULTRA-DELUXE.

No downtown hotel has a more colorful past than the **Horton Grand Hotel**. This 132-room Victorian gem is actually two old hotels that were disassembled piece by piece and resurrected a few blocks away. The two were lavishly reconstructed and linked by an atrium lobby and courtyard. The 1880s theme is faithfully executed in the hotel's antique-furnished rooms, each of which has a fireplace. Such amenities as a concierge and afternoon tea (served Saturday) combine with friendly service and perfect location to make it one of the city's best hotel values. ~ 311 Island Avenue; 619-544-1886, 800-542-1886, fax 619-239-3823; www.hortongrand.com, e-mail horton@connectnet.com. DELUXE TO ULTRA-DELUXE.

Built in 1910 in honor of the 18th president by his son Ulysses S. Grant, Jr., the **U.S. Grant Hotel** reigned as downtown San Diego's premier hotel for decades. The U.S. Grant is a show-

AUTHOR FAVORITE

Don't be put off by its location across the street from a freeway on-ramp—inside, **The Little Italy Inn** is reminiscent of a European boutique hotel and is blissfully quiet. Each of the rooms in this 1910 building is individually decorated in deep earth tones and rich fabrics, while hand-picked artwork that perfectly complements the decor hangs over the original hardwood floors. Rooms range from those with a shared bath to suites complete with whirlpool tubs and San Diego Bay views. ~ 505 West Grape Street; 619-230-1600, fax 619-230-0322; www.littleitalyhotel.com. MODERATE TO ULTRA-DELUXE.

case boasting 285 rooms, a restaurant and a lounge. It is quite possibly the most elegant and certainly the most beautifully restored historic building in the city. There's a marble-floored lobby with cathedral ceilings and enormous crystal chandeliers. Rooms are richly furnished with mahogany poster beds, Queen Anne–style armoires and wingback chairs. ~ 326 Broadway; 619-232-3121, 800-996-3426, fax 619-232-3626; www.usgrant. net. ULTRA-DELUXE.

A recommended Little Italy hotel is the **Best Western Bayside Inn**. Small enough (122 rooms) to offer some degree of personalized service, this modern highrise promises nearly all the niceties you would pay extra for at more prestigious downtown hotels, including a harbor view. Furnishings and amenities are virtually on a par with those in the typical Hilton or Sheraton. There is a pool and spa, plus a restaurant and cocktail lounge. ~ 555 West Ash Street; 619-233-7500, 800-341-1818, fax 619-239-8060; www.baysideinn.com, e-mail tichotels@sandiego.com. MODERATE.

Located in Little Italy and reminiscent of an unpretentious, small European hotel, **La Pensione** is one of San Diego's best values. The 75 rooms may not be spacious, but they are bright and cheery, and the modest furnishings are enhanced by the intriguing photographs from bygone days that serve as the hotel's artwork. ~ 606 West Date Street; 619-236-8000, 800-232-4683, fax 619-236-8088; www.lapensionehotel.com. MODERATE.

DINING

Visitors to Horton Plaza are bombarded with dining opportunities. But for those who can resist the temptation to chow down on pizza, french fries and enchiladas at nearby fast-food shops, there is a special culinary reward. On the plaza's top level sits **Panda Inn**. Here the plush, contemporary design alludes only subtly to Asia with a scattering of classic artwork. But the menu is all Chinese. Three dishes stand out: crispy beef, lemon scallops and chicken with garlic sauce. Lunch and dinner menus together present more than 100 dishes. Dine on the glassed-in veranda for a great view of the harbor. Brunch on Sunday. ~ 506 Horton Plaza; 619-233-7800, fax 619-233-5632; www.pandainn.com. BUDGET TO DELUXE.

There is no shortage of restaurants in the Gaslamp, either, with the majority offering sidewalk tables from which to watch the passing parade of horse-drawn carriages, bike taxis and pedestrians.

Asti Ristorante, with its exposed red-brick walls, plenty of old photos and other Italian-inspired wall decorations, is a warmly lighted, cozy Italian restaurant serving creative southern Italian fare. Traditional dishes such as osso buco are fork tender, while seafood specialties, such as *gamberoni* (jumbo prawns wrapped in pancetta), are unfailingly fresh and flavorful—and the tiramisu is to die for. On a balmy night the patio is a great place for Gaslamp Quarter people-watching, including the comings and goings at the USA Hostels San Diego next door. ~ 728 5th Avenue; 619-232-8844, fax 619-232-9898; www.astisandiego.com. MODERATE TO DELUXE.

The red-light district was called the Stingaree, after the dangerous sting rays in San Diego Bay—in either place, you were bound to get badly stung.

Fans of the late Jim Croce ("Bad, Bad Leroy Brown," "Time in a Bottle") will surely enjoy a visit to **Croce's Restaurants and Bars**. Located in the heart of the Gaslamp Quarter and managed enthusiastically by Jim's widow, Ingrid Croce, the restaurants feature an eclectic mix of dishes served in a friendly setting. Daily dinner specials vary and are best described as contemporary American, ranging from salads to pasta, beef, chicken and fresh fish. No breakfast or lunch on weekdays. ~ 802 5th Avenue; 619-233-4355, fax 619-232-9836; www.croces.com, e-mail ingrid@croces.com. MODERATE TO DELUXE.

Just down the block, **Dakota Grill & Spirits** occupies two floors of San Diego's first skyscraper (1914). Clad in black, bolo ties in place, the staff bustles around, serving wood-fired pizza, hearty rotisserie meats and grilled seafood whipped up by the cooks in the open kitchen. Among the offerings: grilled pork prime rib with apricot-mustard glaze, chicken breast with honey-mustard sauce and seafood fettuccini in cream sauce. There's piano music Wednesday through Saturday. ~ 901 5th Avenue; 619-234-5554; www.cohnrestaurants.com, e-mail info@cohnrestaurants.com. MODERATE TO DELUXE.

Though **The Gaslamp Strip Club** bills itself as a "21-years-and-up establishment," it's not a girlie joint. But it is patterned after the dark, moody steakhouses of bygone days. Artwork by famous 1940s pinup artist Alberto Vargas hangs on the exposed red-brick walls, while customers sip martinis in cozy semicircular black-leatherette booths. What makes the club unique, however, is that the choice cuts of prime beef are cooked by diners over the gas-fired grills dotted around the restaurant. Not only does this assure you that the meat is just as you like it, but there's no telling who you might meet over a hot grill. Dinner only. ~ 340 5th Avenue; 619-231-3140, fax 619-231-3119; www.gas lampstripclub.signonsandiego.com. MODERATE TO DELUXE.

History, atmosphere and great cooking combine to make dining at **Ida Bailey's Restaurant** a memorable experience. Located in the Horton Grand Hotel, Ida's was once a brothel, operated back in the 1890s by a madam of the same name. Things are tamer now, but the rich Victorian furnishings serve as a reminder of San Diego's opulent past. The chef serves a varied menu highlighted by old-fashioned American fare, including Victorian pot roast, rack of lamb, and tenderloin. Breakfast, lunch and dinner are served. ~ 311 Island Avenue; 619-544-1886, fax 619-239-3823; www.hortongrand.com, e-mail horton@connectnet.com. MODERATE TO DELUXE.

With its proximity to the border, San Diego is flush with Mexican restaurants, but few are as elegant and authentic as **Las Fajitas**, which is really more Mexico City than Tijuana. The decor includes an antique wooden bar and mahogany-framed mirrors, accented by brightly colored table linens. Though fajitas are the house specialty, the Mexican-style seafood dishes are also delicious. Try the *camarones al chipotle*, large shrimp sautéed in a creamy sauce made with chipotle chili, green tomatillo, onion and garlic, or the fresh fish, shrimp and scallop ceviche. ~ 628 5th Avenue; 619-232-4242, fax 619-531-7474; www.diningonfifth.com. MODERATE TO DELUXE.

Twinkling candlelight dances over walls covered in murals of life in rural India, the music is pure Bombay and the smells are richly spiced and exotic. At **Monsoon**, the staff breezes around in Nehru jackets, serving the very tastiest Indian cuisine, which relies heavily on tandoori cooking flavored with coconut milk, cumin and curry. In cozy booths and high-back chairs, patrons dine on such succulent entrées as shrimp simmered in cream, cardamom and ginger and lamb combined with vegetables, rice, homemade cheese, pistachios and almonds. ~ 729 4th Avenue; 619-234-5555, 800-666-7666; www.monsoonrestaurant.com. MODERATE.

Mister Tiki Mai Tai Lounge is a Polynesian restaurant with flair. Liquor-laden umbrella drinks are accompanied by updated versions of traditional *pupus* and entrées such as lemongrass shrimp tempura and cashew-crusted chicken chow mein. Blown-glass lights in the shape of fish dangle over the tables and giant wooden tikis lurk in the corners. ~ 801 5th Avenue; 619-233-1183; www.cohnrestaurants.com. MODERATE TO DELUXE.

For the richly flavored tastes of Persia, head for **Sadaf** in the Gaslamp Quarter. Copies of classic Persian art hang on the walls of this simply furnished restaurant where secret family recipes are cooked to perfection. Thanks in part to their high-temperature grill, meat, chicken and fish are perfectly seared on the outside, tender and juicy within. The saffron-infused chicken kabobs melt in your mouth and are perfectly complemented by basmati rice mixed with lentils, raisins, dates and saffron. Start with an appetizer like the stuffed grape leaves or the sautéed eggplant with onion, garlic, yogurt and fried mint, and end with Persian ice cream. On weekends, a belly dancer adds to the Middle Eastern experience. ~ 828 5th Avenue; 619-338-0008, fax 619-338-0009; www.sadafrestaurants.com. MODERATE.

A suit of armor marks the entrance to **Sevilla**. Inside, clouds float across the ceiling, red-tiled roofs and striped awnings extend from walls with shuttered windows and gaslamps dot the dining room, evoking the festive atmosphere of a Spanish plaza. Over glasses of sangria, diners combine plates of *tapas* (*bocadillos*, marinated lamb, empanadas) or indulge in full-size traditional meals such as *zarzuela* (a savory seafood stew) and paella. Save room for the equally marvelous desserts. Dinner only. ~ 555 4th Avenue; 619-233-5979; www.cafesevilla.com. MODERATE TO DELUXE.

The Tin Fish, conveniently located across from the Convention Center, serves the freshest fish at easy-on-the-wallet prices. Orders for specialties such as fish-and-chips and tacos made with cod, swordfish, salmon or halibut are taken at the counter and the generous portions devoured al fresco, in front of a periodically erupting fountain. No dinner Monday through Friday. ~ 170 6th Avenue; 619-238-8100; www.thetinfish.net, tin.man@thetinfish.net. BUDGET TO MODERATE.

HIDDEN ►   To say that **Pokez Mexican Restaurant**'s clientele is diverse would be an understatement. This is a local favorite with everyone from purple-haired punk rockers with multiple body piercings to corporate attorneys in three-piece suits. It is certainly not the place to come for the service, which is slipshod at best, nor for atmosphere, which, with its formica tables, plastic plants and a few Mexican wall decorations, could best be described as south of the border meets funk. But it is the place to come for top-notch Mexican cuisine at bargain prices. While the traditional dishes, such as *carne asada* and enchiladas, are great, the real standouts are the vegetarian entrées. There are more than 30 veggie dishes on the menu, including fake "chorizo" burritos and tofu tostada salad, and many can be made vegan upon request. ~ 947 E Street; 619-702-7160. BUDGET.

An environmentally friendly restaurant, **Orbit Earth Cafe** is short on atmosphere but long on healthy and creative sandwiches, such as caesar salad, tomato and turkey wrapped in a spinach tortilla or raw veggies on warm pita bread. The best place to watch Little Italy's passing parade is at an outside table. Breakfast and lunch Monday through Friday. Closed weekends. ~ 610 West Ash Street #100; 619-595-0322, fax 619-595-0350; www.orbit earthcafe.com, e-mail chefsteve@orbitearthcafe.com. BUDGET.

◄ HIDDEN

Sitting in **Vincenzo Ristorante**'s cozy dining room, with its yellow-ochre walls, trompe l'oeil window and door murals and blue-clothed, flower-decked tables is like being transported to a small Italian trattoria. Appropriately located in Little Italy, adjacent to La Pensione hotel, this award-winning family-owned restaurant serves Italian specialties such as a paella risotto and osso buco at reasonable prices. No lunch on Saturday and Sunday. ~ 1702 India Street; 619-702-6180. MODERATE.

AUTHOR FAVORITE

Hob Nob Hill is the kind of restaurant where motherly waitresses in uniforms and aprons know all the regulars by name, may just call you honey and never let your coffee cup reach empty. They've been serving up hearty homecooked meals from this Midtown location since 1946. The dark wooden booths and patterned carpets are reminiscent of the 1950s, as are some of the better-than-your-mother-cooked, stick-to-your-ribs specialties, such as chicken and dumplings, roast beef hash and meatloaf with mashed potatoes. This is a primo place for breakfast, which may include warm cinnamon and pecan rolls fresh from the onsite bakery. Open for breakfast, lunch and dinner. ~ 2271 1st Avenue; 619-239-8176, fax 619-239-5856; www.hobnobhill.com. BUDGET TO MODERATE.

SHOPPING   The **Westfield Shoppingtown Horton Plaza** is anchored by three department stores, and a flood of specialty and one-of-a-kind shops complete the picture. Along the tiled boulevard are shops and vendors peddling their wares. ~ Between Broadway and G Street, 1st and 4th avenues; 619-239-8180; www.westfield.com.

On the second level, the **San Diego City Store** (619-238-2489) sells retired street signs, key chains and the like. There are men's apparel shops, shoe stores, jewelry shops and women's haute couture boutiques, dozens of stores in all.

The **Gaslamp Quarter** is a charming 16-block assemblage of shops, galleries and sidewalk cafés in the downtown center. Faithfully replicated in the quarter are Victorian-era street lamps, red-brick sidewalks and window displays thematic of turn-of-the-20th-century San Diego.

A favorite spot for antique lovers is **The Cracker Factory**, which offers three floors of antiques and collectibles in the restored 1913 Bishop Cracker Factory. Legend has it that there is a resident ghost here named "Crunch" who shuffles through mounds of broken crackers searching for a small brass cookie cutter. ~ 448 West Market Street; 619-233-1669.

Other intriguing Gaslamp Quarter shops include **Le Travel Store**, which sells innovative and hard-to-find travel gear, packs and luggage, guidebooks, maps and travel accessories—there's even a travel agency inside the store. ~ 745 4th Avenue; 619-544-0005; www.letravelstore.com. **Palace Loan & Jewelry** offers top-of-the-line pre-owned merchandise at bargain prices in a building that once housed a saloon and gambling parlor owned by Wyatt Earp. Closed Sunday. ~ 951 4th Avenue; 619-234-3175.

You can watch Cuban exiles roll *panatelas, toropedos, presidentes* and *robustos* from Cuban-seed tobacco grown in other parts of the Caribbean at the **Cuban Cigar Factory**. ~ 551 5th Avenue; 619-238-2429; www.cubancigarfactory.com.

HIDDEN ▶   Chocolaholics won't want to miss **Chi Chocolat** in Little Italy. Whether you're popping creamy bonbons or sipping a chocolate-sweetened espresso drink, a trip to this upscale chocolatier is a thrill for your sweet tooth. ~ 2021 India Street; 619-501-9215, fax 619-501-9216; www.chichocolat.com.

NIGHTLIFE   The sun is certainly the main attraction in San Diego, but the city also features a rich and varied nightlife, offering the night owl everything from traditional folk music to high-energy discos. There are piano bars, singles bars and a growing number of jazz clubs.

Call the **San Diego Performing Arts League** for its monthly arts calendar and information about inexpensive events. ~ 619-238-0700; www.sandiegoperforms.com. KIFM Radio (98.1 FM) hosts **Jazz Hotline**, a 24-hour information line that provides the latest in jazz happenings. ~ 619-543-1401.

THE BEST BARS   In the Gaslamp Quarter, **5th Quarter** has live entertainment nightly, usually featuring house bands. Occasional cover. ~ 600 5th Avenue; 619-236-1616; www. 5quarter.com.

Lawman Wyatt Earp once ran three gambling halls in the Gaslamp Quarter.

4th & B features national musical acts and well-known comedians. ~ 345 B Street; 619-231-4343; www.4thandb.com.

It's a nonstop party at the **Bitter End**, a three-level bar and nightclub that has something to offer everyone. Top-40 music complete with videos is blasted on the first level, high-energy dance music can be found on the second and a more mellow crowd kicks back to jazz on the top level. Cover. ~ 770 4th Avenue; 619-338-9300; www.bitterend.com.

Fans of the immortal Jim Croce will love **Croce's Jazz Bar** (619-233-4355), built as a memorial to the late singer-songwriter by his wife, Ingrid. Family mementos line the walls in tribute to a talented recording artist. Live entertainment nightly. Just next door, **Croce's Top Hat Bar** (619-233-6945) is a snazzy New Orleans–style club featuring live R&B. Closed Sunday through Thursday. Cover. ~ 802–820 5th Avenue; www.croces.com.

Though it boasts more than 54 imported beers and is called **Henry's Pub**, this club is actually owned by transplants from Finland. Dance to live music Tuesday through Thursday, or hog the spotlight on Sunday, karaoke night. If you dare, try a Finnish Guinness, a lethal combination of vodka, Kahlua and Guinness. ~ 618 5th Avenue; 619-238-2389, fax 619-557-0538; www.henryspub.com.

Live bands play nightly at **Jimmy Love's**, located in a historic, late-1800s "Old City Hall" building and appealing to young professionals. The emphasis is on jazz and blues, with a little disco thrown in for good measure. ~ 672 5th Avenue; 619-595-0123, fax 619-233-7056; www.jimmyloves.com.

Karl Strauss Restaurant and Brewery Downtown may well have the best beer in town—San Diego's original microbrew. ~ 1157 Columbia Street; 619-234-2739; www.karlstrauss.com.

A tony place, the **Onyx and Thin** are two dimly but warmly lighted rooms, one with a piano player crooning lounge tunes, the other offering live jazz or a deejay. Dozens of colored bottles line the bar, while music fans sit around small tables in red chairs. Cover on Friday and Saturday. ~ 852 5th Avenue; 619-235-6699, fax 619-702-6699.

Plaza Bar, at the distinctive Westgate Hotel, is a graceful period-French lounge where prominent locals and visitors enjoy classy piano entertainment nightly. ~ 1055 2nd Avenue; 619-238-1818, www.westgatehotel.com.

HIDDEN ► The stark warehouse setting tells you that **Dizzy's** is strictly about the music. This East Village club offers no bar, no gimmicks and not much ambience, just quality music by serious jazz, folk, blues or world beat artists. Closed Sunday through Tuesday. Cover. ~ 344 7th Avenue; 858-270-7467.

HIDDEN ► There's no hard liquor served, but the young hip clientele seems quite happy swilling sangria, beer or sake in **The Rosary Room** where, surrounded by dark-red glazed walls, original art and rosary beads by the score, they listen to live indie and punk bands. ~ 947 E Street; 619-702-7160.

The action at the **Chee Chee Club,** a local cruise bar and the oldest gay establishment in San Diego, revolves around shooting pool and playing pinball. Occasional performers present shows for the mostly male crowd. ~ 929 Broadway; 619-234-4404.

A young, hip, mixed crowd patronizes Little Italy's **Six Degrees** on any given night, as well as for weekday happy hours and Sunday barbecue. Customers enjoy karaoke on Wednesday and Sunday. Entertainment is split between live bands and deejays playing Top-40 and hip-hop. Occasional cover. ~ 3175 India Street; 619-296-6789.

The Casbah has hosted the likes of Nirvana and Smashing Pumpkins, among others, before they made it big. Rock, punk, rockabilly and pop bands rock out nightly at this San Diego institution for live alternative music. Cover. ~ 2501 Kettner Boulevard; 619-232-4355; www.casbahmusic.com.

THEATER   In addition to performances of the San Diego Opera, the **San Diego Civic Theatre** presents a variety of entertainment ranging from pop artists to plays to dance performances. ~ 1100 3rd Avenue; 619-570-1100; www.sandiegotheatres.org.

The **San Diego Repertory Theatre** performs dramas, comedies and musicals. ~ At the Lyceum, 79 Horton Plaza; 619-544-1000; www.sandiegorep.com.

The **Asian American Repertory Theatre** produces three or four plays a year, performed in several locations. Though many are by Asian-American authors, non-Asian plays are also performed so that audiences may experience Asian Americans simply as actors. ~ 888-568-2278; www.asianamericanrep.org.

> If you're a culture vulture with a limited pocketbook, try Times Arts Tix, a 24-hour recording listing half-price theater, music and dance tickets. ~ 619-497-5000.

OPERA AND DANCE   With performances at the San Diego Civic Theatre, the **San Diego Opera** presents such international stars as Patricia Racette, Ferruccio Furlanetto and Anja Henteros. The season runs from January through May. ~ 1100 3rd Avenue; 619-232-7636, fax 619-231-6915; www.sdopera.com.

California Ballet Company and School presents a diverse repertoire of contemporary and traditional ballets at area theaters. ~ 4819 Ronson Court; 858-560-5676; www.californiaballet.org.

East Village's **Sushi Performance & Visual Art** is committed to the most contemporary performance, dance and visual art. Not afraid to take risks and push boundaries, these artists are encouraged to perform groundbreaking and controversial works. ~ Until 2006, Sushi is performing at other venues until their performance space at 320 11th Avenue is renovated; 619-235-8466; www.sushiart.org.

◄ HIDDEN

Balboa Park and the San Diego Zoo

It's unclear as to whether it was intelligent foresight or unbridled optimism that prompted the establishment of Balboa Park. Certain that a fine neighborhood would flourish around it, city fathers in 1868 set aside 1400 acres of rattlesnake-infested hillside above "New Town" as a public park. The park's eventual development, and most of its lovely Spanish Baroque buildings, came as the result of two world's fairs—The Panama–California Exposition of 1915–16 and the California–Pacific International Exposition of 1935–36.

Today, Balboa Park ranks among the largest and finest of America's city parks. Wide avenues and walkways curve through luxurious subtropical foliage leading to nine major museums, three art galleries, four theaters, picnic groves, the world's largest zoo, a golf course and countless other recreation facilities. Its verdant grounds teem with cyclists, joggers, skaters, picnickers, weekend artists and museum mavens.

SIGHTS   The main entrance is from 6th Avenue onto Laurel Street, which becomes El Prado as you cross Cabrillo Bridge. Begin your visit at the **Balboa Park Visitors Center**, located on the northeast corner of Plaza de Panama. You'll find plenty of free pamphlets and maps on the park. ~ House of Hospitality, 1549 El Prado; 619-239-0512; www.balboapark.org.

From here you can stroll about, taking in Balboa Park's main attractions. To the right, as you head east on the pedestrian-only section of El Prado, is the **Casa de Balboa**. This building houses several worthwhile museums, including the **San Diego Model Railroad Museum** (619-696-0199, fax 619-696-0239; www.sd modelrailroadm.com, e-mail sdmodrailm@abac.com), which features the largest permanent model railroad layouts in North America. Children under 15 enter free. Closed Monday. Here, too, is the **San Diego Historical Society**'s extensive collection of documents and photographs spanning the urban history of San Diego. Closed Monday and Tuesday. The **Museum of Photographic Arts** (619-238-7559, fax 619-238-8777; www.mopa.org, e-mail info@mopa.org) has exhibits of internationally known photographers. Admission, except on the second Tuesday of the month.

Continuing east to the fountain, you'll see the **Reuben H. Fleet Science Center** on your right. Among the park's finest attractions, it features one of the largest planetariums and the world's first IMAX dome theater. The galleries offer various hands-on exhibits and displays dealing with modern phenomena. Admission. ~ 619-238-1233, fax 619-685-5771; www.rhfleet.org.

Across the courtyard is the **San Diego Natural History Museum**, with displays devoted mostly to the natural heritage of Southern California and Baja. Traveling exhibitions and giant-screen films cover more global topics. Admission. ~ 619-232-3821, fax 619-232-0248; www.sdnhm.org, e-mail lenstad@sdnhm.org.

Going back along El Prado, take a moment to admire your reflection in the **Lily Pond**, with the old, latticed **Botanical Building** in the background. The scene is a favorite among photographers. The fern collection inside is equally striking.

Next is the **Timken Museum of Art,** considered to have one of the West Coast's finest collections of European and early American paintings. The displays include works by Rembrandt and Copley, as well as an amazing collection of Russian icons. Closed Monday and the month of September. ~ 619-239-5548, fax 619-531-9640; www.timkenmuseum.org, e-mail info@timkenmuseum.org.

Right next door on the plaza is the **San Diego Museum of Art,** with an entrance facade patterned after the University of Salamanca in Spain. The museum's treasures include a permanent collection of Italian Renaissance, Dutch and Spanish Baroque paintings and sculpture, a display of Asian art, a gallery of Impressionist paintings, contemporary art and an American

collection, as well as touring exhibitions. Closed Monday. Admission. ~ 619-232-7931, fax 619-232-9367; www.sdmart.com, e-mail info@sdmart.org.

HIDDEN ►

Across El Prado from the Museum of Art is the **Mingei International Museum**. The Mingei (which means "art of the people" and is pronounced min-gay), has a superb collection of folk art, crafts and design from countries around the world. Closed Monday. Admission. ~ 1439 El Prado; 619-239-0003, fax 619-239-0605; www.mingei.org, e-mail mingei@mingei.org.

The grandest of all Balboa Park structures, built as the centerpiece for the 1915 Panama–California Exposition, is the 200-foot Spanish Renaissance **California Tower**. The **San Diego Museum of Man**, at the base of the tower, is a must for anthropology buffs and those interested in Egyptian mummies and American Indian cultures. Admission. ~ 619-239-2001, fax 619-239-2749; www.museumofman.org.

Balboa Park's museums charge an admission fee, but every Tuesday select museums can be visited free.

The southern portion of the park hosts more intriguing structures. The teahouse created for the Panama–California Exposition was expanded over the years into the lovely, two-acre **Japanese Friendship Garden**. Take a meditative stroll along its winding paths, past a Zen garden, a koi-filled pond, a bonsai exhibit and various works of art. Tea is still served in the Tea Pavilion. Closed Monday from Labor Day to Memorial Day. Admission. ~ 2215 Pan American Way; 619-231-0048; www.niwa.org.

Practically next door is the **Spreckels Organ Pavilion**. Those 4416 pipes make it the world's largest outdoor instrument of its kind.

The **San Diego Aerospace Museum**, several blocks south of the plaza, is not to be missed. It contains over 65 aircraft, including a replica of Charles Lindbergh's famous *Spirit of St. Louis*, the original of which was built in San Diego. Also on display is *Black Bird*, the world's fastest plane. Admission. ~ 619-234-8291; www.aerospacemuseum.org, e-mail info@aerospace museum.org.

Sports fans will want to take in the **Hall of Champions Sports Museum** in the historic Federal Building. It houses the Breitbard Hall of Fame and exhibits that feature world-class San Diego athletes from more than 40 sports. The museum also has an interactive sports center. Admission. ~ 2131 Pan-American Plaza; 619-234-2544, fax 619-234-4543; www.sandiegosports.org.

You'll want to attend a play at the **Old Globe** to absorb the full greatness of this Tony Award–winning stage, but for starters you can stroll around the 581-seat theater, famed for its annual Shakespeare festival. Located in a grove on the north side of California Tower, the Old Globe is part of the trio of theaters that includes the Cassius Carter Centre Stage and the outdoor Lowell Davies Festival Theatre. Admission. ~ 619-239-2255; www.oldglobe.org, e-mail tickets@theoldglobe.org.

Designed by San Diego architects William Hebbard and Irving Gill in 1905, **Marston House** sits on five acres of landscaped grounds in Balboa Park. The furnishings rely heavily on artifacts from the American Arts and Crafts Movement, which are in harmony with the function and simplicity of the house's design. ~ 3525 7th Avenue; 619-298-3142, 858-292-0455; www.sandiegohistory.org/mainpages/locate3.htm.

SAN DIEGO ZOO   North of the Balboa Park museum and theater complex is the **San Diego Zoo**, which needs no introduction. It quite simply is the world's top-rated zoo. The numbers alone are mind-boggling: 4000 animals, representing 800 species, spread out over 100 acres. Most of these wild animals live in surroundings as natural as human beings can make them. Rather than cages there are glass enclosures where orangutans roam free on grassy islands and multihued birds fly through tropical rainforests. All around is a manmade jungle forest overgrown with countless species of rare and exotic plants.

Of particular merit is "Polar Bear Plunge." Here you can watch the polar bears as they gracefully swim underwater in their deep saltwater bay. At "Ituri Forest," hippos Funani and Kiboko delight all with their infamous underwater ballet. The zoo's state-of-the-art primate exhibit, the "Gorilla Tropics," is a two-and-a-half-acre African rainforest that is home to eight lowland gorillas and hundreds of jungle birds. Within this area is "Pygmy Chimps at Bonobo Road," home to frolicsome troupes of pygmy chimps and Angolan colobus monkeys. At the nearby "Sun Bear Forest," an equatorial rainforest, you'll encounter Bornean sun bears and lion-tailed macaques. One of the first pandas to be born and survive in captivity can be seen at the "Panda Research Station."

At the Children's Zoo, where there are just as many adults as kids, you can watch a large variety of bugs crawling around, and there's a petting zoo. Don't miss the pygmy marmosets. They are the world's smallest monkeys, weighing in at only four ounces when full grown. For a bird's-eye view of the entire San Diego Zoo, you can take the "Skyfari," an aerial tramway. Admission. ~ Located off Park Boulevard; 619-234-3153, fax 619-231-0249; www.sandiegozoo.org.

LODGING   My vote for the prettiest and most hospitable of San Diego's bed and breakfasts goes to the **Keating House**. This historically designated 1888 Victorian home in a sunny hillside residential neighborhood between Balboa Park and downtown offers nine comfy-cozy rooms—seven in the main house and two in the cottage out back. The cottage rooms feature private baths. Beneath its gabled roof, hexagonal turreted window and conical peak, this beautifully restored Queen Anne is every bit as nice inside. A garden completes the homey scene. ~ 2331 2nd Avenue; 619-239-8585, 800-995-8644, fax 619-239-5774; www.keatinghouse. com, e-mail inn@keatinghouse.com. MODERATE TO DELUXE.

The best value for your dollar among reasonably priced hotels in the area is the 67-room **Comfort Inn**. It features wood furniture, designer color schemes, and high-grade carpeting. The inn has a pool-size jacuzzi and serves a continental breakfast. It's conveniently located near Balboa Park, just a few blocks from the city center. ~ 719 Ash Street; 619-232-2525, 800-404-6835, fax 619-687-3024; www.comfortinnsandiego.com. MODERATE TO DELUXE.

Dmitri's Guesthouse offers five rooms, two with shared bath. Each suite comes with a ceiling fan and a refrigerator (one includes a full kitchen). Feel free to shed your clothing on the sundeck and immerse yourself in the hot tub or swimming pool. Situated in a century-old house, Dmitri's serves a continental breakfast poolside every morning. Reservations recommended. ~ 931 21st Street; 619-238-5547; www.dmitris.com, e-mail dmitrisbb@aol.com. MODERATE TO DELUXE.

An old hotel with a colorful past, including its popularity with the Hollywood film community of in the 1920s, **Park Manor Suites Hotel** is a definite throwback. Old-fashioned clubby furniture from the mid-20th century decorates the large rooms. A generous continental breakfast and parking are free. ~ 525 Spruce Street; 619-291-0999, 800-874-2649; www.park manorsuites.com. MODERATE.

A cozy little red tile–roofed retreat in a residential neighborhood, **Casa-Granada** consists of three individually furnished suites, which can either be rented out separately or opened up to turn the whole house into one unit. Each suite has a separate entrance, full kitchen or kitchenette, separate sitting or living room and cable TV. ~ 1720 Granada Avenue; 619-501-5911, 866-524-2312, fax 619-501-5912; www.casa-granada.com. MODERATE TO DELUXE.

◀ HIDDEN

DINING

When you're visiting the San Diego Zoo, consider **Albert's Restaurant**. Named for the gorilla that once occupied the area, this sit-down eatery offers a variety of salads, sandwiches, fresh pastas and fish and meat entrées. No dinner except in summer (late June through Labor Day). ~ 2920 Zoo Drive, the San Diego Zoo; 619-685-3200, fax 619-685-3204; www.sandiegozoo.org. MODERATE TO DELUXE.

Lovers of tea who need a break from Balboa Park museumhopping will find 90 varieties on hand in **The Tea Pavilion** at the Japanese Friendship Garden. Sit at a patio table and get as adventurous as you dare with teas that range from Earl Grey to kelp with plum. Traditional Japanese dishes and sushi are also available. Closed Monday from Labor Day to Memorial Day. ~ 2215 Pan American Way; 619-231-0048; www.niwa.org. MODERATE.

AUTHOR FAVORITE

Located in Balboa Park's House of Hospitality is the **Prado Restaurant**, surrounded by lovely Spanish terraces and burbling fountains. Pasta, seafood, poultry and meat dishes here blend Latin and Italian flavors. For lunch, you may find fancy panini sandwiches, pasta and fish tacos, while dinner choices might include wild-mushroom risotto, grilled jumbo prawns in coconut broth and honey chipotle–marinated ribeye steak; the dessert menu is equally mouth-watering. Patio seating and a pitcher of sangria are a must during the warm months. No dinner on Monday. ~ 1549 El Prado; 619-557-9441, fax 619-557-9170; www.pradobalboa. com. MODERATE TO ULTRA-DELUXE.

A couple of San Diego's better restaurant finds lie just west of the park. **Fifth and Hawthorn** is a neighborhood sensation, but not many tourists find their way to this chic little room. The owners present an array of tasty Pacific Rim dishes, and specialize in fresh seafood such as sea bass, halibut and salmon. Usually available is filet mignon with green peppercorn and cabernet sauce. No lunch on weekends. ~ 515 Hawthorn Street at 5th Avenue; 619-544-0940, fax 619-544-0941. MODERATE TO DELUXE.

As its name suggests, **Liaison** is an intimate bistro with beautiful French doors, a wood-burning fireplace and a patio with a waterfall. Add candlelight and superb French cuisine and you're talking about the perfect place for a rendezvous. The five- or six-course, prix-fixe dinner varies and may include lamb curry served with rice, medallions of filet mignon with béarnaise sauce and salmon served in a crayfish-butter sauce. Or select dishes à la carte. For a romantic dinner, this place comes highly praised. Reservations are recommended. Dinner only. Closed Sunday and Monday. ~ 2202 4th Avenue; 619-234-5540; www.liaisonsandiego.com. MODERATE TO DELUXE.

Laurel Restaurant & Bar is definitely a splurge eatery. This is where San Diego's movers and shakers dine in elegant surroundings on gourmet entrées such as duck confit and chicken provençal roasted in a clay pot. It has a buzzing bar and top-notch jazz musicians performing live. Dinner only. ~ 505 Laurel Street; 619-239-2222, fax 619-239-6822; www.laurelrestaurant.com. ULTRA-DELUXE.

SHOPPING A haven for art-lovers is **Spanish Village Art Center**. Over 35 studios are staffed by artists displaying their work and giving daily demonstrations. For sale are original paintings, sculpture, hand-blown glass and fine jewelry. ~ 1770 Village Place, near the San Diego Zoo entrance; 619-233-9050, fax 619-239-9226; www.spanishvillageart.com.

NIGHTLIFE The **Globe Theatres** present classic and contemporary plays, including Shakespeare with innovative twists, in three Balboa Park theaters. ~ Balboa Park; 619-239-2255; www.theoldglobe.org.

To the west of Balboa Park is **Bertrand at Mr. A's**, the critics' choice for "best drinking with a view." The atmosphere at this

elegant restaurant is one of monied luxury, and gentlemen are expected (but not required) to wear a jacket. ~ 2550 5th Avenue,
12th floor; 619-239-1377.

You'll likely find a line out the door at **Extraordinary
Desserts**. The reason? An agonizing array of decadent, French-
style creations that will sate any sweet tooth. Tables, both indoor
and patio, are often in short supply, so don't be shy about nab-
bing the first one you see. Located on a quiet block at the western edge of the park. ~ 2929 5th Avenue; 619-294-7001.

Reminiscent of the 1960s, when the Rat Pack hung around
lounges like this, the **Imperial House** is the place to sip a perfectly
blended martini in aristocratically wood-paneled surroundings.
The place is a hangout for 40- and 50-something regulars, who
trip the light fantastic on the tiny dance floor to live music on the
weekends. Closed Monday. ~ 505 Kalmia Street; 619-234-3525,
fax 619-239-5406; www.imperialhouse.net.

Hillcrest & Uptown

Ironically, it's thanks to the strong presence of
the U.S. Navy that San Diego has such a significant gay scene. After World War II, thousands of newly discharged men and women who had discovered
their sexual identities during their military service opted to remain in places like San Diego and San Francisco instead of returning home. The longtime military presence contributed to the
fairly conservative personality of San Diego's gay community,
but a more liberalizing effect began to take place in the 1960s
with the arrival of the University of California–San Diego in La
Jolla. Today, San Diego's gay and lesbian community is more out

URBAN IMPROVEMENT

Since the **Utility Art Box Project** began, more than 80 utility boxes
around town have been transformed by local artists. This innovative project
encourages volunteer artists to use the utility boxes that house the
switches, fuses and cables for streetlights and stoplights as blank canvases
for self-expression, turning these gray and green eyesores into brightly
colored works of art. Check out "Cow-mouflage" on 6th Avenue between University and Robinson Avenues. ~ www.uptownpartner
ship.org/projects.htm

than it's ever been, and the center of attention is the section of town just to the northwest of Balboa Park called Hillcrest.

The '50s architecture and neon signage give the area a campy feel (an actual neon sign, which works intermittently, hangs across University Avenue at 5th Avenue and signals your entrance into Hillcrest). Bookstores, trendy boutiques and coffee shops line University Avenue, 5th Avenue and Robinson Street—all within easy walking distance of one another. And because Hillcrest boasts some of the best movie houses and restaurants in San Diego, you'll see everyone there: gay yuppies, leather-clad lesbians, stylish hipsters and Ozzie and Harriet look-alikes.

LODGING   Since many of its guests hail from outside the U.S., the **Hillcrest Inn** considers itself an international hotel. Right at the hub of Hillcrest activity, the 45 modestly furnished rooms, outfitted with microwaves and refrigerators, provide guests with a comfortable stay. Fatigued wayfarers will appreciate the sunning patio and spa after long days of sightseeing. ~ 3754 5th Avenue; 619-293-7078, 800-258-2280, fax 619-293-3861; www.hillcrest inn.net, e-mail hillcrestinn@juno.com. BUDGET TO MODERATE.

The **Balboa Park Inn** is a popular caravansary with gays and straights alike. Like Balboa Park nearby, the four-building inn was built in 1915 for the Panama–California Exposition. Its 26 rooms are decorated in different themes; you can choose to luxuriate in *Gone With the Wind*'s "Tara Suite," get sentimental in "1930s Paris" or go wild in "Greystoke." Some suites boast jacuzzi tubs, kitchens and faux fireplaces, and everyone can request a continental breakfast served in bed. A courtyard and sun terrace round out the facilities at this winsome getaway. Reservations recommended. ~ 3402 Park Boulevard; 619-298-0823, 800-938-8181, fax 619-294-8070; www.balboaparkinn.com, e-mail info@balboaparkinn.com. MODERATE TO ULTRA-DELUXE.

DINING   Although it's located in a nondescript strip mall, **Bai Yook** has been declared to be the most authentic Thai restaurant in the city.

HIDDEN ►   Entrées can be made with beef, chicken or shrimp, or left vegetarian, and the table trays of chilis and spices mean you can satisfy your palate, whether mild or hot, hot, hot. ~ 1260 University Avenue; 619-296-2700; www.baiyookthaicuisine.com. BUDGET.

Lovers of thin-crust pizza and plenty of New York attitude won't be disappointed at **Bronx Pizza**. The joint is tiny, the music is deafening and the guys behind the counter are in constant motion. Buy it by the slice or whole, and don't forget to load on the garlic powder, oregano, parmesan cheese and pepper flakes. Closed Sunday. ~ 111 Washington Street; 619-291-3341. BUDGET.

Anyone looking for an easy-on-the-wallet but crazily creative meal won't want to miss **Cafe on Park**. Large portions of healthy-California meets greasy-spoon fare include such unusual offerings as peanut butter and jelly quesadillas, pancakes stuffed with Cap'n Crunch cereal and blackberries and meatloaf spaghetti with roasted tomatoes. No dinner on Sunday. Closed Monday. ~ 3831 Park Boulevard; 619-293-7275, fax 619-293-7275. BUDGET.

Judging by the name itself, you'd think **Hamburger Mary's** was a typical burger joint. It peddles burgers, yes, but with washboards, surfboards and murals decorating the walls, it definitely ain't typical. Besides hamburgers, you'll find steak and halibut dinners, vegetarian plates and salads, which can be eaten outdoors on the patio. Afterward, you'll want to join the festivities at Kickers, the gay country-and-western bar in the same building. Sunday brunch is also served. ~ 308 University Avenue; 619-

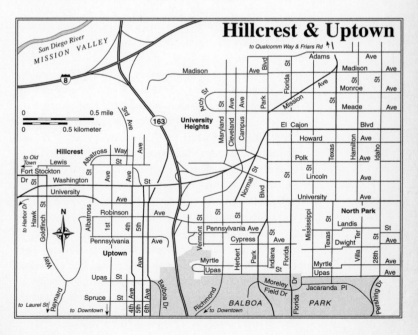

491-0400, fax 619-491-0160; www.hamburgermarys.com, e-mail mary@hamburgermarys.com. BUDGET TO MODERATE.

HIDDEN ▶

Bread-lovers will think they have landed in paradise when they enter **Bread & Cie**. The aroma of fig, jalapeño, cheese and rosemary breads lingers in this amazing bakery, which also serves sandwiches, pastries and cappuccinos. Be prepared to wait at lunchtime. ~ 350 University Avenue; 619-683-9322, fax 619-683-9299; e-mail kaufworld@earthlink.net. BUDGET.

How can you not like a cabaret-style restaurant that bills itself as "The Ultimate in Drag Dining," with cross-dressing waiters lip-syncing racy hits by divas such as Bette Midler and Cher? At **Lips**, amidst over 500 yards of colored velvet and seven disco balls, diners gobble up dishes honoring famous drag queens. The chicken roulade is listed on the menu as "Chest Rockwell—a butch breast." The place is a kick! Dinner and Sunday brunch. Closed Monday. ~ 2770 5th Avenue; 619-295-7900; www.lips show.biz. MODERATE TO DELUXE.

Attracting attention has never been a problem for the **Corvette Diner**. Although it's usually crammed full of families and high school kids, the decor is not to be missed. Cool 1950s music, a soda fountain (complete with resident jerks), rock-and-roll memorabilia, dancing waitresses and a classy Corvette are this Hillcrest haven's magic formula. The place is jammed for lunch and dinner. Simple "blue-plate" diner fare includes meatloaf, chicken-fried steak and hefty burgers named for 1950s notables like Dion, Eddie and Kookie. ~ 3946 5th Avenue; phone/fax 619-542-1001; www.cohnrestaurants.com/corvette.html. MODERATE.

Around the corner and up the block is another diner complete with black-and-white tile, neon, shiny chrome and Naugahyde booths. **City Delicatessen & Bakery**, however, whips up Jewish deli treats such as matzo ball soup, lox and bagels and beef brisket. You'll also find burgers, steaks, salads and sandwiches; breakfast is served all day. A popular late-night spot. ~ 535 University Avenue; 619-295-2747, fax 619-295-2129. BUDGET TO MODERATE.

Located in the heart of Hillcrest, **California Cuisine** offers sumptuous dishes for your discriminating palate. Beef tenderloin and loin of New Zealand lamb are among the many items on their ever-changing menu, as are pasta, salads and vegetarian fare. You also get a taste of the promising local artists whose original work adorns the walls. No lunch Saturday and Sunday. Closed Monday. ~ 1027 University Avenue; 619-543-0790, fax 619-543-0106; www.californiacuisine.cc, e-mail info@california cuisine.cc. MODERATE TO DELUXE.

Be transported to France without the airfare at **La Vache**, a neighborhood bistro that serves up French delicacies in a romantic setting. Velvet window coverings, mirrored walls and wooden wine racks surround diners who savor such creative dishes as salmon with crayfish sauce and a salad of walnuts, pears, olives, Roquefort, parmesan and goat cheese. A three-course prix-fixe dinner is offered Tuesday and from 5 p.m. to 6 p.m. the rest of the week and is a bargain. ~ 420 Robinson Avenue; 619-295-0214; www.lavacheandco.com. MODERATE TO DELUXE.

Parallel 33's eclectic menu draws on a wonderful blend of flavors gathered from cuisines of countries whose global latitude is the same as San Diego's. Moroccan, Lebanese, Indian, Chinese and Japanese influences result in such specialties as breaded softshell crab crusted in black sesame seeds, duck in Asian five-spice sauce and curried lamb. Dinner only. Closed Sunday. ~ 741 West Washington Street; 619-260-0033, fax 619-260-1039. MODERATE TO DELUXE.

SHOPPING

Aromas wafting out of **Cathedral** make venturing inside hard to resist. Treat yourself to a beautifully textured candle, some bath salts and milk lotion, then run back to your hotel room and soak in a hot tub by candlelight. ~ 435 University Avenue; 619-296-4046, fax 619-296-4420.

Obelisk carries gay, lesbian and bisexual reading material, as well as gift items to tickle your fancy—jewelry, shirts and cards, to name a few. ~ 1029 University Avenue; 619-297-4171.

AUTHOR FAVORITE

Searching high and low for that Betty Page calendar? How about some sweater-girl paper dolls? **Babette Schwartz**, the local drag queen, has a store that carries an array of novelty items and retro toys. Besides such treasures as I Love Lucy lunchboxes, Barbies and pink flamingos, there's a drag queen doll that is almost as off-the-wall as Babette him/herself. ~ 421 University Avenue; 619-220-7048, fax 619-220-7049; www.babette.com.

Everyone from retro-dressing gen-Xers to drag queens will find endless possibilities at **Wear It Again Sam**. Racks are jammed with vintage clothing that runs the gamut from beautifully made hand-beaded gowns to men's black-and-white wingtips and Prohibition-era fedoras. ~ 3823 5th Avenue; 619-299-0185.

Appeasing vinyl junkies and casual listeners alike, **Off the Record** is jam-packed with new, used and out-of-print CDs, LPs and singles (both vinyl and plastic). You'll also find T-shirts, posters, books, magazines and other music-related paraphernalia. ~ 3849 5th Avenue; 619-298-4755.

It's hard to imagine that any store anywhere has such a diverse selection of hats as the **Village Hat Shop**. Enter the store under a bowler hat awning and marvel at the amount and variety within. Besides the regulation straw, felt, knit and cloth hats, caps and skullies, you can buy such esoteric numbers as a Viking helmet or a Harry Potter Gryffindor beanie. ~ 3821 4th Avenue; 619-683-5533; www.villagehatshop.com.

NIGHTLIFE

HIDDEN ►

Longtime **Nunu's Cocktail Lounge** regulars are no doubt both amused and bewildered to find that their time-warp saloon has been rediscovered by the youngsters. This old-time drinking establishment has a long, winding bar, Naugahyde booths, a 1960s brown and orange color scheme and appropriately tacky decorating touches, such as mirrored walls, faux Tiffany lamps and plastic ivy. Amazingly, the place has become hip with a crowd

CROSSING THE CANYONS

Some of San Diego's best-kept public secrets are the historic footbridges that were built to allow pedestrians to traverse the deep canyons in the Hillcrest and Banker's Hill neighborhoods. The **Vermont Street Bridge**, which crosses over Washington Street, has incorporated into its 400-foot structure murals by local artists depicting the walking experience. The **Quince Street Bridge**, built in 1905, is a wooden trestle bridge spanning Maple Canyon. Where 1st Avenue crosses the canyon there's an arched bridge whose steel girders loom 104-feet above the canyon floor. And for brave souls who don't mind a little swaying, the **Spruce Street suspension bridge** floats over Kate Sessions Canyon, named for the horticulturist who started some of the plantings visible from the bridge's footpath.

that wasn't even born when Nunu's was in its original heyday. ~ 3537 5th Avenue; 619-295-2878.

The **Brass Rail**, which opened in 1958, is one of San Diego's oldest gay bars. The bartenders' famed congeniality keeps the primarily male clientele coming back year after year for more— more drinks and more dancing (which is in full swing every weekend). Saturday is Latino night. Cover on weekends. ~ 3796 5th Avenue; phone/fax 619-298-2233.

A few doors down from the Brass Rail and next to the Hillcrest Inn is **David's Coffee House**. Designed to look like a living room, with a couch and antique furniture, this popular coffeehouse is a home away from home for travelers and locals alike; pets are also welcome. Aside from knocking back espresso and admiring the passing scenery, you can engage your neighbor in a board game or surf the web. David's Coffee House donates a portion of its proceeds to local AIDS organizations. ~ 3766 5th Avenue; 619-296-4173.

Also in this same stretch of 5th Avenue, **The Loft** is a gay bar offering jukebox music and a pool table. ~ 3610 5th Avenue; 619-296-6407.

Not for the uptight or prudish, the avant-garde **6th@Penn Theatre** specializes in plays that shock. While this tiny black-box theater is not exclusively a gay and lesbian venue, the cutting-edge shows that are performed here often draw on gay and lesbian themes. ~ 3704 6th Avenue; 619-688-9210; www.sixthat penn.com.

The short trek to University Avenue brings you to Hamburger Mary's restaurant, home of **Kickers**. This C&W bar keeps gay, lesbian and straight folks kickin' with free line-dancing and two-step lessons Thursday through Saturday. On Sunday, disco is the soundtrack for the tea dance. Cover for tea dance. ~ 308 University Avenue; 619-491-0400; www.hamburgermarys.com.

The real action on University Avenue is over at the Rainbow Block, a strip of gay-oriented establishments. First there's **Flicks**, a video bar that flashes visual stimuli on its six big screens while playing dance and progressive music. Depending on the evening, you might catch some live music, or you could pop in for a Monday night round of The Dating Game. Occasional cover. ~ 1017 University Avenue; 619-297-2056; www.sdflicks.com.

At the far end of the block, **Rich's** heats up Friday through Sunday with high-energy dancing until 2 a.m. The deejay-mixed music sets the beat: groove, techno, house and tribal rhythms. Music isn't the only stimulation; your eyes will be dazzled by the specially created visual effects. Each night has a different theme. On Friday nights Rich's go-go boys "work it." Saturdays boast varied themes and are about good music (a deejay host) and dancing. To finish off the weekend, there is The Tea on Sunday, with the doors opening at 9 p.m. Cover. ~ 1051 University Avenue; 619-295-2195; www.richs-sandiego.com.

Beyond the Rainbow Block you can take a pleasant stroll along the north side of Balboa Park to **The Flame**. Touted as "San Diego's hottest women's nightclub," this postmodern apocalypse features a dancefloor, pool tables and darts. Although men are always welcome here, Tuesday is officially "Boys' Night." Dancing runs seven nights a week, with deejays spinning everything from Top 40 to Gothic trance. No cover Tuesday through Thursday. ~ 3780 Park Boulevard; 619-295-4163; www.theflame-sd.com.

HIDDEN ►

Just up the street, there's plenty to entertain **Numbers** customers, thanks to pool tables, arcade games, two huge wraparound bars and a wall-size video screen and accompanying televisions that play the latest "gay divas" dance mix. Besides the dancefloor in the back, there's a makeshift stage where anyone can strut their stuff; some good, some ghastly. ~ 3811 Park Boulevard; 619-294-9005, fax 619-294-9005.

Other gay bars around town include **Bourbon Street**, a French Quarter–style bar that features an outdoor patio and nightly entertainment. Live music Thursday through Sunday. ~ 4612 Park Boulevard; 619-291-0173; www.bourbonstreetsd.com.

Inland Neighborhoods

Northeast of downtown and adjoining the Hillcrest area is a cluster of neighborhoods, each of which, though it appears to tumble into the next, has its own unique character.

Golden Hill, which backs up to Balboa Park, was a classy area in Victorian times, as evidenced by the remaining spectacular gingerbread mansions.

In neighboring **South Park**, modest early-20th-century, Craftsman-style bungalows house yuppies with toddlers and emerging artists, while the tiny commercial district favors eclectic businesses that cater to locals.

Conversely, **North Park**'s slightly gritty commercial district is sprawling and full of businesses such as auto repair shops and fast-food emporiums.

To the east, **City Heights** is an inner-city neighborhood probably best avoided after dark.

Head north and run into **Normal Heights**, a smaller version of North Park that, while still having plenty of practical business, also has neighborhood establishments, including an impressive number of specialty bookstores.

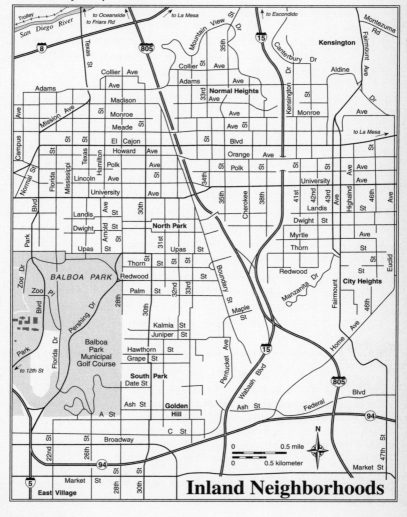

Inland Neighborhoods

East of Normal Heights, **Kensington** is the toniest of the neighborhoods, full of older houses lovingly cared for. The one-block-long commercial district tends toward the upscale.

LODGING

An attractive bed and breakfast in North Park, on the north-eastern side of Balboa Park, is **Carole's B&B Inn**, built in 1904 and situated on a quiet residential street. The main house has eight antique-furnished guest rooms (some with shared bath), while an annex across the street contains two garden studio apartments with private bath and kitchenette, a one-bedroom cottage and a two-bedroom apartment. In addition to a sitting room, with its player piano, and the conference room, the inn has a swimming pool. ~ 3227 Grim Avenue; 619-280-5258, 800-975-5521. MODERATE TO ULTRA-DELUXE.

DINING

My guess is that the exterior of the **Turf Supper Club** looked exactly the same when it opened, years ago, and the dark interior, with faux leather booths and vintage San Diego photos on the wall, isn't all that much different, either. This is the place to have a martini, cook a steak over the communal grill and be transported back to the 1950s, when gin and beef were in. ~ 1116 25th Avenue, Golden Hill; 619-234-6363. MODERATE TO DELUXE.

Owned by the same folks as the Turf Supper Club next door, **Krakatoa** is a pleasant, neighborhoody kind of place where locals enjoy coffee and a light meal on the tree-shaded deck or in the retro interior, surrounded by South Pacific masks. ~ 1128 25th Street, Golden Hill; 619-230-0272. BUDGET.

Big Kitchen is a hole-in-the-wall neighborhood coffee shop with panache, thanks mostly to Judy the Beauty, who runs the place. It's not surprising to learn that Whoopi Goldberg once

AUTHOR FAVORITE

A San Diego institution, the **San Diego Chicken Pie Shop** has been turning out freshly made chicken pot pies since 1938. Gobble up this richly crusted, savory classic, served with mashed potatoes and gravy, in the town hall–like dining room or get an order to go, either baked or unbaked, but don't forget to bring cash. They don't accept plastic. ~ 2633 El Cajon Boulevard, North Park; 619-295-0156. BUDGET.

waited tables at this idiosyncratic establishment, where regulars from blue-collar workers to edgy artists come to wolf down hearty portions of standard American grub, accompanied by as much coffee as the nerves can stand. Breakfast and lunch only. ~ 3003 Grape Street, South Park; 619-234-5789. BUDGET.

Ranchos Cocina serves up healthy Mexican fare in a cheerfully bright setting. Vegetarians will be delighted by the meatless options, including blue-corn enchiladas and tofu burritos, and vegans and the lactose intolerant are happily accommodated. Entrées, such as chicken in chocolatey mole sauce and turkey chorizo and eggs, are cooked in olive oil rather than lard, but be forewarned—the portions are enormous. ~ 3910 30th Street, North Park; 619-574-1288. BUDGET.

For fresh and delicious vegetarian cuisine in peaceful, Zen-infused surroundings, head for **Jyoti Bihanga**. Enjoying a homemade vegan soup, a smoothie or a curry dish in the sparkling blue-and-white dining room to the strains of relaxing music is almost enough to transport you to Nirvana. No dinner Wednesday and Sunday. ~ 3351 Adams Avenue, Normal Heights; 619-282-4116; www.jyotibihanga.com. BUDGET.

◄ HIDDEN

Kensington's **Green Tomato Restaurant** is old-timey elegant, with high-backed, brocade-covered chairs, candelabra and dark wood accents. The food tends toward traditional Continental with a twist, such as seafood linguine with garlic and caper seasoning and herb-crusted lamb chops in a mole sauce. No lunch on Saturday. ~ 4090 Adams Avenue, Kensington; 619-283-7546, fax 619-283-0116. MODERATE TO DELUXE.

A sophisticated little sidewalk café, **Just Fabulous Kensington** specializes in trendy entrées such as Kobe beef burgers with truffle cheese and crab cakes on ciabatta, and to-die-for desserts like flourless chocolate cake drizzled with warm chocolate and brandy-soaked cherries. Brunch Saturday and Sunday. ~ 4116 Adams Avenue, Kensington; 619-584-2929. MODERATE TO DELUXE.

While you can buy all sorts of music at **M-Theory Music**, they have perhaps the best selection of work by San Diego musicians available anywhere. Besides buying and selling CDs, LPs and DVDs, the store is often the venue for live music performances. ~ 3004 Juniper Street, South Park; 619-269-2963; www.mtheorymusic.com.

SHOPPING

The Grove is more than simply a neighborhood book, card and gift shop—it's a sort of artistic community center, which hosts prose readings, artists' shows, and book club events. ~ 3010 Juniper Street, South Park; 619-284-7684.

For lovers of felines, **Cat Alley** is bound to enchant. There are all sorts of items geared to cataholics, as well as presents for their furry friends. ~ 2807 University Avenue, North Park; 619-683-7877; www.catalley.net.

HIDDEN ► Located in the Book Row portion of Adams Avenue, **The Prince & the Pauper** specializes in collectible children's books. This is the place to come for those hard-to-find, beautifully illustrated juvenile books of the past. ~ 3201 Adams Avenue, Normal Heights; 619-249-4380.

HIDDEN ► If cookbooks are more your thing, check out the **Cookbooks & Paperbacks** strip-mall shop, stuffed with cookbooks. ~ 4112½ Adams Avenue, Kensington; 619-281-8962.

NIGHTLIFE   **Coffee House on Broadway**'s decor is early thrift shop meets college dorm. The service is haphazard, the place is messy, but it's
HIDDEN ► where emerging artists, whether they're musicians, painters or poets, can showcase their talents ~ 2991 Broadway, Golden Hill; 619-557-0156; www.coffeehouseonbroadway.com.

Conversely, **Claire de Lune** is a stylish coffeehouse with high ceilings, brightly colored couches, easy chairs and original artwork. Creative coffee drinks, sandwiches, salads, soups and sweets are served from early in the morning until late at night, and there's live entertainment on the weekends. ~ 2906 University Avenue, North Park; 619-688-9845, fax 619-795-3630; www.clairedelune.com.

Shooterz, a popular sports bar, boasts two large-screen TVs, five pool tables, pinball and video games. The Odyssey Club, lo-

AUTHOR FAVORITE

It may have taken over space formerly occupied by a dive bar, but **Air Conditioned** is definitely way cool now. This is one of the most happening places in town, where an eclectic mix of people hang out on retro-modern vinyl barstools and deep sofas, sip cocktails and listen to deejay-spun tunes. ~ 4673 30th Avenue, Normal Heights; 619-501-9831, fax 619-546-0208.

cated inside, is a danceclub that appeals to both a gay and straight clientele. Occasional cover. ~ 3815 30th Street, North Park; 619-574-0744; www.shooterzbar.com.

Lestat's decor is unusual, but one would hardly expect less of a place named for Anne Rice's fictional vampire. In keeping with its gothic theme, gargoyles leer down on patrons snuggled into comfortable plush seats. There's live music most nights and insomniacs can hang around drinking coffee until the sun comes up. Open 24 hours. ~ 3343 Adams Avenue, Normal Heights; 619-282-0437; www.lestats.com.

A neighborhood bar that goes hip at night, the **Kensington Club** is the place to go to sip the perfect 1950s-style martini. A separate room is where the entertainment is—deejays spinning hip-hop during the week, live bands (C&W, techno, swing) on weekends. ~ 4079 Adams Avenue, Kensington; 619-284-2848.

Kensington is just the place you'd expect to run across a retro neighborhood movie theater like **Ken Cinema**. Specializing in foreign films and classics from the past, this intimate little place is a welcome change from today's multiplexes. ~ 4061 Adams Avenue, Kensington; 619-283-5909.

Old Town Area

Back in 1769, Spanish explorer Gaspar de Portolá selected a hilltop site overlooking the bay for the mission that would begin the European settlement of California. A town soon spread out at the foot of the hill, complete with plaza, church, school and the tile-roofed adobe *casas* of California's first families. Through the years, Spanish, Mexican and American settlements thrived until an 1872 fire destroyed much of the town, prompting developers to relocate the commercial district nearer the bay.

SIGHTS

Some of the buildings and relics of the early era survived and have been brought back to life at **Old Town San Diego State Historic Park**. Lined with adobe restorations and brightened with colorful shops, the six blocks of Old Town provide a lively and interesting opportunity for visitors to stroll, shop and sightsee. ~ Park headquarters, 4002 Wallace Street; 619-220-5422, fax 619-220-5421.

The state historic park sponsors a free walking tour at 11 a.m. and 2 p.m. daily, or you can easily do it on your own by picking up a copy of the *Old San Diego Gazette*. The paper, which comes out once a month and includes a map of the area, is free at local stores. You can also hop aboard the Old Town Trolley for a delightful two-hour narrated tour of Old Town and a variety of other highlights in San Diego and Coronado. It makes eight stops, and you're allowed to get on and off all day long. Fee. ~ 4010 Twiggs Street; 619-298-8687, 800-868-7482, fax 619-298-3404; www.historictours.com.

As it has for over a century, everything focuses on **Old Town Plaza**. Before 1872, this was the social and recreational center of the town: political meetings, barbecues, dances, shootouts and bullfights all happened here. ~ San Diego Avenue and Mason Street.

Casa de Estudillo is the finest of the original adobe buildings. It was a mansion in its time, built in 1827 for the commander of the Mexican Presidio. ~ Located at the Mason Street corner of the plaza.

Casa de Bandini was built in 1829 as a one-story adobe but gained a second level when it became the Cosmopolitan Hotel in the late 1860s. **Seeley Stables** next door is a replica of the barns and stables of Albert Seeley, who operated the stage line. Nowadays, it houses a collection of horse-drawn vehicles and Western memorabilia and has a video presentation. ~ At Mason and Calhoun streets.

The **San Diego Union building** was Old Town's first frame building and the place where the *San Diego Union* was first printed in 1868. It has been restored as a 19th-century printing office. ~ Located at San Diego Avenue.

Shoppers seem to gravitate in large numbers to the north side of the plaza to browse the unusual shops comprising **Bazaar del Mundo**. Built in circular fashion around a tropical courtyard, this complex also houses several restaurants.

Within earshot of the original jail in Old Town, the **San Diego Sheriff's Museum** celebrates more than 150 years of service by the men and women of the city's sheriff's department. Housed in a Spanish adobe-style building, the museum has all sorts of exhibits and memorabilia, including historic photographs and a 1970s patrol car. ~ 2384 San Diego Avenue; 619-260-1850, fax 619 260-1862; www.sheriffmuseum.org.

The original mission and Spanish Presidio once stood high on a hill behind Old Town. This site of California's birthplace now houses **Junipero Serra Museum**, a handsome Spanish Colonial structure containing an excellent collection of American Indian and Spanish artifacts from the state's pioneer days and relics from the Royal Presidio dig sites. Open Friday through Sunday. Admission. ~ Presidio Drive; 619-297-3258, fax 619-297-3281; www.sandiegohistory.org.

Within five years after Father Serra dedicated the first of California's 21 missions, the site had become much too small for the growing numbers it served. So **Mission San Diego de Alcalá** was moved from Presidio Hill six miles east into Mission Valley. Surrounded now by shopping centers and suburban homes, the "Mother of Missions" retains its simple but striking white adobe facade topped by a graceful *campanario*, or bell wall. There's a library (open 10 a.m. to 12 p.m., Tuesday and Thursday) containing mission records in Junípero Serra's handwriting and a lovely courtyard with gnarled pepper trees. Admission. ~ 10818 San Diego Mission Road; 619-281-8449; www.missionsan diego.com, e-mail info@missionsandiego.com.

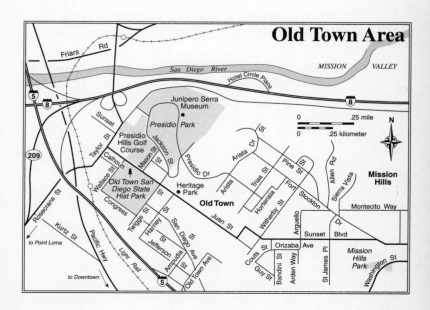

LODGING   A good bet in the lower-price categories is the appropriately
named **Old Town Inn**. Strolling distance from Old Town and
across from the Old Town Trolley and Transit Center (the transportation hub), this spiffy little 84-room family-owned motel has
two types of rooms: the economy units and the handicapped-ac-
cessible deluxe rooms, some of which have full kitchens. A guest
laundry is available, as is a heated outdoor pool and a complimentary deluxe breakfast buffet every morning. ~ 4444 Pacific
Highway; 619-260-8024, 800-643-3025, fax 619-296-0524;
www.oldtown-inn.com. MODERATE.

For the romantic, **Heritage Park Inn**, a storybook 1889
Queen Anne mansion with a striking turret, is an enchanting bed
and breakfast. Set on a grassy hillside, it provides a tranquil es-
cape. Choose from 12 distinctive chambers (all with private
bath), each furnished with museum-quality antiques. Most feature ornate brass or four-poster canopy beds and old-fashioned
quilts; three have jacuzzi tubs. ~ 2470 Heritage Park Row; 619-
299-6832, 800-995-2470, fax 619-299-9465; www.heritage
parkinn.com, e-mail innkeeper@heritageparkinn.com. DELUXE
TO ULTRA-DELUXE.

For a choice of motels with a variety of prices, try looking for
accommodations along Hotel Circle, on the north side of Presidio Park. The road loops under a portion of Route 8. Most
properties around the circle are large chain hotels designed for
vacation travelers, with resort facilities including large pools,
tennis courts and spas or fitness centers; many share the use of
the 27-hole Riverwalk Golf Club. Rates here are generally lower
than at downtown hotels.

Among them is the 417-room **Red Lion Hanalei Hotel**,
whose tall palm trees, courtyard and tiki-style bar aim for a Polynesian ambience. ~ 2270 Hotel Circle North; 619-297-1101,

OLD TOWN VICTORIANA

About one and a half blocks east of Old Town lies **Heritage Park**, an area
dedicated to the preservation of the city's Victorian past. Seven historic
1880s-era houses and an old Jewish temple have been moved to the hillside site and beautifully restored. ~ Juan and Harney streets.

800-733-5466, fax 619-297-6049; www.redlion.com, e-mail sales@hanaleihotel.com. DELUXE.

The **Handlery Hotel Resort** is a lowrise 217-room complex adjacent to the golf course, with an outdoor pool, a jacuzzi and a poolside gym. ~ 950 Hotel Circle North; 619-298-0511, 800-676-6567, fax 619-298-9793; www.handlery.com, e-mail sales@handlery.com. DELUXE.

The **Town and Country Hotel** is geared to travelers who mix business with pleasure, featuring its own convention center as well as four swimming pools and an adjacent shopping mall. ~ 500 Hotel Circle North; 619-291-7131, 800-772-8527, fax 619-291-3584; www.towncountry.com. ULTRA-DELUXE.

Hawthorn Suites San Diego has 50 one-bedroom and two-bedroom, two-bath suites ideal for traveling families, as well as an outdoor barbecue area. ~ 1335 Hotel Circle South; 619-299-3501, 800-527-1133, fax 619-294-7882; www.hawthornsuites sandiego.com. MODERATE TO DELUXE.

The 280 rooms at **Days Inn–Hotel Circle**, which holds the distinction of being the largest Days Inn in California, feature Nintendo for kids, as well as ironing boards and irons; some rooms have kitchenettes. ~ 543 Hotel Circle South; 619-297-8800, 800-227-4743, fax 619-298-6029; www.daysinnhc.com. MODERATE.

DINING

Mexican food and atmosphere abound in Old Town, especially in the Bazaar del Mundo. Here five restaurants lure a steady stream of diners into festive, flowered courtyards. **Casa de Pico** is a great place to sit and munch cheese nachos and sip a margarita. Mexican entrées are served outside or in one of the hacienda-style dining rooms. ~ 2754 Calhoun Street; 619-296-3267, fax 619-296-3113; www.casadepico.com. BUDGET TO MODERATE.

Next door, in a magnificent 1829 hacienda, **Casa de Bandini**, you will find the cuisine a bit more refined. The seafood is good here, especially the crab enchiladas, and the health-conscious will like the low-fat menu. Mariachis often play at both restaurants. ~ Mason and Calhoun streets; 619-297-8211, fax 619-297-2557; www.casadebandini.com. MODERATE.

Two Old Town charmers provide satisfying diversions from a Mexican diet. **Berta's** specializes in Latin American cuisine. *Vatapa* (coconut sauce over mahimahi, scallops and shrimp) and *cansado* (a plate of pinto beans, rice, salsa, plantain and green salad) are wonderfully prepared. Closed Monday. ~ 3928 Twigg Street; phone/fax 619-295-2343. MODERATE.

Fresh, innovative seafood is the calling card at **Café Pacifica**, where a billion points of light sparkle from the wood-beamed ceiling and candles create a warm, intimate setting. California cuisine meets Pacific Rim panache, with preparations such as ginger-stuffed seared halibut and swordfish with a soy-peanut glaze. Seating is also available at the bar and, in warm weather, the patio with removable roof. Dinner only. ~ 2414 San Diego Avenue; 619-291-6666, fax 619-291-0122; www.cafepacifica. com, e-mail info@cafepacifica.com. MODERATE TO ULTRA-DELUXE.

HIDDEN ▶

Less than a mile from Old Town are a pair of excellent ethnic take-out shops that few visitors ever find. **El Indio** opened in 1940 as a family-operated *tortillería*, then added an informal restaurant serving quesadillas, enchiladas, tostadas, burritos, tacos and taquitos. Quality homemade Mexican food at Taco Bell prices; you can sit indoors or out on the patio, or order to go. Open for breakfast, lunch and dinner. ~ 3695 India Street; 619-299-0333; www.el-indio.com. BUDGET.

The other one-of-a-kind fast-food operation, with an equally fervent following, is **Saffron Chicken**, which turns out zesty Thai-grilled chicken on a special rotisserie. The aroma is positively exquisite and so is the chicken, served with jasmine rice, Cambodian salad and five tangy sauces. Eat on an adjacent patio or take a picnic to the beach. Also, next door is **Saffron Noodles**, owned by the same restaurateurs. ~ 3731-B India Street; 619-574-0177. BUDGET TO MODERATE.

SHOPPING

Historic Old Town is blessed with several exciting bazaars and shopping squares. By far the grandest is the **Bazaar del Mundo**, Old Town's version of the famous marketplaces of Spain and Mexico. Adobe casitas house a variety of international shops. Here **Fabrics and Finery** (619-296-3161) unfurls cloth, buttons and craft accessories from around the world, and **Ariana** (619-296-4989) features clothing and wearable art. ~ Calhoun Street between Twiggs and Juan streets.

Unlike other antique stores in the area, **Circa a.d.** offers anything but American antiques. It proudly displays a vast assortment of Asian, European and African art, jewelry, textiles and pottery, specializing in goods from around the Pacific Rim. It

Meandering through
Mission Hills

Nestled between Old Town and Hillcrest, Mission Hills is a hilly area filled with older homes that range from palatial mansions to Craftsman-style bungalows. Though this is an upscale neighborhood, businesses tend to be low-key, friendly and unpretentious, and plenty of food deals can be found.

For example, who'd have thought this would be the area to get retro favorites such as creamed chipped beef on toast or biscuits with gravy for a mere $4? At **The Huddle**, a tiny throwback to the 1950s diner, loyal regulars sit surrounded by faded photos of TV stars such as Jackie Gleason and Jack Webb and devour old-time food at old-time prices. ~ 4023 Goldfinch Street; 619-291-5950. BUDGET.

Just up the street, the aromas alone are enough to entice at **A La Francaise**, a French-style *patisserie* that serves light meals and irresistible pastries. Enjoying a sandwich on freshly baked French bread on the outside patio is like being transported to Provence. Open for breakfast and lunch. ~ 4029 Goldfinch Street, Mission Hills; 619-294-4425. BUDGET TO MODERATE.

Appropriately located across the street from A La Francaise, **Maison en Provence** carries all the lovely pottery and linens one associates with this sunny part of France. ~ 820 Fort Stockton, Mission Hills; 619-298-5318.

For truly tasty Mexican food at bargain prices head for **Jimmy Carter's Mexican Cafe**. No, it's not owned by the ex-president, but by a cheerful fellow who claims his restaurant serves some of the best Mexican food outside the barrio. The menu emphasizes what Carter calls San Diego border food, tortillas, enchiladas, tacos, burritos, rice and beans, as well as less familiar daily specials. ~ 807 West Washington Street, Mission Hills; 619-296-6952. BUDGET.

even carries bonsai trees. ~ 5355 Grant Street; 619-293-3328, fax 619-293-7488; www.circaad.com, e-mail info@circaad.com.

On the fringes of Old Town, **Artist & Craftsman Supply** stocks everything a professional or aspiring artist could want, from color wheels to sketch pads, as well as paint for every conceivable surface, from silk to tile. ~ 1911 San Diego Avenue; 619-688-1911.

From Friday through Sunday, **Kobey's Swap Meet** converts the parking lot of the San Diego Sports Arena into a giant flea market where over 1000 sellers hawk new and used wares. Admission. ~ Sports Arena Boulevard; 619-226-0650.

NIGHTLIFE The prevailing culture in Old Town is Mexican, as in mariachis and margaritas. The **Old Town Mexican Café y Cantina**, a festive, friendly establishment, has a patio bar. ~ 2489 San Diego Avenue; 619-297-4330, fax 619-297-8002; www.oldtownmex cafe.com.

Built to resemble an old-fashioned barn, **The Theatre in Old Town,** located right in the heart of this historic district, specializes in productions of long-running musicals and comedies like *Forever Plaid*. With only 250 seats, there is not a bad one in the house. ~ 4040 Twiggs Street; 619-688-2494, fax 619-688-0960; www.theatreinoldtown.com.

O'Hungry's, a nearby restaurant, features an acoustic guitarist every night but Monday. ~ 2547 San Diego Avenue; 619-298-0133.

For country-and-western dancing, try **In Cahoots**, which has free dance lessons every night but Wednesday. There are also occasional live acts. Closed Monday. Cover Wednesday through Saturday. ~ 5373 Mission Center Road; 619-291-8635, fax 619-291-1723; www.incahoots.com.

THREE

San Diego's Waterfront

One of San Diego's most appealing features is its proximity to the Pacific Ocean. The waterfront area runs from the almost-island of Coronado, with its tony homes and hotels, to Pacific Beach, popular with students, surfers and middle-class beach lovers. The downtown harbor area is filled with boats of every description, from simple fishing vessels to historic ships, and is the launching site for commercially run harbor and whale-watching cruises. For landlubbers, Seaport Village is the place to shop and dine within view of the harbor. Across San Diego Bay, Point Loma and Ocean Beach are two distinctly different beach communities, Point Loma being more upscale and Ocean Beach more modest and eccentric. Traveling north, Mission Bay is fronted by resorts, condominiums and marinas, and home to world-renowned SeaWorld San Diego, while Mission Beach consists of beachy dwellings, restaurants and a small-scale amusement park. Pacific Beach is the most sprawling of the beach towns, with the most businesses and a population that tends toward the young, hip and laid-back.

An isolated and exclusive community in San Diego Bay, Coronado is almost an island, connected to the mainland only by the graceful San Diego–Coronado Bay Bridge and by a long, narrow sandspit called the Silver Strand. Coronado has long been a playground of the rich and famous, and its hotels reflect this ritzy heritage.

Coronado

Once known as the "Nickel Snatcher," the Coronado Ferry for years crossed the waters of San Diego Harbor between the Embarcadero and Coronado. All for five cents each way. That's

SIGHTS

history, of course, but the 1940s-vintage, double-decker *Silvergate* still plies the harbor's waters. The **San Diego Bay Ferry** leaves from the Bay Café on North Harbor Drive at the foot of Broadway on the hour and docks 15 minutes later at the Ferry Landing Marketplace on the Coronado side. ~ San Diego Harbor Excursion; 619-234-4111, fax 619-522-6150; www.sdhe.com.

The town's main attraction is the **Hotel del Coronado**, a red-roofed, Victorian-style, wooden wonder and a National Historic Landmark. Explore the old palace and its manicured grounds, discovering its intricate corridors and cavernous public rooms. It was Elisha Babcock's dream, when he purchased 4100 acres of barren, wind-blown peninsula in 1888, to build a hotel that would be the "talk of the Western world." Realizing Babcock's dream from the beginning, it attracted presidents, dignitaries and movie stars. You might even recognize it from the movie *Some Like It Hot*. ~ 1500 Orange Avenue; 619-435-6611, fax 619-522-8262; www.hoteldel.com, e-mail delinquiries@hoteldel.com.

Although overshadowed by its noted neighbor, the **Glorietta Bay Inn** is a worthy landmark in its own right. It was built in 1908 as the private mansion of sugar scion John D. Spreckels. From here you can cruise the quiet neighborhood streets that radiate off Orange Avenue between the bay and the ocean, enjoying the town's handsome blend of cottages and historic homes. ~ 1630 Glorietta Boulevard; 619-435-3101, 800-283-9383, fax 619-435-6182; www.gloriettabayinn.com, e-mail info@glorietta bayinn.com.

You can learn all about the town at the **Coronado Museum of History and Art**. Besides mounting exhibits of photos and memorabilia, twice a week, the museum sponsors hour-long docent-led walking tours (fee) through Coronado's architectural past. Tours leave from the lobby. Reservations required for walking tours. ~ 1100 Orange Avenue; 619-435-7242, fax 619-435-8504.

LODGING   **El Cordova Hotel** is in the heart of Coronado. Originally built as a private mansion in 1902, El Cordova's moderate size (40 rooms) and lovely Spanish-hacienda architecture make it a relaxing getaway spot. A pool and patio restaurant, as well as 20 boutique shops, are added attractions. ~ 1351 Orange Avenue; 619-435-4131, 800-229-2032, fax 619-435-0632; www.elcordo vahotel.com. DELUXE TO ULTRA-DELUXE.

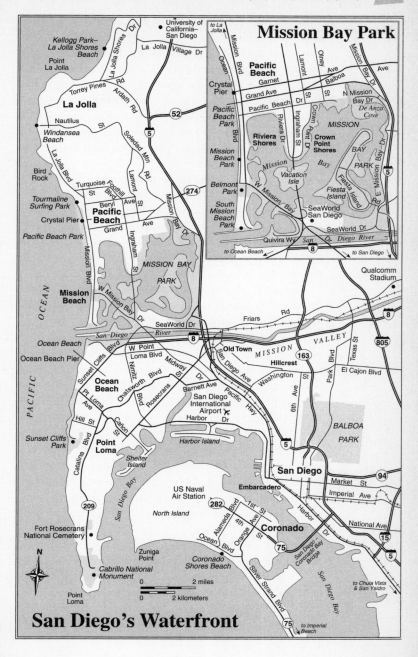

Mission Bay Park

San Diego's Waterfront

Nothing can detract from the glamour of the **Hotel del Coronado**. With its turrets, cupolas and gingerbread facade, it is one of the great hotels of California. The last in a proud line of extravagant seaside resorts, the Hotel del Coronado has long been the place where Hollywood stars—and 14 United States presidents—have come to relax. Remember, however, this celebrated Victorian landmark is a major tourist attraction, so in addition to guests, who usually fill its 688 rooms to capacity, a large number of visitors crowd the lobby, grounds and shops every day. Be aware, too, that many rooms are in the two structures adjacent to the original building and though more comfortable are not the real thing. The "Hotel Del" has two pools, a long stretch of beach, nine eating areas, three tennis courts, a fitness center, a spa and a gallery of shops. Reservations recommended. ~ 1500 Orange Avenue; 619-522-8000, 800-435-6611, fax 619-522-8262; www.hoteldel.com, e-mail delinquiries@hoteldel.com. ULTRA-DELUXE.

Across the street rises the **Glorietta Bay Inn**, the 1908 Edwardian mansion of sugar baron John D. Spreckels, which has been transformed into an elegant 100-room hotel. Rooms and suites in the mansion reflect the grandeur of Spreckels' time; more typical accommodations are available in the contemporary inn buildings that surround the mansion. Continental breakfast, ladies and gentlemen, is served on the mansion's terrace. ~ 1630 Glorietta Boulevard; 619-435-3101, 800-283-9383, fax 619-435-6182; www.gloriettabayinn.com, e-mail info@gloriettabayinn.com. DELUXE TO ULTRA-DELUXE.

The **Coronado Victorian House** is quite possibly the only hotel anywhere to offer dance, exercise and gourmet cooking classes with a night's stay. Located in a historic 1894 building near the beach and downtown Coronado, this seven-room bed and breakfast includes amenities such as Persian rugs, stained-glass windows and private baths with clawfoot tubs; rooms are named after artists and dancers. Those guests not interested in the extracurricular activities are invited to relax and enjoy such healthy home-cooked specialties as baklava, stuffed grape leaves and homemade yogurt. Two-night minimum. ~ 1000 8th Street; 619-435-2200, 888-299-2822; www.coronadovictorian.com. ULTRA-DELUXE.

Rooms at the **Coronado Inn** may be basic and the decor a bit   ◄ *HIDDEN*
worn, but on the plus side there's a nice pool area, a complimentary continental breakfast, a helpful staff and reasonable (for
Coronado) rates. ~ 266 Orange Avenue; 619-435-4121, 800-598-
6624; www.coronadoinn.com. MODERATE.

DINING

Visitors crossing over to Coronado invariably tour the famous
Hotel del Coronado, and many are lured into the **Crown-Coronet
Room**. Its grand Victorian architecture and enormous domed
ceiling (the chandeliers were designed by *Wizard of Oz* author
L. Frank Baum) set a tone of elegance and style unmatched anywhere on the Pacific Coast. The place is so magnificent that the
food seems unimportant. Most food critics, in fact, assert that
dinner (served every night except Monday; reservations recom-

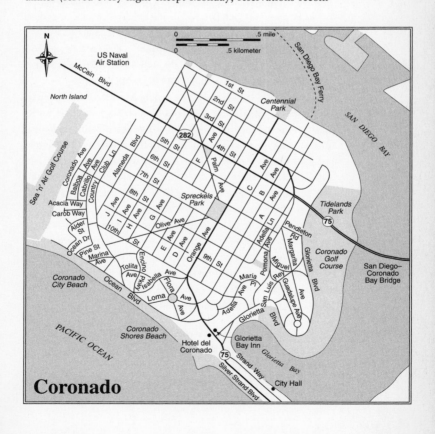

Coronado

mended) in the hotel's **Prince of Wales Room** is better, but the Sunday brunch at the Crown-Coronet Room will never disappoint. Reservations recommended for Sunday brunch. ~ 1500 Orange Avenue; 619-435-6611, fax 619-522-8262; www.hotel del.com. ULTRA-DELUXE.

Locals looking to avoid the crowds at the "Hotel Del" usually head for **Chez Loma**. Set in a charming 1889 Victorian house, it serves a lovely Continental/French dinner—excellent *canard rôti* (traditional roast duck with cherry, green peppercorn and burnt orange sauce). Dine inside or out. Dinner only. ~ 1132 Loma Avenue; 619-435-0661, fax 619-435-3770; www.chezloma.com, e-mail chef@chezloma.com. DELUXE TO ULTRA-DELUXE.

Sitting in the courtyard of the El Cordova Hotel sipping a hand-shaken margarita at **Miguel's Cocina Coronado**—what could be more idyllic? Besides all the expected Mexican dishes, there are some interesting creations, such as a calamari *relleno*, a sautéed calamari steak wrapped around a *chile relleno*. ~ 1351 Orange Avenue; 619-437-4237, fax 619-437-8478; www.miguel cocina.signonsandiego.com. BUDGET TO MODERATE.

Peohe's, located at the Ferry Landing Marketplace, is primarily praised for its panoramic views of San Diego Bay and for its tropical decor. The dining room features green palms and rushing cascades of water flowing into ponds of live fish. The dinner menu is mostly fresh fish plus lobster, shrimp and a daily featured "catch." There are also prime rib, chicken and lamb. Sunday brunch is another option. ~ 1201 1st Street; 619-437-4474; www.peohes.com. DELUXE TO ULTRA-DELUXE.

Also at the Ferry Landing, **Bay Beach Cafe** is your typical casual California beach restaurant. On a warm day sun worshipers vie for a table on the patio, where they gobble up burgers and fish specials, along with lovely views of San Diego Bay and the city skyline. ~ 1201 1st Street; 619-435-4900, fax 619-435-6641; www.baybeachcafe. MODERATE.

SHOPPING   Coronado's fancy Orange Avenue in the village center harbors an assortment of unusual shops in the **El Cordova Hotel**. ~ 1351 Orange Avenue; 619-435-4131; www.elcordovahotel.com.

The **Ferry Landing Marketplace** is a modern shopping area complete with boutiques, specialty shops, galleries and eateries.

A farmer's market is held on Tuesday afternoons. ~ 1201 1st Street; 619-435-8895.

A Ferry Landing favorite for Anglophiles is **Scottish Treasures Celtic Corner,** a store that specializes in all things English, Irish and Scottish. Besides traditional kilts and accessories, you can get everything from mushy peas to family crest key chains. ~ 1201 1st Street #213; 619-435-1880, 888-728-8737; www.scottish treasures.net.

For those who tend more toward American Indian goods, **Southwestern Indian Den** carries a terrific assortment of authentic American Indian art, jewelry and music, including Navajo baskets and pottery from the Southwest and CDs of pure, evocative flute music. ~ 1201 1st Street #104; 619-435-3561.

The **Hotel del Coronado** is a city within a city and home to many intriguing specialty shops, such as the Babcock & Story Emporium, which has a selection of bath and body products, kitchenware and gardening accessories. ~ 1500 Orange Avenue; 619-435-6611; www.delshop.com.

NIGHTLIFE

If you're out Coronado way, stop for a cocktail in the Hotel del Coronado's **Babcock & Story Bar.** Live entertainment Wednesday through Sunday night. ~ 1500 Orange Avenue; 619-435-6611; www.hoteldel.com.

Check out the boisterous Irish scene at **McP's,** a full, swinging bar and grill with shamrock-plastered walls and a bartender with the gift of gab. McP's is a Navy SEAL hangout, so, as one glib bartender noted, it's the most likely place in town to pet a seal. Entertainment includes live rock and jazz bands on a nightly basis. ~ 1107 Orange Avenue; 619-435-5280; www.mcpspub.com.

AUTHOR FAVORITE

The Hotel Del's **Palm Court Lounge** is an elegant place to sip a specialty martini and listen to a pianist tickling the ivories. Such potentially lethal concoctions as the California Blonde (Bombay Sapphire gin with a touch of Dubonnet) are delivered in individual carafes, quick-chilled in glass and steel ice buckets and poured into icy martini glasses. Surprisingly, the prices are not bad, considering the tony surroundings and generous portions. ~ 1500 Orange Avenue; 619-435-6611.

The historic Spreckels Building in Coronado is a vintage-1917 opera house that has been restored to a 347-seat venue called the **Lamb's Players Theatre.** ~ 1142 Orange Avenue; 619-437-0600; www.lambsplayers.org.

The **Coronado Players,** the town's resident company, has been turning out plays year-round since 1946. Sadly, they have lost their home theater, the Coronado Playhouse, which was pieced together from WWII barracks, but that hasn't stopped them from performing at a temporary pavilion at the Ferry Landing. ~ 1335 1st Street; 619-435-4856; www.coronadoplayhouse.com.

BEACHES & PARKS

CORONADO SHORES BEACH 🏖️ 🏄 ⚓ It's the widest beach in the county but hardly atmospheric, backed up as it is by a row of towering condominiums. Still, crowds flock to this roomy expanse of clean, soft sand, where gentle waves make for good swimming and surfing. The younger crowd gathers at the north end, just south of the Hotel del Coronado. There are lifeguards. ~ Located off Ocean Boulevard.

CORONADO CITY BEACH 🏖️ 🏄 ⚓ That same wide sandy beach prevails to the north. Here, the city has a large, grassy picnic area known as **Sunset Park**, where frisbees and the aroma of fried chicken fill the air. Facilities include firepits, restrooms and lifeguards. The beach offers good fishing and swimming. Surfing is restricted to the north end during the busy summer months; it's generally safe, but be wary of unpredictable breaks. ~ On Ocean Boulevard north of Avenue G.

▼▼▼▼▼▼▼▼▼▼▼▼▼▼

San Diego Harbor

San Diego's beautiful harbor is a notable exception to the rule that big-city waterfronts lack appeal. Here, the city embraces its bay and presents its finest profile along the water.

SIGHTS

The best way to see it all is on a harbor tour. A variety of vessels dock near Harbor Drive at the foot of Broadway. **San Diego Harbor Excursion** provides leisurely trips around the 22-square-mile harbor, which is colorfully backdropped by commercial and naval vessels as well as the dramatic cityscape. Ferry service to Coronado from downtown is also operated by Harbor Excursion. Fee. ~ 1050 North Harbor Drive; 619-234-4111, fax 619-

522-6150; www.sdhe.com. My favorite sunset harbor cruises are aboard the 150-foot yacht *Spirit of San Diego*. Admission. ~ 1050 North Harbor Drive; 619-234-8687; 800-442-7847; www. sdhe.com, e-mail george@sdhe.com.

All along the city side of the harbor, from the Coast Guard Station opposite Lindbergh Field to Seaport Village, is a lovely landscaped boardwalk called the **Embarcadero**. It offers parks where you can stroll and play, a floating maritime museum and a thriving assortment of waterfront diversions.

The **Maritime Museum of San Diego** consists of four vintage ships and one visiting ship on loan from Fox Studios until 2005; most familiar is the 1863 *Star of India*, the world's oldest iron-hulled merchant ship still afloat. Visitors go aboard for a hint of what life was like on the high seas more than a century ago. You can also visit the 1898 ferry *Berkeley*, which helped in the evacuation of San Francisco during the 1906 earthquake, and the 1904 steam yacht *Medea*. Admission. ~ 1492 North Harbor Drive;

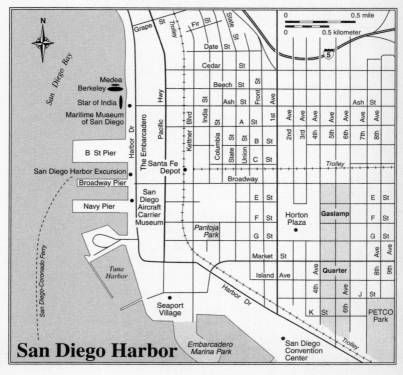

San Diego Harbor

619-234-9153, fax 619-234-8345; www.sdmaritime.com, e-mail info@sdmaritime.com.

Nautical buffs and anyone concerned about American naval power will be interested in the presence of the **U.S. Navy** in San Diego Harbor. As headquarters of the Commander Naval Base, San Diego hosts one of the world's largest fleets of fighting ships—from aircraft carriers to nuclear submarines. Naval docks and yards are off-limits but you'll see the sprawling facilities and plenty of those distinctive gray-hulled ships during a harbor cruise. Naval vessels moored at the Broadway Pier hold open house on weekends.

The Marine Center presents colorful **military reviews** most Fridays. Marching ceremonies begin at exactly 10 a.m. at the Marine Corps Recruiting Depot (619-524-1772). ~ The center may be reached from downtown by going north on Pacific Highway to Barnett Avenue, then following the signs.

The city's newest harbor attraction is the **San Diego Aircraft Carrier Museum**. *Midway*, the nation's longest serving aircraft carrier, with active service since the late 1950s, has been turned into a naval aviation museum. Visitors can check out the many exhibits, wander around the second hangar and flight decks, and experience an airplane's lift-off from the carrier in a flight simulator. ~ 910 North Harbor Drive; 619-544-9600, fax 619-544-9188; www.midway.org.

Near the south end of the Embarcadero sits the popular shopping and entertainment complex known as **Seaport Village**. Designed to replicate an early California seaport, it comprises 14 acres of bayfront parks and promenades, shops, restaurants and galleries. You'll also find a carousel, free weekend concerts and magicians and musicians to entertain the masses. ~ Kettner Boulevard and West Harbor Drive; 619-235-4013, fax 619-696-0025; www.seaportvillage.com, e-mail info@seaportvillage.com.

On the south side, overlooking the water, is the 45-foot-high **Mukilteo Lighthouse**, the official symbol of the village, a re-creation of a famous lighthouse located in Washington state. Nearby is the **Broadway Flying Horses Carousel**, a hand-carved, turn-of-the-20th-century model that originally whirled around on Coney Island.

Nearby, the **San Diego Convention Center** looks like an Erector set gone mad. An uncontained congeries of flying buttresses, giant tents and curved glass, it is fashioned in the form of a ship, seemingly poised to set sail across San Diego Harbor. This architectural exclamation mark is certainly worth a drive-by or a quick tour. ~ 111 West Harbor Drive; 619-525-5000, fax 619-525-5005; www.sdcc.org.

DINING

You'd be remiss to visit San Diego without enjoying a fresh seafood feast at a spot overlooking the harbor. Why not go first class at **Star of the Sea**? This place wears more awards than a Navy admiral. Dramatically set over the water and elegantly decorated, Star of the Sea presents a remarkable seasonal seafood menu. Live jazz on Thursday. Reservations are recommended. Dinner only. ~ 1360 North Harbor Drive; 619-232-7408, fax 619-232-1877; www.starofthesea.com, e-mail starmail@afg corp.com. ULTRA-DELUXE.

If your budget can't handle the "Star," check out the place next door—**Anthony's Fish Grotto**, whose menu includes fresh catch-of-the-day, seafood kabobs and lobster thermidor. ~ 1360 North Harbor Drive; 619-232-5103, fax 619-232-1877; www. gofishanthonys.com. BUDGET TO DELUXE.

A macho kind of establishment, famous for being used as a location in the movie *Top Gun*, **Kansas City Barbeque** is one of San Diego's most happening places. It is also *the* place in the city to eat barbecue, whether it's huge platters of chicken or ribs with all the sides or enormous barbecue beef sandwiches. ~ 610 West Market Street; 619-231-9680. BUDGET TO MODERATE.

SHOPPING

Seaport Village was designed to capture the look and feel of an early California waterfront setting. Its 57 shops dot a 14-acre village and include the usual mix of boutiques, galleries, clothing

AUTHOR FAVORITE

It may be in touristy Seaport Village, but **Greek Islands Cafe** is not your typical tourist joint; rather, it's a family-owned business that's been in the same location since 1980. The traditional Greek dishes, such as spanikopita (spinach and cheese pie) and dolmades (beef and rice stuffed grape leaves), are aromatic and savory and may just leave you longing for a trip to Greece. ~ 879 West Harbor Drive, Seaport Village; 619-239-5216; www.greekislandscafe.com. BUDGET TO MODERATE.

stores and gift shops. ~ Kettner Boulevard and West Harbor Drive; 619-235-4013; www.seaportvillage.com, e-mail info@ seaportvillage.com.

Feline-fancying visitors to Seaport Village shouldn't miss **Whiskers**, with its amazing assortment of cat-related goods and gifts. Those who can't have the real thing can adopt a ceramic counterpart called a Phlat Cat, each of which is one of a kind and comes with a family history and a name. The ultimate cat shop. ~ 863 West Harbor Drive; 619-234-6300; www.shop whiskers.com.

Seaport Village hosts a variety of open-air entertainments, from blues, jazz and salsa bands to wandering magicians and mimes.

Whether you like your hot sauce mild or volcanic, **Hot Licks** can fill the bill. The names alone, such as Da Bomb or Salsa From Hell, give you a clue as to the temperature reading. They actually have some sauces here that are so explosive that patrons must sign a waiver before purchasing a bottle. ~ 865 West Harbor Drive; 619-235-4000, 888-766-6468; www.2hot licks.com.

NIGHTLIFE   There's a wonderful view of San Diego Bay from the Seaport Village restaurant **Edgewater Grill**, where a tropical setting creates a lovely relaxed atmosphere. ~ 861 West Harbor Drive; 619-232-7581.

The Hilton Hotel's **Sierra Pacific Restaurant and Lounge** is a good place to kick back in front of the fireplace or on the patio, sipping a glass of wine and watching the yachts skimming through the marina. ~ 1960 Harbor Island Drive; 619-291-6700; www.sierrapacificrestaurant.com.

Aside from being a popular restaurant and lounge, **Tom Ham's Lighthouse** is a real lighthouse and the official Coast Guard–sanctioned beacon of Harbor Island. This scrimshaw-filled nautical lounge is a piano bar Wednesday through Friday. ~ 2150 Harbor Island Drive; 619-291-9110; www.tomhamslight house.com.

BEACHES & PARKS   **EMBARCADERO MARINA PARKS**   The center city's only real waterfront park is a breezy promenade situated on the bay and divided into two sections. The northern part has a nicely landscaped lawn and garden, picnic tables and benches. The southern half features a fishing pier, basketball courts and an athletic

course. Restrooms are available. ~ At the southern end, enter at
Harbor Drive and 8th Street; at the northern end, from Seaport
Village shopping center; 619-686-6225, fax 619-686-6200;
www.portofsandiego.org.

▼▼▼▼▼▼▼▼▼▼▼▼

Point Loma Area

The Point Loma peninsula forms a high promontory that shelters San Diego Bay from the Pacific.
It also provided Juan Rodríguez Cabrillo an excellent place from which to contemplate his 16th-century discovery
of California. For those of us who are interested in contemplating life today—or just zoning out on a view—Point Loma peninsula presents the perfect opportunity. While Point Loma seems to
appeal to young parents, professionals and an old guard who live
in tony dwellings, its northern neighbor, Ocean Beach, is a tie-dye-
and-dreadlocks-meets-gray-hair-and-sensible-shoes kind of town.

SIGHTS

Heading down Catalina Boulevard, you'll enter Cabrillo National Monument through the U.S. Navy's Fort Rosecrans, home
to a variety of sophisticated military facilities and the haunting
Fort Rosecrans National Cemetery. Here, thousands of trim
white markers march down a grassy hillside in mute testimony
to San Diego's fallen troops and deep military roots.

Naturally, **Cabrillo National Monument** features a statue of
the navigator facing his landing site at Ballast Point. The sculpture itself, a gift from Cabrillo's native Portugal, isn't very impressive, but the view is outstanding, with the bay and the city
spread out below. You can often see all the way from Mexico to
the La Jolla mesa. The visitors center includes a small museum.
The nearby **Old Point Loma Lighthouse** guided shipping from
1855 to 1891. Admission. ~ 1800 Cabrillo Memorial Drive, Point
Loma; 619-557-5450, fax 619-557-5469; www.nps.gov/cabr.

On the ocean side of the peninsula is **Whale Watch Lookout
Point**, where, during winter months, you can observe the southward migration of California gray whales. Close by is a superb
network of tidepools.

Heading north on Catalina Boulevard, you'll eventually pass
through Point Loma to **Ocean Beach**. Typical of this quirkily
eclectic beach community are the businesses along Newport
Avenue, the town's main drag. On one side of the street sits The
Electric Chair, perhaps the city's edgiest hairdressing salon, dec-

orated in wild African motif, with a staff that tends toward improbable hair color and multiple body piercings, while, across the street, the Pacific Shores Cocktail Lounge serves aging regulars, just as it has for decades. One of San Diego County's most dramatic coastlines then unfolds as you follow Sunset Cliffs Boulevard south.

LODGING   A rare beachfront find in residential Point Loma is the **Inn at Sunset Cliffs**. This trim, white, two-story, 25-room apartment hotel sits right on the seaside cliffs. Rooms are neat and clean but very basic. You can practice your swing on a miniature putting green, or lounge by the pool. There are also bachelor and studio apartments (with kitchenettes). ~ 1370 Sunset Cliffs Boulevard, Point Loma; 619-222-7901, 866-786-2543, fax 619-222-4201; www.innatsunsetcliffs.com, e-mail info@innatsunsetcliffs.com. DELUXE TO ULTRA-DELUXE.

Manmade Shelter and Harbor Islands jut out into San Diego Bay, providing space for several large resorts. For a relaxing, offbeat alternative to these mammoth hotels try **Humphrey's Half Moon Inn**. Surrounded by subtropical plants, this nautical, 182-room complex overlooks the yacht harbor and gives you the feeling that you're staying on an island. The rooms are tastefully decorated with a Polynesian theme. There is a pool, spa, putting green, concert venue and restaurant. ~ 2303 Shelter Island Drive, Point Loma; 619-224-3411, 800-542-7400, fax 619-224-3478; www.halfmooninn.com, e-mail res@halfmooninn.com. DELUXE TO ULTRA-DELUXE.

Ensconced in a plain-vanilla, two-story former church building, **Hostelling International—San Diego Point Loma** is filled up with 61 economy-minded guests almost every night during the summer. Comfortable bunk beds are grouped in 13 rooms housing from two to eight persons, youth-hostel fashion. Family rooms and private rooms are also available, and there is a common kitchen and dining area. The courtyard has Ping-Pong and other recreational activities. ~ 3790 Udall Street, Point Loma; 619-223-4778, fax 619-223-1883; www.sandiegohostels.org, e-mail pointloma@sandiegohostels.org. BUDGET.

For budget travelers who want to hang out in a quirky Southern California beach town, the **OB International Hostel** is a cheap, bare-bones place to crash. The front porch is usually

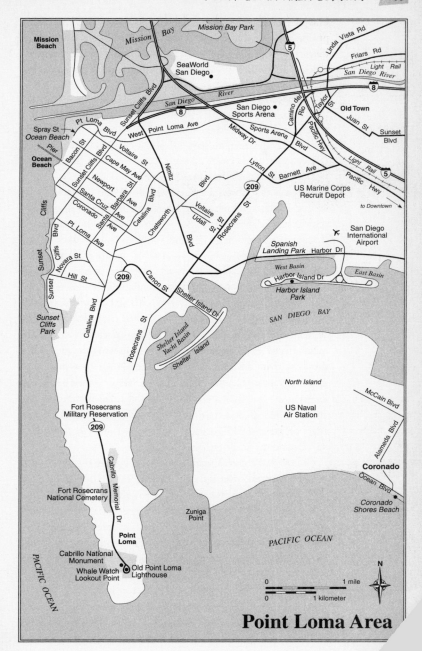

Point Loma Area

filled with youngish backpackers from various countries trading tips on the best places to find bargain-priced brews and grub. ~ 4961 Newport Avenue, Ocean Beach; 619-223-7873, 800-339-7263, fax 619-223-7881; www.californiahostel.com. BUDGET.

DINING

A marine view and whirling ceiling fans at **Humphrey's by the Bay** suggest Casablanca. California coastal cuisine is the fare, which means lots of fresh seafood. Breakfast, lunch and dinner are served. ~ Adjacent to the Half Moon Inn, 2241 Shelter Island Drive, Point Loma; 619-224-3577, fax 619-224-9438; www.humphreysbythebay.com. DELUXE TO ULTRA-DELUXE.

It seems that no matter when you go to **Point Loma Seafoods** there's a line, and rightly so. Forget the frills, this marinaside restaurant and fish market serves no-nonsense food using the freshest fish available. The clam chowder comes either red or white, and the sandwiches and seafood plates are piled high with fish, crab, squid, scallops or oysters. Grab an outside table and eat in the shadow of fishing boats and multimillion-dollar yachts. ~ 2805 Emerson Street, Point Loma; 619-223-1109; www.plsf.com. BUDGET TO MODERATE.

The air at **South Beach Bar & Grille** is decidedly salty, with fishing trophies, a long wooden bar overlooking the pier and a fun-loving, sun-bronzed crowd. It's the perfect environment in which to enjoy grilled fish tacos (mahi, shark, wahoo), steamed clams and mussels, seafood burritos and other mouthwatering choices—and wash them down with a selection from the dozen beers on tap. ~ 5059 Newport Avenue, Ocean Beach; 619-226-4577. BUDGET.

HIDDEN ►

The **O.B. People's Organic Foods Co-op** has been an Ocean Beach fixture since the early 1970s. The downstairs is tidily filled with groceries, while the second floor is occupied by a deli that specializes in fresh soup daily, organic juices and vegetarian entrées, all of which can be taken away or eaten at tables surrounding the counter, on the tiny balcony or on stools overlooking the bustling store below. ~ 4765 Voltaire Street, Ocean Beach; 619-224-1387; www.obpeoplesfood.coop. BUDGET.

One of the newest additions to Ocean Beach, and its only Portuguese restaurant, is **Portugalia**. Specialties include roast pork cooked with a sweet red-pepper paste and codfish cakes with lemon and garlic. The restaurant is on the second floor, and a gourmet Portuguese market is planned for the ground floor. Closed Monday. ~ 4835 Newport Avenue, Ocean Beach; 619-222-7678; www.sdportugalia.com. MODERATE TO DELUXE.

SHOPPING

Newport Avenue in Ocean Beach is the area's best bet for shopping. The street has a 1950s downtown feel, with slightly shabby storefronts housing old-time coffee shops and dive bars sitting next to newer, more upscale jewelry stores and restaurants. The blocks closest to the beach are lined with stores exuding a bohemian air: eclectic clothing and jewelry, black-light posters, smoking paraphernalia. Farther down is arguably San Diego County's largest antique district, with most of the stores leaning toward collectibles and retro clothing rather than pricey antiques.

Even for someone who has no intention of ever making beaded jewelry **Black Bead** is intriguing. Bins are filled with beads of every conceivable shape, size and color, and, while experts whiz around filling up bags with treasures, beginners can get advice from the helpful staff. ~ 5003 Newport Avenue, Ocean Beach; 619-222-2115.

In addition to the established shops, the 4900 block of Newport Avenue hosts a **farmer's market** every Wednesday afternoon.

NIGHTLIFE

Even musicians head outdoors during San Diego summers. **Humphrey's by the Bay** hosts the city's most ambitious series of jazz, comedy, funk and mellow rock shows, which include an impressive lineup of name artists in a beautiful oceanview concert venue. ~ 2241 Shelter Island Drive, Point Loma; 619-224-3577.

Alternative rock and pop bands, mainly local, perform Wednesday through Saturday to a young crowd at **Dream Street**. Cover. ~ 2228 Bacon Street, Ocean Beach; 619-222-8131; www.dream streetlive.com.

AUTHOR FAVORITE

Of all of Newport Avenue's used clothing and collectibles shops, **The Retro** gets my vote for the most colorful facade—bright chartreuse, purple and yellow—and the whackiest window displays—mannequins lolling around in wild getups looking like part of a Middle Eastern orgy. This is a great place to buy retro clothes or find way-out costumes. ~ 4879 Newport Avenue, Ocean Beach; 619-222-0220.

HIDDEN ▶   Red Sox and Patriots fans will be in heaven at **OB Grille**. This ultimate sports bar and restaurant has TVs galore and a rowdy, adoring crowd. Not only is New England the main event sportswise, the place even has East Coast food specials, such as a fresh Maine lobster dinner on the weekends. And while they'll serve anyone, if you go on a night the Red Sox are playing, you'd better be a fan. ~ 1956 Bacon Street, Ocean Beach; 619-269-2380.

A mellower mood can be had nightly at nearby **Winston's**, where live blues, rock and reggae are the preferred sounds. Cover. ~ 1921 Bacon Street, Ocean Beach; 619-222-6822.

BEACHES & PARKS

OCEAN BEACH 🏄 🏊 🎣 🛶 Where you toss down your towel at "OB" will probably depend as much on your age as your interests. Surfers, sailors and what's left of the hippie crowd hang out around the pier; farther north, where the surf is milder and the beach wider, families and retired folks can be found sunbathing and strolling. At the far north end is San Diego's first and only dog beach, complete with a doggie drinking fountain. There are picnic areas, restrooms and restaurants. Fishing is good from the surf or the fishing pier. Swimming and surfing are very popular here. ~ Take Ocean Beach Freeway (Route 8) west until it ends; turn left onto Sunset Cliffs Boulevard, then right on Voltaire Street; 619-235-1100.

SUNSET CLIFFS PARK 🚶 🏄 🎣 🛶 The jagged cliffs and sandstone bluffs along Point Loma peninsula give this park a spectacular setting. High-cresting waves make it popular with expert surfers, who favor the rocky beach at the foot of Ladera Avenue. Tidepools evidence the rich marine life that attracts many divers. Winding staircases (at Bermuda and Santa Cruz avenues) and steep trails lead down to some nice pocket beaches. ~ Located off of Sunset Cliffs Boulevard south of Ocean Beach; 619-235-1100.

SHELTER ISLAND 🏄 🚤 🛥 🛶 Like Harbor Island, its neighbor to the northeast, Shelter Island functions primarily as a boating center, but there's a beach facing the bay for swimming, fishing and picnicking. A landscaped walkway runs the length of the island. There are picnic areas, a children's playground, restrooms, a fishing pier and restaurants. ~ Located on Shelter Island Drive near Rosecrans Street; 619-235-1100.

HARBOR ISLAND There are no sandy beaches on this manmade island, but there is a walkway bordered by lawn, with benches along its entire length. You'll get fabulous views of the city. Facilities here include restrooms and restaurants. ~ Located south of San Diego International Airport on Harbor Island Drive; 619-686-6200, fax 619-686-6400.

SPANISH LANDING PARK 🏊 This is a slender sandy beach with walkways, a grassy picnic area and a children's playground. Situated close to San Diego International Airport, the park overlooks the Harbor Island marina and offers lovely views of the bay and city. Restrooms are available. ~ Located just west of the airport on North Harbor Drive; 619-686-6200, fax 619-686-6400.

Mission Bay Park Area

Dredged from a shallow, mosquito-infested tidal bay, 4600-acre Mission Bay Park is the largest municipal aquatic park in the world. For San Diego's exercise enthusiasts it is Mecca, a recreational paradise dotted with islands and lagoons and ringed by 27 miles of sandy beaches.

Here, visitors join with residents to enjoy swimming, sailing, windsurfing, waterskiing, fishing, jogging, cycling, golf and tennis. Or perhaps a relaxing day of kite flying and sunbathing.

SIGHTS

More than just a playground, Mission Bay Park features a shopping complex, resort hotels, restaurants and the popular marine park **SeaWorld San Diego**. This 189-acre park-within-a-park is one of the world's largest oceanariums. Admission. ~ SeaWorld Drive; 619-226-3901, fax 619-226-3996; www.seaworld.com.

Among the attractions are killer whales; one of the largest penguin colonies north of Antarctica; a "Forbidden Reef" inhabited by bat rays and over 100 moray eels; and "Rocky Point Preserve," an exhibit boasting a wave pool, pettable dolphins and a colony of California sea otters. "Manatee Rescue," only one of three U.S. manatee exhibits outside of Florida, is a venture designed to relieve the Florida SeaWorld of its overflowing supply of rehabilitating manatees. The exhibit provides over 800 feet of underwater viewing. The park also includes "Journey to Atlantis," a wild

Mission Bay Park was a vast tidal marsh until 1944, when the city converted the land into an aquatic park.

ride that takes thrill seekers on a tour of Poseidon's watery island nation; a Sky Tower that lifts visitors nearly 300 feet above Mission Bay; a helicopter simulator dubbed the "Wild Arctic" that takes visitors to an Arctic research station to explore two capsized century-old sailing ships and see native Arctic mammals; and "Shipwreck Rapids," a wet and winding ride in a raft-like innertube.

One of the best bargains at SeaWorld is the guided tour of the park (fee). It's expert guides take the guests on adventures that may include the Shark Laboratory, the animal care area and the killer whale facility. I prefer simply to watch the penguins waddle about on their simulated iceberg and zip around after fish in their glass-contained ocean, or to peer in at the fearsome makos at "Shark Encounter." The park's magnificent marine creatures are all the entertainment I need.

Down along the oceanfront, **Mission Beach** is strung out along the narrow jetty of sand that protects Mission Bay from the sea. Mission Boulevard threads its way through this eclectic, wall-to-wall mix of shingled beach shanties, condominiums and luxury homes.

The historic 1925 "Giant Dipper" has come back to life after years of neglect at **Belmont Park**. One of only two West Coast seaside coasters, this beauty is not all the park has to offer. There's also a carousel, a video arcade, a large indoor swimming pool and a host of shops and eateries along the beach and board-walk. ~ 3146 Mission Boulevard or on the beach at Mission Boulevard and West Mission Bay Drive; 858-228-9283; www.belmontpark.com, e-mail info@belmontpark.com.

Pacific Beach, which picks up at the northern edge of the bay, is the liveliest of the city beaches, an area packed with high school and college students. Designer shorts, a garish Hawaiian shirt, strapped-on sunglasses and a skateboard are all you need to fit in perfectly along the frenetic boardwalk at "PB." If you're missing any or all of these accoutrements, Garnet Avenue is the city's core, lined with skate and surf shops and funky boutiques, as well as colorful bars and taco eateries.

Stop and see the 1920s **Crystal Pier**, with its tiny hotel built out over the waves. Or take a stroll along the boardwalk, check-ing out the sunbathers, skaters, joggers and cyclists. ~ Located at the end of Garnet Avenue.

There aren't many beachfront facilities along Pacific Beach, **LODGING**
Mission Beach and Ocean Beach, except for condominiums. One
particularly pretty four-unit condominium, **Ventanas al Mar**,
overlooks the ocean in Mission Beach. Its contemporary two-
and three-bedroom units feature fireplaces, jacuzzis, kitchens
and washer-dryers. They sleep as many as eight people. In the
summer, these rent by the week only. ~ 3631 Ocean Front Walk,
Mission Beach; 858-488-1580, 800-869-7858, fax 858-488-
1584; www.billluther.com, e-mail vacation@billluther.com.
ULTRA-DELUXE.

Pacific Beach boasts the San Diego County lodging with the
most character of all. **Crystal Pier Hotel** is a throwback to the
1930s. Fittingly so, because that's when this quaint-looking assemblage of 29 cottages on Crystal Pier was built. This blue-and-
white woodframe complex, perched over the waves, features tiny
little cottages. Each comes with a kitchen and patio-over-the-sea,
not to mention your own parking place on the pier. A unique discovery indeed. ~ 4500 Ocean Boulevard, Pacific Beach; 858-483-
6983, 800-748-5894, fax 858-483-6811; www.crystalpier.com.
ULTRA-DELUXE.

The 23 rooms at the **Beach Haven Inn** may be furnished in
an eclectic mix of garage sale–type furniture, but most come with
kitchens, there's an inviting pool area with a communal barbecue, it's only a block from the beach and the price is right. ~ 4740

AUTHOR FAVORITE

Only one Mission Bay resort stands out as unique—the **San Diego Paradise
Point Resort & Spa**. Over 40 acres of lush gardens, lagoons and white-sand
beach surround the bungalows of this 462-room resort. Except for some
fancy suites, room decor is basic and pleasant, with quality furnishings. But
guests don't spend much time in their rooms anyway. At Paradise Point
there's more than a mile of beach, catamaran and bike rentals, a spa, a fitness center, five tennis courts, five pools, a basketball court, sand volleyball, two restaurants and an 18-hole putting course. A stay at this self-
contained island paradise is as close as you can get to a Hawaiian
vacation without actually crossing the Pacific. ~ 1404 West Vacation
Road, Mission Beach; 858-274-4630, 800-344-2626, fax 858-581-5929;
www.paradisepoint.com, e-mail reservations@paradisepoint.com.
ULTRA-DELUXE.

Mission Boulevard, Pacific Beach; 858-272-3812, 800-831-6323, fax 858-272-3532; www.beachhaveninn.com. MODERATE.

A real bargain is **Banana Bungalow**, a privately run hostel right on Pacific Beach. The accommodations are of the co-ed bunk-bed variety, for those of the backpacker persuasion who don't mind sharing rooms with strangers. You must be a traveler with an out-of-state license or a foreign passport. A complimentary breakfast is served every morning. Accommodations are on a first-come, first-served basis. ~ 707 Reed Avenue, Pacific Beach; 858-273-3060, 800-546-7835, fax 858-273-1440; www.bananabungalow.com. BUDGET.

DINING

The **Mission Cafe** is a casual neighborhood restaurant where folks are likely to chat with whoever is dining next to them. The ambience is funky, the furniture eclectic, and the walls are enlivened with local art. Blending Asian and Latin influences, the cuisine emphasizes food that is healthy, tasty and original. There are breakfast standards with a twist—the French toast is served with berries and blueberry purée. If you're in the mood for something more Mexican, order the *plata verde con huevos* (slightly sweet tamales with eggs, roasted chile verde and cheese). For lunch there are such creations as the ginger-sesame chicken roll-up and the Baja shrimp wrap. You can also choose from several soups, salads and sandwiches. No dinner. ~ 3795 Mission Boulevard, Mission Beach; 858-488-9060. BUDGET.

Critic's choice for the area's best omelettes is **Broken Yolk Café**. Choose from nearly 30 of these eggy creations or invent your own. If you can eat it all within an hour, the ironman/

AUTHOR FAVORITE

When **Saska's Restaurant** opened in 1951, it was dedicated to providing diners with the choicest cuts of meat and salads with real roquefort dressing. It is still owned and operated by the Saska family. The steaks are still top-quality and the roquefort remains, but entrées have expanded to include pasta and fresh seafood dishes. The atmosphere is still 1950s, cozily dark with comfy booths, a fireplace and a bar filled with regulars. In keeping with the times, the family has opened up High Tide Sushi next door. ~ 3768 Mission Boulevard, Mission Beach; 858-488-7311. MODERATE TO DELUXE.

woman special—including a dozen eggs, mushrooms, onions, cheese, etc.—costs only $1.98. Faint or fail and you pay much more. They make soups, sandwiches and salads, too. Outdoor patio seating is available. Breakfast and lunch only. ~ 1851 Garnet Avenue, Pacific Beach; 858-270-0045, fax 858-270-4745; www.brokenyolkcafe.com. BUDGET.

For the best sandwiches, head for **The Chalkboard**. Regulars' photos paper the walls, plastic action figures dangle over the few stools and the sandwiches are enormous. Using high-quality Boar's Head brand meats and the freshest veggies, this hole-in-the-wall mom-and-pop sandwich shop turns out humorously named creations such as "Bill Clinton"—honey-roasted turkey (a.k.a. the cooked goose). No dinner. Closed Sunday. ~ 1146 Garnet Avenue, Pacific Beach; 858-274-8819. BUDGET.

The most creative restaurant in Pacific Beach is **Château Orleans**, one of the city's finest Cajun-Creole restaurants. Tasty appetizers fresh from the bayou include Louisiana crab cakes and Southern-fried 'gator bites. Yes, indeed, they eat alligators down in Cajun country, and you should be brave enough to find out why. Mardi Gras gumbo chock-full of crawfish, Uncle Bubba's prime rib steak, chicken sauce piquant and colorful jambalaya are typical menu choices. Everything is authentic except the decor, which, thankfully, shuns board floors and bare bulbs in favor of carpets, original New Orleans artwork and a patio seating in a New Orleans–style garden. Live jazz and blues Thursday through Saturday. Dinner only. Closed Sunday. ~ 926 Turquoise Street, Pacific Beach; 858-488-6744, fax 858-488-6745; www.chateauorleans.com. MODERATE TO DELUXE.

All the pasta at **Pasta Expresso** is homemade, and every day there is a selection of six or seven types that can be paired with marinara, Italian sausage, alfredo or pesto sauce. The generous portions of pasta and sauce come with salad and garlic bread and are a real bargain for only $6. Closed Sunday. ~ 4480 Haines Street, Pacific Beach; 858-272-9448. BUDGET.

SHOPPING

Commercial enterprises in these beach communities cater primarily to sun worshipers. Beachie boutiques and rental shops are everywhere. A shopping center on the beach, **Belmont Park** has a host of shops and restaurants. ~ 3146 Mission Boulevard, Mission Bay Park.

Though it's tiny, **La Sandale**'s colorful muraled exterior is bound to catch your eye. Inside, the shop is crammed with beach footwear for both surfers and beach bunnies. ~ 3761 North Mission Boulevard, Mission Beach; 858-488-1134.

The **Promenade Mall at Pacific Beach**, a modern, Mediterranean-style shopping complex, houses a dozen or so smartly decorated specialty shops and restaurants. A farmer's market is held here on Saturday. ~ Located on Mission Boulevard between Pacific Beach Drive and Reed Street, Pacific Beach; 858-490-9097.

Garnet Avenue is the place in "PB" to hook up with laid-back street styles, skintight clubwear, one-of-a-kind outfits and tattoos. **Anatomic Rag** carries vintage wear that'll tickle the fancy of modern-day hep cats and kittens. ~ 1336 Garnet Avenue, Pacific Beach; 858-274-3597.

HIDDEN ►   Shipments of the very latest in Hawaiian-designed duds arrive at the **Aloha Shirt Shop** several times a month. Little off-the-beaten-track Aloha positively overflows with the print shirts and accessories that typify the beach lifestyle. ~ 3460 Ingraham Street, Pacific Beach; 866-746-7256; www.alohashirtshop.com.

NIGHTLIFE   The **Pennant** is a Mission Beach landmark where local beachies congregate on the deck en masse to get rowdy and watch the sunset. The entertainment here is the clientele. ~ 2893 Mission Boulevard, Mission Beach; 858-488-1671.

The **Cannibal Bar** features a variety of live music Wednesday through Sunday. Bands may play blues, ska, rock or even jazz. Closed Monday and Tuesday. Cover. ~ Catamaran Hotel, 3999 Mission Boulevard, Pacific Beach; 858-488-1081; www.catamaranresort.com.

Blind Melons, beside the Crystal Pier, is best described as a Chicago beach bar featuring punk rock on Tuesday, a national blues act twice a month and local acts the other nights of the week. Cover. ~ 710 Garnet Avenue, Pacific Beach; 858-483-7844; www.home.fan.rr.com/melonsx.

HIDDEN ►   **Javanican Coffee House** is hard to miss since it's painted deep purple and has a flowering bright-pink bougainvillea crawling up the side. Inside, the place is strictly a retro 1950s coffee house. They serve up organic coffees and light snacks, as well as serendipitous live entertainment. There's no schedule, but the owner is a musician, so no telling who will show up to jam. ~ 4338 Cass Street, Pacific Beach; 858-483-8035; www.sluka.com.

MISSION BAY PARK 🏊 🦅 🏄 ⛴ 🚣 🛥 🛶 ⛵ One of the nation's largest and most diverse city-owned aquatic parks, Mission Bay has something to suit just about everyone's recreational interests. Key areas and facilities are as follows: **Dana Landing** and **Quivira Basin** make up the southwest portion of this 4600-acre park. Most boating activities begin here, where port headquarters and a large marina are located. Adjacent is **Bonita Cove**, used for swimming, picnicking and volleyball. There is a softball field at **Mariner's Point.** Mission Boulevard shops, restaurants and recreational equipment rentals are within easy walking distance. **Ventura Cove** houses a large hotel complex but its sandy beach is open to the public. Calm waters make it a popular swimming spot for small children.

BEACHES & PARKS

Fiesta Island is a favorite spot for fishing from the quieter coves and for kite flying.

Vacation Isle and **Ski Beach** are easily reached via the bridge on Ingraham Street, which bisects the island. The west side contains public swimming areas, boat rentals and a model yacht basin. Ski Beach, on the east side, is the best spot in the bay for waterskiing. **Fiesta Island** is situated on the southeast side of the park. It's ringed with soft-sand swimming beaches and laced with jogging, cycling and skating paths. On the south side of Fiesta Island sits **South Shores**, a large boat-launching area.

Over on the **East Shore**, you'll find landscaped picnic areas, a physical fitness course, playgrounds, a sandy beach for swimming and the park information center. **De Anza Cove**, at the extreme northeast corner of the park, has a sandy beach for swimming plus a large private campground. **Crown Point Shores** provides a sandy beach, a picnic area, a nature study area, a physical fitness course and a waterski landing.

Sail Bay and **Riviera Shores** make up the northwest portion of Mission Bay and back up against the apartments and condominiums of Pacific Beach. Sail Bay's beaches aren't the best in the park and are usually submerged during high tides. Riviera Shores has a better beach, with waterski areas.

Santa Clara and **El Carmel points** jut out into the westernmost side of Mission Bay. They are perfect for water sports: swimming, snorkeling, surfing, waterskiing, windsurfing and boating. Santa Clara Point is of interest to the visitor, with its recreation center, tennis courts and softball field. A sandy beach fronts San Juan Cove, between the two points.

Just about every facility imaginable can be found somewhere in Mission Bay Park. There are also catamaran and windsurf rentals, playgrounds and parks, frisbee and golf, restaurants and groceries. ~ Located along Mission Boulevard between West Mission Bay Drive and East Mission Bay Drive; 619-221-8900, fax 619-581-9984.

▲ The finest and largest of San Diego's commercial campgrounds is **Campland On The Bay** (2211 Pacific Beach Drive; 800-422-9386; www.campland.com), featuring 600 hookup sites for RVs, vans, tents and boats; $30 to $155 per night.

MISSION BEACH PARK 🚲 🏊 🏃 The wide, sandy beach at the southern end is a favorite haunt of high school and college students. The hot spot is at the foot of Capistrano Court. A paved boardwalk runs along the beach and is busy with bicyclists, joggers and roller skaters. Farther north, up around the old Belmont Park roller coaster, the beach grows narrower and the surf rougher. The crowd tends to get that way, too, with heavy-metal teens, sailors and bikers hanging out along the sea wall, ogling and sometimes harassing the bikini set. This is the closest San Diego comes to Los Angeles' colorful but funky Venice Beach. Facilities include restrooms, lifeguards and a boardwalk lined with restaurants and beach rentals. Surfing is popular along the jetty. ~ Located along Mission Boulevard north of West Mission Bay Drive.

PACIFIC BEACH PARK 🚲 🏊 🏃 ⛵ At its south end, "PB" is a major gathering place, its boardwalk crowded with teens and assorted rowdies, but a few blocks north, just before Crystal Pier, the boardwalk becomes a quieter concrete promenade that follows scenic, sloping cliffs. The beach widens here and the crowd becomes more family-oriented. The surf is moderate—fine for swimming and bodysurfing. Pier and surf fishing are great for corbina and surf perch. South of the pier, Ocean Boulevard becomes a pedestrian-only mall with a bike path, benches and picnic tables. Amenities include restrooms, lifeguards and restaurants. ~ Located near Grand Avenue and Pacific Beach Drive.

FOUR

La Jolla

A certain fascination centers around the origins of the name "La Jolla." It means "jewel" in Spanish, but according to Indian legend it means "hole" or "caves." Both are fairly apt interpretations: this Mediterranean-style enclave perched on a bluff above the Pacific is indeed a jewel; and its dramatic coves and cliffs are pocked with sea caves. Choose your favorite interpretation, but for goodness sake don't pronounce the name phonetically—it's "La Hoya."

According to artifacts found in the area, American Indian settlements may have flourished along La Jolla's shoreline more than 3000 years ago, but it wasn't until the middle of the 19th century that the modern-day town began to develop. Things really started booming when the railroad extended to La Jolla in the 1890s, causing developers to see the benefit of constructing resorts along the shoreline, to attract visitors from neighboring San Diego. Shortly thereafter, luckily for La Jolla, newspaper heiress Ellen Browning Scripps moved to town. Her considerable financial gifts to the community are obvious in the number of institutions bearing her name, most notably the Scripps Institute of Oceanography, whose first building was constructed in 1909.

Throughout the first few decades of the 20th century, tony hotels began popping up around La Jolla, some of which, such as the Grande Colonial and La Valencia, still reign as the town's most popular and beautiful hostelries. These resorts appealed to many people in the Hollywood film-making community, who started coming to La Jolla in the 1930s. They helped to start a local theater, The Summer Playhouse, which developed into the now-famous La Jolla Playhouse.

Today La Jolla is a community within the city of San Diego, though it considers itself something more on the order of a principality—like Monaco. Locals call it "The Village" and boast that it's an ideal walking town, which is another way of saying La Jolla is a frustrating place to drive in. Narrow, curvy 1930s-era streets are jammed with traffic and hard to follow. A parking place in The Village is truly a jewel within the jewel.

The beauty of its seven miles of cliff-lined sea coast is La Jolla's raison d'être. Spectacular homes, posh hotels, chic boutiques and gourmet restaurants crowd shoulder to shoulder for a better view of the ocean. Each of the area's many beaches has its own particular character and flock of local devotees. Though most beaches are narrow, rocky and not really suitable for swimming or sunbathing, they are the best in the county for surfing and skindiving.

SIGHTS   To get the lay of the land, wind your way up **Mount Soledad** (east on Nautilus Street from La Jolla Boulevard), where the view extends across the city skyline and out over the ocean. That large white cross at the summit is a memorial to the war dead and the setting for sunrise services every Easter Sunday.

Ah, but exploring The Village is the reason you're here, so head back down Nautilus Street, go right on La Jolla Boulevard and continue until it leads into **Prospect Street**. This is La Jolla's hottest thoroughfare and the intersection with **Girard Avenue**, the town's traditional "main street," is the town's epicenter. Here, in the heart of La Jolla, you are surrounded by the elite and elegant.

Although Girard Avenue features as wide a selection of shops as anyplace in San Diego, Prospect Street is much more interesting and stylish. By all means, walk Prospect's curving mile from the cottage shops and galleries on the north to the **Museum of Contemporary Art San Diego** on the south. The museum, by the way, is a piece of art in itself, one of many striking contemporary structures in La Jolla, originally designed by noted architect Irving Gill. The museum's highly regarded collection focuses on Minimalist, California, Pop, and other avant-garde developments in painting, sculpture and photography. Closed Wednesday. Admission. ~ 700 Prospect Street; 858-454-3541, fax 858-454-6985; www.mcasd.org, e-mail info@mcasd.org.

During this stroll along Prospect Street, also visit the lovely **La Valencia Hotel**, a very pink, very prominent resting place nicknamed "La V." This pink lady is a La Jolla landmark and a local institution, serving as both village pub and town meeting hall. You can feel the charm and sense the rich tradition of the place the moment you enter. While "La V" has always been a

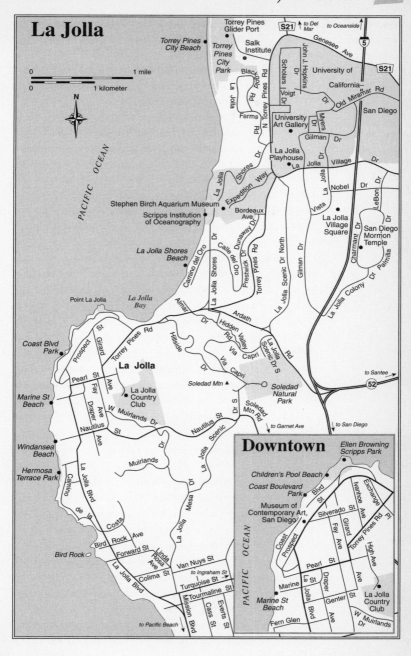

La Jolla

0 _____ 1 mile
0 _____ 1 kilometer

N

PACIFIC OCEAN

Torrey Pines Glider Port

S21 to Del Mar   to Oceanside

Torrey Pines City Beach

Salk Institute

Torrey Pines City Park

John J. Hopkins

Genesee Ave

5

Black Gold Rd

La Jolla Farms Rd

Scholars Dr

N Torrey Pines Rd

Voigt Dr

University of California–

San Diego

Old Miramar Rd

University Art Gallery

Myers Dr

S21

La Jolla Playhouse

Gilman Dr

La Jolla Shores Dr

Expedition Way

La Jolla Village Dr

La Jolla Village Dr

Stephen Birch Aquarium Museum

Bordeaux Ave

Nobel Dr

LeBon Dr

Scripps Institution of Oceanography

Dunaway Dr

La Jolla Village Square

San Diego Mormon Temple

Palmilla Dr

La Jolla Shores Beach

Camino del Oro

Calle del Oro

La Jolla Shores Dr

Prestwick Dr

N Torrey Pines Rd

La Jolla Scenic Dr North

Gilman Dr

Charmant Dr

La Jolla Colony Dr

Point La Jolla

La Jolla Bay

Almar

Ardath

Hidden Valley Rd

La Jolla Rd

to Santee

52

Coast Blvd Park

Prospect St

Girard

Torrey Pines Rd

Hillside Dr

Via Capri

Via Capri

La Jolla Scenic Dr S

La Jolla

Pearl St

Fay Ave

Draper Ave

W Muirlands Dr

Soledad Mtn ▲

Soledad Natural Park

to Garnet Ave

to San Diego

Marine St Beach

La Jolla Country Club

Nautilus St

Nautilus St

Soledad Mtn Rd

Windansea Beach

La Jolla Scenic Dr

Muirlands

Hermosa Terrace Park

Camino de la Costa

La Jolla Blvd

La Jolla Mesa Dr

Bird Rock Ave

Bird Rock

Forward St

Linda Rosa Ave

Van Nuys St

to Ingraham St

PACIFIC OCEAN

Colima St

Turquoise St

Tourmaline St

Everts St

Cass St

Mission Blvd

to Pacific Beach

Downtown

Ellen Browning Scripps Park

Children's Pool Beach

Coast Boulevard Park

Exchange Pl

Ivanhoe Ave

Coast Blvd

Museum of Contemporary Art, San Diego

Silverado St

Girard Ave

Torrey Pines Rd

High Ave

Prospect

Fay Ave

Pearl St

Marine

La Jolla Blvd

Draper Ave

Genter St

W Muirlands Dr

La Jolla Country Club

Marine St Beach

Fern Glen

haven for the gods and goddesses of Hollywood, the Gregory Peck and Olivia de Haviland gang of old has been replaced by a client roster of current stars like Will Smith and Jada Pinkett. ~ 1132 Prospect Street; 858-454-0771, 800-451-0772, fax 858-456-3921; www.lavalencia.com, e-mail info@lavalencia.com.

The Museum of Contemporary Art San Diego's modern lines belie the fact that it was designed as a private villa back in 1915.

Another center of interest lies at the northern end of La Jolla. The best beaches are here, stretching from the ritzy La Jolla Shores to the scientific sands of Scripps Beach.

Driving along North Torrey Pines Road you will undoubtedly cross the **University of California–San Diego** (858-534-2230) campus, a sprawling 1200 acres set on a mesa above the Pacific Ocean. Home to over 22,000 undergraduate and graduate students, the university boasts natural chaparral canyons, green lawns and eucalyptus groves, contrasted with urban student plazas and buildings. Spread throughout this expansive campus is the **Stuart Collection of Sculpture**, featuring permanent outdoor sculptures by leading contemporary artists. Maps are available at the information kiosk. ~ 858-534-2117, fax 858-534-9713; stuartcollection.ucsd.edu.

While you're on campus, consider checking out the **University Art Gallery,** dedicated to delivering high-quality exhibits ranging from works of international contemporary artists to touring exhibitions. ~ 9500 Gilman Drive; 858-822-3547, fax 858-822-3548; universityartgallery.ucsd.edu.

Another interesting campus attraction is the **Mandeville Special Collections Library**, which offers periodic exhibits of its rare books, manuscripts, maps, photographs and art works. Recent exhibits include displays of some of the library's large collection of drawings by Theodor Seuss Geisel, better known as Dr. Seuss, and a retrospective of the books published by Ninja Press over its 20-year history. ~ 9500 Gilman Drive; 858-534-2533, fax 858-534-5950; orpheus.ucsd.edu/speccoll.

Also part of the university is the **Scripps Institution of Oceanography**, the oldest institution in the nation devoted to oceanography and the home of the **Birch Aquarium at Scripps**. Here you'll find 60 marine life tanks, a manmade tidepool, breathtaking exhibits of coastal underwater habitats, interactive displays for children and adults and displays illustrating recent advances in oceanographic research. Admission. ~ 2300 Expedition Way; 858-534-3474, fax 858-534-7114; www.aquarium. ucsd.edu, e-mail aquariuminfo@ucsd.edu.

Another research center, the **Salk Institute**, created by the man whose vaccine helped vanquish polio, is renowned not only for its research but its architecture as well. The surrealistic concrete structure was designed by Louis Kahn in 1960 to be an environment that would stimulate original thinking. It is a stunning site, perched on the lip of a high canyon overlooking the Pacific. A daily tour, by appointment only, is conducted in the morning. ~ 10010 North Torrey Pines Road, just north of the University of California–San Diego campus; tour information, 858-453-4100 ext. 1200, fax 858-625-2404; www.salk.edu.

Next to the institute is the **Torrey Pines Glider Port**, where you can watch hang-gliding and paragliding masters soar over the waves from atop a 360-foot cliff. ~ 2800 Torrey Pines Scenic Drive; 858-452-9858, 877-359-8326, fax 858-452-9983; www.flytorrey.com, e-mail aircal@ix.netcom.com.

Trails leading down to the notorious **Black's Beach** begin here. Black's is San Diego's unofficial, illegal, ever-loving nude beach. And a beautiful strip of natural landscape it is.   ◄ HIDDEN

Bordering Black's on the north is **Torrey Pines State Reserve and Beach**, whose 1750-acre preserve was established to protect one of the world's rarest pine trees, the Torrey Pine. The tree itself is a gnarled and twisted specimen. Centuries ago these pines covered the southern coast of California; today they are indigenous only to Santa Rosa Island, off the coast of Santa Barbara, and to this reserve. A network of trails through this blufftop reserve makes hiking sheer pleasure. Among the rewards are the views, extending along the cliffs and ocean, and the chance to walk quietly among La Jolla's rare treasures. ~ Located west of North Torrey Pines Road, two miles north of Genesee Avenue.

Driving along Route 5, you'd have to be blind to miss the **San Diego Mormon Temple**. It looks like a gleaming white ice palace, with spires that reach to the clouds; the impressive structure is 190 feet tall and covers 59,000 square feet. While you have to be a member of the Church of Jesus Christ of Latter-day Saints to go inside the temple, anyone can wander around the grounds and investigate the awe-inspiring structure, up close and personal. ~ 7474 Charmant Drive; 858-622-0991.

LODGING   Like a Monopoly master, La Jolla possesses the lion's share of "Park Place" accommodations in the San Diego area. Understandably, there are no budget hotels in this fashionable village by the sea.

Sands of La Jolla is a small, 39-room motel on a busy thoroughfare just a quick drive away from the bustle of Girard Avenue and Prospect Street. Rooms (kitchenettes are available) are not exactly designer showcases, but they are tastefully appointed and neatly maintained. Amenities include a heated pool and minifridges. ~ 5417 La Jolla Boulevard; 858-459-3336, 800-643-0530, fax 858-454-0922; www.sandsoflajolla.com, e-mail sandsoflajolla@aol.com. MODERATE.

Small, European-style hotels have always been popular in La Jolla, and the granddaddy of them all is the **The Grande Colonial**. Established in 1913, the 75-room establishment features rooms lavishly decorated with historically inspired furnishings. Oceanfront rooms provide matchless views. There's a restaurant on-site. ~ 910 Prospect Street; 858-454-2181, 800-826-1278, fax 858-454-5679; www.thegrandecolonial.com, e-mail info@thegrandecolonial.com. ULTRA-DELUXE.

More than just a hotel, **La Valencia** is a La Jolla institution and one of the loveliest hotels in San Diego. Resplendent in pink stucco and Spanish tile, it is perched on a breezy promontory overlooking the coves and sea cliffs of La Jolla. From the moment guests enter via a trellis-covered tile loggia into a lobby that could pass for King Juan Carlos' living room, they are enveloped in elegance. The 106 private accommodations reflect the European feel—that is, they tend to run on the small side and are furnished in reproduction antiques. Ah, but out back there's a beautiful garden terrace opening onto the sea and tumbling down to a free-form swimming pool edged with lawn. Facilities include a gym, sauna, whirlpool and three distinctive restaurants. ~ 1132 Prospect Street; 858-454-0771, 800-451-0772, fax 858-456-3921; www.lavalencia.com, e-mail info@lavalencia.com. ULTRA-DELUXE.

Also smack dab in The Village is the **Empress Hotel**, a five-story, L-shaped building set on a quiet street just a stone's throw from both the beach and the bustle of Prospect Street. A contemporary establishment blending Victorian and European boutique styles, it has 73 spacious rooms and suites that offer amenities such as minifridges, bathrobes, coffeemakers and high-speed internet; two "green" suites have filtered air and water. If you're looking to splash out, you probably can't get any fancier than one of the two jacuzzi suites outfitted with a baby grand piano and ocean views. There are also fitness facilities, a sauna, a spa and a restaurant. Enjoy complimentary continental breakfast on the flower-lined patio. ~ 7766 Fay Avenue; 858-454-3001, 888-369-9900, fax 858-454-6387; www.empress-hotel.com, e-mail reservations411@empress-hotel.com. ULTRA-DELUXE.

Tucked away on the north fringe of The Village is **Andrea Villa Inn**, a classy-looking 49-unit motel that packs more amenities than some resorts. There is a pool, a jacuzzi and continental breakfast service. The rooms are spacious and professionally decorated with quality furniture. Be forewarned, however, that some guests have complained that the inn was not as clean as they would have liked. ~ 2402 Torrey Pines Road; 858-459-3311, 800-411-2141, fax 858-459-1320; www.andrea villa.com, e-mail info@andreavilla.com. DELUXE.

A great stop for picnic supplies is the La Jolla Farmers Market, held Sunday at the La Jolla Elementary School. ~ Center and Girard streets.

Just as The Village boasts San Diego's finest selection of small hotels, it can also claim a well-known bed and breakfast. **The Bed and Breakfast Inn at La Jolla**, listed as a historical site, was designed as a private home in 1913 by the architect Irving Gill. The John Phillip Sousa family resided here in 1921. Faithfully restored by its present owners as a 15-room inn, it stands today as Gill's finest example of Cubist-style architecture. Ideally situated a block and a half from the ocean, this inn is the essence of La Jolla. Each guest room features an individual decorative theme carried out in period furnishings. Some have a fireplace and an ocean view. All have private bath. Bicycles are available for guests' use. ~ 7753 Draper Avenue; 858-456-2066, 800-582-2466, fax 858-456-1510; www.innlajolla.com, e-mail bed+breakfast@innlajolla.com. ULTRA-DELUXE.

La Jolla's only true beachfront hotel is **Sea Lodge on La Jolla Shores Beach**. Designed and landscaped to resemble an old California hacienda, this 128-room retreat overlooks the Pacific on a mile-long beach. With its stuccoed arches, terra-cotta roofs, ceramic tilework, fountain and flowers, Sea Lodge offers a relaxing south-of-the-border setting. Guest rooms are large; most feature balconies, some have kitchens and all have access to the usual amenities: fitness room, sauna, jacuzzi, pool and tennis courts. ~ 8110 Camino del Oro; 858-459-8271, 800-237-5211, fax 858-456-9346; www.sealodge.com. ULTRA-DELUXE.

La Jolla Travelodge may belong to a chain, which doesn't make it exactly hidden or exciting, but it's about the best deal you're likely to find in pricey La Jolla. It's only a block from the beach, and, for most of the year, room rates start at $70, which makes it a real bargain in this neck of the woods. ~ 6750 La Jolla Boulevard; 858-454-0716, 800-454-4361, fax 858-454-1075; www.lajollatravelodge.com. MODERATE TO DELUXE.

Built on 9.5 acres that were formerly part of an equestrian ranch across from the UCSD campus, the Estancia La Jolla Hotel & Spa is the newest addition (opened in June 2004) to La Jolla's luxury properties. The modern Spanish rancho-style resort has all the upscale amenities you'd expect, and the courtyards are planted in a wide variety of plants and succulents befitting the building style. The meeting facilities are state of the art, and the spa has plenty of treatment rooms where the harried business traveler can be massaged into tranquility. ~ 9700 North Torrey Pines Road; 858-550-1000, 877-437-8262, fax 858-550-1001; www.estancialajolla.com. ULTRA-DELUXE.

Just north of UCSD, the Hilton La Jolla Torrey Pines, adorned with marble and polished wood, is an outstanding white-glove establishment. Here, art deco visits the 21st century in a series of terraces that lead past plush dining rooms, multitiered fountains, a luxurious swimming pool and a fitness center. Avid golfers will appreciate its location—overlooking the 18th fairway of the Torrey Pines Golf Course, and the site of the 2008 U.S. Open. ~ 10950 North Torrey Pines Road; 858-558-1500, 800-762-6160, fax 858-450-4584; www.lajollatorreypines.hilton.com, e-mail santp-reservations@hilton.com. ULTRA-DELUXE.

DINING

Just as it is blessed with many fine hotels, La Jolla is a restaurant paradise. George's at the Cove based its climb to success on its knockout view of the water, a casual, contemporary environment, fine service and a trend-setting regional menu. Daily menus incorporate the freshest seafood, beef, lamb, poultry and pasta available. Downstairs in the fine-dining room are selections such as sesame-crusted tuna with eggplant-miso purée, roasted loin of lamb and braised lamb shoulder with spicy Medjool date couscous. The food presentation alone is a work of art. ~ 1250 Prospect Place; 858-454-4244, fax 858-454-5458; www.georgesat thecove.com. MODERATE TO ULTRA-DELUXE.

For no-frills sushi and *bento* boxes, head for **Yummy Maki Yummy Box**, located in a nondescript strip mall. The seafood is fresh, and the service is courteous and attentive. No lunch. Closed Sunday. ~ 3211 Holiday Court #101; 858-587-9848. BUDGET.   ◄ *HIDDEN*

Jose's Court Room, a noisy, down-to-earth Mexican pub, is the best place in town for quick, casual snacks. They offer all the typical taco, tostada and enchilada plates plus tasty sautéed shrimp and chicken *ranchero* dinners. There's also a Mexican-style weekend breakfast. ~ 1037 Prospect Street; 858-454-7655. BUDGET TO MODERATE.

Just down the street, the aptly named **Living Room** has an eclectic mix of chairs and couches that probably started out as somebody's living room furniture. The comfy atmosphere and excellent coffee drinks attract a lively crowd that hang around chatting, reading and getting a caffeine fix while munching on pastries and sandwiches. ~ 1010 Prospect Street; 858-459-1187, fax 858-551-0973; www.livingroomcafe.com. BUDGET.   ◄ *HIDDEN*

Illuminated only by the flickering of candles and the incandescent glow of fish tanks, the **Manhattan** at the Empress Hotel features cozy booths, boisterous patrons and a singing maître d', successfully replicating a New York City family-style Italian restaurant. Popular dishes include cannelloni, veal marsala and chicken piccata; in addition, there are wonderful caesar salads and tiramisu. No lunch Sunday or Monday. ~ Empress Hotel, 7766 Fay Avenue; 858-459-0700, fax 858-454-4741. MODERATE TO ULTRA-DELUXE.

AUTHOR FAVORITE

Spice & Rice Thai Kitchen is popular both for its tasty Thai cuisine and its atmosphere. Besides the standard Thai dishes there are house specialties, such as "Gold Bags," a combination of minced pork, roast duck or calamari, herbs and veggies wrapped in rice paper. Grab a table on the romantic gardenlike patio and watch the passing parade. No lunch on Sunday. ~ 7734 Girard Avenue; 858-456-0466, fax 858-451-9515.

Set in an early-1900s bungalow surrounded by a white picket fence, **The Cottage** serves up breakfast and lunch fare melding California, Southwest and Mediterranean flavors: French toast, Mediterranean omelette, vegetable frittata, fish tacos, penne pesto and Napa Valley beef stew. Dinner brings Santa Fe shrimp brochettes, meatloaf, Cajun jambalaya pasta and steak. A shady patio table is ideal when the sun's out (which is often). No dinner from October through May. ~ 7702 Fay Avenue; 858-454-8409, fax 858-454-0284; www.cottagelajolla.com. BUDGET TO MODERATE.

HIDDEN ►

If, during your shopping foray down Girard Avenue, you come across a line of locals snaking out of a small, unassuming eatery, you've no doubt reached **Girard Gourmet**. You may have to wait to partake of the deli goods (salads, quiches, sandwiches, pastries), but it's worth it. Take it to go, or dine out on the sidewalk or inside, in an alpinelike setting. ~ 7837 Girard Avenue; 858-454-3321, fax 858-454-2325; www.funcookies.com, e-mail info@funcookies.com. BUDGET.

HIDDEN ►

Who'd have thought that in the middle of upscale Girard Avenue you'd find a place like **Harry's Coffee Shop**. Catering to a group of loyal regulars, Harry's dishes up good old American coffee shop food in a decidedly untrendy atmosphere, just like it did when it first opened in 1960. Breakfast and lunch only. ~ 7545 Girard Avenue; 858-454-7381; www.harryscoffeeshop.com. BUDGET.

With its modern-minimalist Japanese-inspired decor and large streetside patio, **Fresh** is a relaxing place to enjoy the fruits of the sea. Though there are landlubber entrées, fish is the main attraction, with creative dishes running the gamut from coriander-crusted mahimahi to scallop ceviche in a three-citrus marinade. ~ 1044 Wall Street; 858-551-7575; www.freshseafoodrestaurant.com. DELUXE TO ULTRA-DELUXE.

Right around the corner, **Karl Strauss Brewing Company** showcases San Diego's local brew. This big, bustling brewpub serves up heaping platters of standards with an appropriate twist, such as beer-battered fish-and-chips and beer-brined pork chops, which are accompanied by mugs of frosty Karl Strauss beers. ~ 1044 Wall Street; 858-551-2739, fax 858-551-9812; www.karlstrauss.com. MODERATE.

Once a secluded seaside village, La Jolla has emerged as a world-famous resort community that offers style and substance. The shopping focuses on Girard Avenue from Torrey Pines Road to Prospect Street, and along Prospect. Both are lined with designer boutiques, specialty shops and art galleries. Generally, Girard Avenue tends to have more affordable shops than Prospect Street, where the price tags are over the top for most of us. Girard also has more shops than any other La Jolla street and boasts a variety of businesses that sell everything from secondhand designer clothes to knitting materials.

SHOPPING

For two levels of hip and stylish designer duds and shoes, stop by **Let's Go**. ~ 7863 Girard Avenue; 858-459-2337; www.houseofstyle.com.

Also on Girard Avenue is **myownspace**. This is the place to buy high-quality, minimalist Scandinavian home furnishings in bold bright colors and gleaming steel. ~ 7840 Girard Avenue; 858-459-0099, fax 858-459-0069; www.mosmyownspace.com.

Just walking into **Neroli Lingerie** is enough to make you feel sexy. This store sells some of the most seductive and luscious silk, satin and lace underpinnings anywhere, as well as swimsuits and nightwear. ~ 7944 Girard Avenue; 858-456-9618, fax 858-456-9618; www.neroli.com.

For those who prefer easily mixed and matched wardrobes, the **White House** is a find. This shop sells only fashions that are black, white or a combination of the two, so making sure you are color coordinated is a no-brainer. ~ 7927 Girard Avenue; 858-459-2565.

Even if you're way past toy store age, it's hard not to be enchanted by **Geppetto's**. Open the door and you're assailed by a burst of primary colors and a tumble of toys in all shapes and

AUTHOR FAVORITE

Housed as it is in a landmark 1903 cottage covered with wisteria, **John Cole's Book Shop** provides a refuge from those slick, chic La Jolla boutiques. Its nooks and crannies are lined with books ranging from best sellers to rare editions. Closed Sunday and Monday. ~ 780 Prospect Street; 858-454-4766.

sizes, toys of every description. The store atmosphere is pure fun, and the toys are high-quality, whether they're strictly educational or not. ~ 7850 Girard Avenue; 858-456-4441.

HIDDEN ►

Fido and Fluffy can shop on Girard as well. To say that **Muttropolis**, billing itself as catering to "haute dogs and cool cats," is an animal-friendly place would be an understatement. The sign in the window states "Dogs Welcome, Owners Must be Leashed," and inside everything from elaborate collars to gourmet treats are available to pamper the pet. ~ 7755 Girard Avenue; 858-459-9663; www.muttropolis.com.

In La Jolla's numerous galleries, traditional art blends with contemporary paintings, and rare Oriental antiques complement 20th-century bronze sculpture. The **Tasende Gallery** has a large display area and patio garden that pack in contemporary art by big names like Henry Moore and Roberto Matta. The gallery showcases sculpture, paintings and drawings as well. Closed Sunday and Monday. ~ 820 Prospect Street; 858-454-3691.

For more reasonably priced one-of-a-kind artistic purchases, **Spirals** sells fun and affordable goodies handcrafted by top-notch artists. Items are creative and whimsical, such as blown-glass animal salt and pepper shakers, crazily painted bird houses and chairs with a veggie motif. ~ 7906 Girard Avenue; 858-551-8199, fax 858-551-8211; www.spiralslajolla.com.

NIGHTLIFE   The dark-red **Whaling Bar** attracts lots of La Jolla's big fish. A fine place to relax and nibble gourmet hors d'oeuvres. ~ La Valencia Hotel, 1132 Prospect Street; 858-454-0771.

Among the most romantic restaurants in town, **Top o' the Cove** features an equally romantic bar, with live entertainment on Saturday. ~ 1216 Prospect Street; 858-454-7779.

A panoramic view of the ocean makes **French Gourmet at the Larias** the perfect place to enjoy live music Tuesday through Saturday. ~ Hotel La Jolla, 7955 La Jolla Shores Drive; 858-459-0541.

Galoka Gallery Restaurant does it all. Besides serving bargain-priced vegetarian Indian fare Thursday through Sunday and showcasing various artists, they offer live music Thursday through Saturday. Thursday is jazz night, Friday is reserved for singer/songwriters, and Saturday there's a live band. Occasional cover. ~ 5662 La Jolla Boulevard; 858-551-8610; www.galoka.com.

Mustangs & Burros at the Estancia Hotel is an upscale Western-themed bar with comfortable manly furniture, a large outside patio and live music by a Spanish guitarist at night. ~ 9700 North Torrey Pines Road; 858-550-1000, 877-437-8262, fax 858-550-1001; www.estancialajolla.com.

The Comedy Store features comedians exclusively, many with national reputations. Closed Monday and Tuesday. Cover. ~ 916 Pearl Street; 858-454-9176; www.thecomedystore.com.

D.G. Wills Books is a tiny literary haven featuring lectures and poetry readings, as well as an occasional jazz night. ~ 7461 Girard Avenue; 858-456-1800.

◄ HIDDEN

The **La Jolla Music Society** hosts year-round performances by such notables as Anne Sophie Von Otter, the Mark Morris Dance Group, and the Royal Philharmonic Orchestra. ~ 858-459-3728; www.ljms.org.

The prestigious **La Jolla Playhouse**, located on the University of California's–San Diego campus, produces innovative dramas and musicals, and spotlights famous actors during the summer and fall. ~ 858-550-1010; www.lajollaplayhouse.com.

TORREY PINES STATE RESERVE AND BEACH 🏃 🏄 🎣 🛶 A long, wide, sandy stretch adjacent to Los Peñasquitos Lagoon and Torrey Pines State Reserve, this beach is highly visible from the highway and therefore heavily used. It is popular for sunning, swimming, surf fishing and volleyball. Nearby trails lead through the reserve with lagoons, rare trees and abundant birdlife. Keep in mind that food is prohibited in the reserve but allowed on the beach. The beach is patrolled year-round, but lifeguards are on duty only in the summer. Restrooms are available. Day-use fee, $4 per vehicle. ~ Located just south of Carmel Valley Road, Del Mar; 858-755-2063, fax 858-509-0981; www.lajollatorreypines.hilton.com, e-mail torreypines@ixpres.com.

BEACHES & PARKS

The spectacular natural beauty of La Jolla Cove makes it one of the most photographed beaches in Southern California.

BLACK'S BEACH 🏄 🚶 🛶 One of the world's most famous nude beaches, on hot summer days it attracts bathers by the thousands, many in the buff. The sand is lovely and soft, and the 300-foot cliffs rising up behind it make for a spectacular setting. Hanggliders and paragliders soar from the glider port above, to add even more enchantment. Swimming is dangerous; beware of

◄ HIDDEN

the currents and exercise caution as the beach is infrequently patrolled. Surfing is excellent; one of the most awesome beach breaks in California. Lifeguards are here in the summer. ~ From Route 5 in La Jolla follow Genesee Avenue west; turn left on North Torrey Pines Road, then right at Torrey Pines Scenic Drive. There's a parking lot at the Torrey Pines Glider Port, but trails to the beach from here are very steep and often dangerous. If you're in doubt, just park at the Torrey Pines State Reserve lot one mile north and walk back along the shore to Black's during low tide.

SCRIPPS BEACH 🏃 ⚓ With coastal bluffs above, a narrow sand beach below and rich tidepools offshore, this is a great strand for beachcombers. Two **underwater reserves** as well as museum displays at the Scripps Institution of Oceanography are among the attractions. There are museum facilities at Scripps Institution. ~ Scripps Institution is located at the 8600 block of La Jolla Shores Drive in La Jolla. You can park at Kellogg Park–La Jolla Shores Beach and walk north to Scripps.

KELLOGG PARK–LA JOLLA SHORES BEACH 🏊 🏄 The sand is wide and the swimming is easy at La Jolla Shores; so, naturally, the beach is covered with bodies whenever the sun appears. Just to the east is Kellogg Park, an ideal place for a picnic, swimming and surfing. There are restrooms, a playground and lifeguards. ~ Off Camino del Oro and Costa Boulevard.

ELLEN BROWNING SCRIPPS PARK AND LA JOLLA COVE 🏊 ⚓ This grassy park sits on a bluff overlooking the cove and is the scenic focal point of La Jolla. The naturally formed cove is almost always free of breakers, has a small but sandy beach and is a popular spot for swimmers and divers. It's also the site of the **La Jolla Ecological Reserve**, an underwater park and diving reserve. There are picnic areas, restrooms, shuffleboard and lifeguards. ~ 1100 Coast Boulevard at Girard Avenue.

CHILDREN'S POOL BEACH 🏊 🎣 At the north end of Coast Boulevard Beach (see below) a concrete breakwater loops around a small lagoon. Harbor seals like to sun themselves on the rock promontories here. Despite its name, the beach's strong rip currents and seasonal rip tides can make swimming hazardous, so check with lifeguards. There are lifeguards and restrooms. Fishing is good from the surf. ~ Located off Coast Boulevard in La Jolla.

COAST BOULEVARD PARK After about a half-mile of wide ◄*HIDDEN*
sandy beach, the bluffs and tiny pocket beaches that character-
ize Windansea (see below) reappear at what locals call "Coast
Beach." The pounding waves make watersports unsafe, but
savvy locals find the smooth sandstone boulders and sandy coves
perfect for reading, sunbathing and picnicking. ~ Paths lead to
the beach at several points along Coast Boulevard.

MARINE STREET BEACH 🏄 Separated from Windansea to the south by towering sandstone bluffs, this is a much
wider and more sandy strand, favored by sunbathers, swimmers,
skindivers and frisbee-tossing youth. The rock-free shoreline is
ideal for walking or jogging. The beach is good for boards and
bodysurfing; watch for rip currents and high surf. ~ Turn west
off La Jolla Boulevard on Marine Street.

WINDANSEA BEACH 🏄 This is surely one of the
most picturesque beaches in the country. It has been portrayed in
the movies and was immortalized in Tom Wolfe's 1968 nonfic-
tion classic, *The Pumphouse Gang*, about the surfers who still
hang around the old pumphouse (part of the city's sewer system),
zealously protecting their famous surf from outsiders. Windansea is rated by experts as one of the best surfing locales on the
West Coast. In the evenings, crowds line the Neptune Place sidewalk, which runs along the top of the cliffs, to watch the sunset.
North of the pumphouse are several sandy nooks sandwiched between sandstone outcroppings. Romantic spot! There are lifeguards in the summer. ~ At the end of Nautilus Street.

HERMOSA TERRACE PARK 🏄 This beach is said to be "sea-
sonally sandy," which is another way of saying it's rocky at
times. Best chance for sand is in the summer, when this is a pretty
good sunning beach. The surfing is good. There are no facilities.
~ Off Winamar Avenue; a paved path leads to the beach.

BIRD ROCK 🏄 Named for a large sandstone boulder
about 50 yards off the coast, this beach is rocky and thus favored
by divers. The surf rarely breaks here, but when it does this spot
is primo for surfing; exercise caution. Fishing is also good.
Facilities are nonexistent. ~ At the end of Bird Rock Avenue.

SOUTH BIRD ROCK 🏄 Tidepools are the attraction along this
rocky, cliff-lined beach. Surfing is best in summer. ~ From Midway or Forward streets in La Jolla follow paths down to the beach.

TOURMALINE SURFING PARK 🏊 🛶 🏄 A year-round reef break and consistently big waves make La Jolla one of the best surfing areas on the West Coast. Tourmaline is popular with surfers. Skindiving is permitted, as is swimming. You'll find picnic areas and restrooms. ~ At the end of Tourmaline Street.

FIVE

North County & Inland San Diego

Stretching along the coast above San Diego is a string of towns with a host of personalities and populations. Residents here range from the county's wealthiest folks in Rancho Santa Fe to Marine privates at Oceanside's Camp Pendleton to yogis in retreat at Encinitas. This part of the county really shines, however, thanks to its many sparkling beaches.

The best way to see North County's fine beaches is to cruise along old Route 101, which preceded Route 5 as the north–south coastal route. It changes names in each beach town along the way, but once you're on it you won't be easily side-tracked.

Touring San Diego County's rugged inland backcountry means wandering through a landscape filled with rambling hills, flowering meadows and rocky peaks. There are old missions and gold mines en route, as well as farms and ranches. More than anything else, exploring this region consists of driving over miles of silent country roads.

North County

The affluent that can't find the perfect property in La Jolla seem to have spilled into the next two towns to the north. Del Mar, probably best known for its racetrack, has a trim, Tudor-style village center and luxurious oceanfront homes that reflect the town's subtle efforts to "keep up with the Joneses" next door. Rancho Santa Fe is La Jolla for the horsey set, where some of America's wealthiest folks reside in hillside mansions and horse ranches parceled out from an old Spanish land grant. North of Del Mar, the oceanside towns wind down in toniness and become more Surfing USA. Solano Beach, Cardiff-by-the-Sea, Encinitas and Leucadia, low-key beach communities with a proliferation of modest beach bungalows, motels and inexpensive eateries, seem to tumble into one another. Carlsbad is a squeaky-clean little beach town, thanks to thoughtful redeveloping. On the other hand, neighboring Oceanside has a slightly rundown, 1950s feel and could use a little sprucing up.

SIGHTS   Although **Del Mar** is inundated every summer by "beautiful people" who flock here for the horse racing, the town itself has retained a casual, small-town identity. On the east side of Route 5, about five miles inland on either Via de la Valle or Lomas Santa Fe Drive, is **Rancho Santa Fe**. If La Jolla is a jewel, then this stylish enclave is the crown itself. Rancho Santa Fe is like Beverly Hills gone country. The area became popular as a retreat for rich industrialists and movie stars in the 1920s, when Douglas Fairbanks and Mary Pickford built their sprawling **Fairbanks Ranch**. To make a looping tour of this affluent community, drive in on Via de la Valle, then return to Route 5 via Linea del Cielo and Lomas Santa Fe Drive.

Encinitas is popularly known as the "Flower Capital of the World" and the hillsides east of the beach are a riot of color. A quick call to the friendly folks at the local **Chamber of Commerce and Visitors Center** will net you information concerning the area. ~ 138 Encinitas Boulevard, Encinitas; 760-753-6041, fax 760-753-6270; www.encinitaschamber.com, e-mail info@encinitaschamber.com.

A self-guided walking tour at **Quail Botanical Gardens** treats visitors to 30 acres of colorful plants and flowers, including the area's natural chaparral and gardens that display rainforest vegetation, orchids and bamboo. A lookout tower provides a 360-degree view of the grounds. Admission. ~ 230 Quail Gardens Drive at Encinitas Boulevard, Encinitas; 760-436-3036; www.qbgardens.com.

Yogis, as well as those of us still residing on terra firma, might want to make a stop at Paramahansa Yogananda's **Self-Realization Fellowship Retreat**. The gold-domed towers of this monastic retreat were built by an Indian religious sect in the 1920s and the compound is still used as a retreat. Although the gardens inside the compound are beautifully maintained and open to the public daily, Yogananda's house is only open on Sunday. The views, overlooking the famous "Swami's" surfing

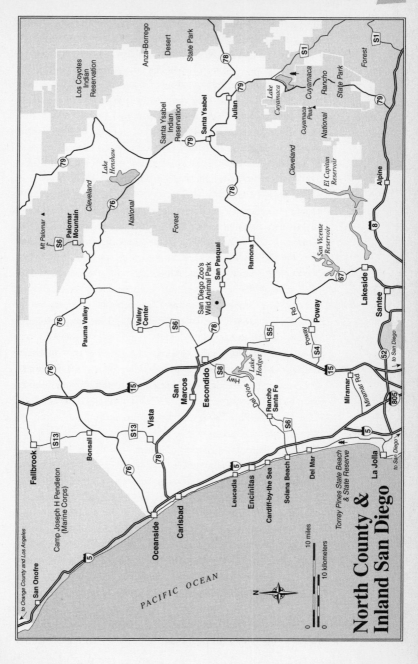

North County & Inland San Diego

PACIFIC OCEAN

to Orange County and Los Angeles
San Onofre
Camp Joseph H Pendleton (Marine Corps)
Fallbrook
Bonsall
Vista
Oceanside
Carlsbad
Leucadia
Encinitas
Cardiff-by-the-Sea
Solana Beach
Del Mar
Torrey Pines State Beach & State Reserve
La Jolla
to San Diego

San Marcos
Escondido
Rancho Santa Fe
Del Dios Hwy
Lake Hodges

Pauma Valley
Valley Center
San Diego Zoo's Wild Animal Park
San Pasqual
Ramona

Mt Palomar
Palomar Mountain

Lake Henshaw

Cleveland National Forest

Santa Ysabel Indian Reservation
Santa Ysabel
Julian

Los Coyotes Indian Reservation

Anza-Borrego Desert State Park

Lake Cuyamaca
Cuyamaca Peak
Cuyamaca Rancho State Park
Cleveland National Forest

El Capitan Reservoir
Alpine

San Vicente Reservoir
Poway
Poway Rd
Lakeside
Santee

Miramar
Miramar Rd
to San Diego
to San Diego

10 miles
10 kilometers

N

to San Diego

beach, are spectacular. Closed Monday. ~ 215 K Street, Encinitas; 760-753-2888, fax 760-753-8156; www.yogananda-srf.org.

North of Encinitas is **Carlsbad**, a friendly, sunny beachfront town that has been entirely redeveloped, right down to its cobblestone streets and quaint shops. Originally, the place established its reputation around the similarity of its mineral waters to the springs of the original Karlsbad in the Czech Republic. But don't waste your time looking for the fountain of youth—the spring has long since dried up. Go to the beach instead.

Added to Southern California's theme park lineup is **LEGO-LAND**, patterned after the park in Denmark where Legos are made. Designed with kids ages two to twelve in mind, attractions include cruises, rides (such as roller coasters) and walkways that take visitors past huge, elaborate constructions made from the colorful plastic snap-together bricks, including models of the Golden Gate Bridge, the New York skyline, the Taj Mahal, 18-foot giraffes, a larger-than-life Albert Einstein, a buffalo herd and much more. Even grown-ups are likely to be amazed. Closed Tuesday and Wednesday except in summer. Admission. ~ LEGOLAND Drive, Carlsbad; 760-918-5346, fax 760-918-5375; www.legoland.com.

Another opportunity for hands-on fun awaits at the **Children's Discovery Museum of North County**. Here, kids can explore the science of light and color, go fishing and spend time in a bubble. Closed Monday. Admission. ~ 2787 State Street, Carlsbad; 760-720-0737, fax 760-720-0336; www.museumforchildren.org, e-mail vaavoom@aol.com.

For hands-on fun of a different sort, stop by the **Museum of Making Music**, which covers the history of musical instruments and how they've shaped American popular music from the 1890s until now. Though their collection of more than 500 vintage instruments is impressive, the fun parts of the museum are the audio and video displays and the interactive area, where anyone can try their hand at playing an instrument. ~ 5790 Armada Drive, Carlsbad; 760-438-5996, 877-551-9976, fax 760-438-8964; www.museumofmakingmusic.org.

The Carlsbad Historical Society's **Magee House Museum** is a turn-of-the-20th-century house originally owned by Carlsbad's early settlers. Furnishings reflect the lifestyle of the period, while displays highlight Carlsbad's history. There are several relocated historic structures on the property, as well as a garden area that includes beds of roses, herbs and native plantings. ~ 258 Beech Street, Carlsbad; 760-434-9189.

Old Route 101 next leads into **Oceanside**, gateway to Camp Pendleton Marine Base. San Diego County's third-largest city is busy renovating its beachfront and image. The refurbished fishing pier is a lengthy one, stretching almost 2000 feet into the Pacific.

If you'd like to learn more about California's "cultural" side, stop by the **California Surf Museum**, which features exhibits on the history of the sport and its early pioneers. On display is the very first surfing trophy, named after Tom Blake, one of the first

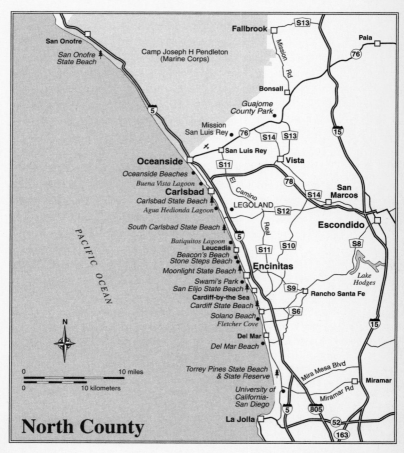

North County

waterproof cameras that was used to capture the sport up close, an exhibit that chronicles the history of surfboard shaping and a collection of wooden boards from the pre-'60s era. A museum shop offers vintage books and videos. Closed Tuesday and Wednesday. ~ 223 North Coast Highway, Oceanside; 760-721-6876; www.surfmuseum.org, e-mail csm@surfmuseum.org.

Housed in a 1930s modernist building designed by California architect Irving Gill, **Oceanside Museum of Art**'s galleries not only display art, but are the venue for regularly scheduled chamber music concerts. Though not to exclusion, this museum's exhibits frequently showcase artists who live or have lived in the San Diego area. ~ 704 Pier View Way, Oceanside; 760-721-2787; www.oma-online.org.

From Oceanside, Mission Avenue, which merges with Route 76, will carry you to **Mission San Luis Rey**. Known as the "King of the Missions" (and named originally after a king of France), this beautifully restored complex was originally constructed in 1798 and represents the largest California mission. Today you can visit the museum, the garden, the chapel and the cemetery while walking these historic grounds. Admission. ~ 4050 Mission Avenue, Oceanside; 760-757-3651, fax 760-757-4613; www.sanluisrey.org.

Continue east on Route 76 to **Guajome County Park**, a 557-acre playground that offers a variety of natural, historical and recreational opportunities. The park is centered around 1850s-era **Rancho Guajome Adobe**, considered one of the region's best examples of early Spanish architecture. Just a few miles away is

TURF AND SURF

While seasonal, **Del Mar Race Track** and companion **Fairgrounds** are the main attractions in Del Mar. The track was financed in the 1930s by such stars as Bing Crosby and Pat O'Brien to bring thoroughbred racing to the Fairgrounds. It was no coincidence that this town, "where the turf meets the surf," became a second home to these and many other top Hollywood stars. Track season is from the end of July to mid-September. The rest of the year you can bet on races televised via satellite. Admission. ~ Route 5 and Via de la Valle, Del Mar; race track 858-755-1141, fairgrounds 858-755-1161; www.delmarracing.com, e-mail marys@dmtc.com.

a 25-acre fishing lake. Hiking and horseback riding trails thread the property, and there are picnic areas, restrooms, a playground and a campground. Parking fee. ~ Guajome Lake Road, south off Route 76, Oceanside; 858-565-3600; www.sdparks.org.

Your last sightseeing opportunity in San Diego County is at **San Onofre State Beach**, about 16 miles north of Oceanside on Route 5. Unique in that it's actually two beaches, North and South, this certainly is one of the county's most scenic beach parks. Its eroded sandstone bluffs hide a variety of secluded sandy coves and pocket beaches. But all this beauty is broken by an eerie and ungainly structure rising from the shoreline. Dividing the park's twin beaches is a mammoth facility, potent and ominous, the **San Onofre nuclear power plant**. Admission. ~ 949-492-0802, fax 949-492-8412.

Many of San Diego's best beaches lie to the north, between Del Mar and Oceanside. Sadly, most of the good hotels do not. But don't worry—among those listed below, all but a handful are either oceanfront or oceanview properties.

LODGING

It's all in the name when it comes to locating **Del Mar Motel on the Beach**, the only motel between Carlsbad and La Jolla that's on the beach. All 48 rooms in this plain stucco building are steps from the sand. That's undoubtedly where you'll spend your time, because there is little about the rooms to enchant you. They are basic in design, equipped with refrigerators, color TVs and air conditioning. Because the hotel is at a right angle to the beach, only two rooms have full views of the water. ~ 1702 Coast Boulevard, Del Mar; 858-755-1534, 800-223-8449, fax 858-259-5403; www.delmarmotelonthebeach.com, e-mail thedelmar motel@cs.com. DELUXE TO ULTRA-DELUXE.

A two-story Spanish Mediterranean inn conveniently situated a few blocks from downtown Del Mar, **Les Artistes** honors several of the world's favorite artists: Diego Rivera, Georgia O'Keeffe, Erté, Claude Monet and Paul Gauguin. The owner, who is an architect from Thailand, designed each room in the style and spirit of the artist. Other architectural delights include a pond filled with water lilies and koi, and a classic Spanish-style courtyard with a fountain. ~ 944 Camino del Mar, Del Mar; 858-755-4646; www.lesartistesinn.com. MODERATE TO ULTRA-DELUXE.

Built on the site of a once-famous Del Mar Beach getaway, **L'Auberge Del Mar Resort and Spa** replicates the old hotel's nostalgic past in the '20s, '30s, and '40s. In fact, L'Auberge Del Mar was frequented by Hollywood greats such as Bing Crosby, Jimmy Durante and Rudolph Valentino. The original Tudor/Craftsman inn's rich lobby is dominated by a replica of the huge original brick fireplace. Along with 120 guest rooms and suites, the inn features a restaurant with patio dining, a bar, a full-service European spa, tennis courts, leisure and lap pools, shops, a park amphitheater and partial ocean views. Each room has its own patio. ~ 1540 Camino del Mar, Del Mar; 858-259-1515, 800-553-1336, fax 858-755-4940; www.laubergedelmar.com, e-mail laubergereservations@destinationhotels.com. ULTRA-DELUXE.

For an elegant country inn, consider **The Inn at Rancho Santa Fe.** Widely known among the world's genteel, it's a country inn consisting of early California–style *casitas* on a 20-acre site. Situated five miles inland from Solana Beach, the inn offers individually decorated guest rooms as well as one-, two-, and three-bedroom cottages. Many rooms and all cottages feature private sun terraces, fireplaces and kitchenettes. Displayed in the homespun lobby is a priceless collection of antique hand-carved model ships. There are tennis courts, a swimming pool, a jacuzzi, an exercise room, croquet and a restaurant. ~ 5951 Linea del Cielo, Rancho Santa Fe; 858-756-1131, 800-843-4661, fax 858-759-1604; www.theinnatrsf.com, e-mail reservations@theinnat rsf.com. ULTRA-DELUXE.

AUTHOR FAVORITE

Affordability and quiet are the order of the day at **Ocean Palms Beach Resort.** This tidy, 57-room mom-and-pop complex is so near the sea that you can hear it, but a row of expensive beach houses blocks the view from all but one beachfront building. Some sections of the rambling ocean manor date back to 1939, and "new" additions have a tropical feel to them, so the general decor could best be described as "beach bungalow." An oldie but goodie in this case, however. The place is clean and lovingly maintained and features a landscaped patio and pool area, complete with two jacuzzis and a sauna. All rooms have fully equipped kitchens. ~ 2950 Ocean Street, Carlsbad; 760-729-2493, 888-802-3224, fax 760-729-0579; www. opalms.com, e-mail info@ocean-palms.net. MODERATE TO ULTRA-DELUXE.

One of the county's leading resorts is **Rancho Bernardo Inn**. World-class golf and tennis aside, this handsome hacienda-style complex is a gracious country retreat. The 287 rooms here are decorated with original artwork and potted palms. There are two pools, seven jacuzzis, a fitness center and a spa. ~ 17550 Bernardo Oaks Drive, Rancho Bernardo; 858-675-8500, 800-542-6096, fax 858-675-8437; www.jcresorts.com, e-mail rancho bernardoinn@jcresorts.com. ULTRA-DELUXE.

Every room is individually decorated at **Cardiff-by-the-Sea Lodge**, with themes such as Old World, Southwest and Mediterranean, and many rooms have ocean views, fireplaces and in-room whirlpools. It's a bed and breakfast, but not of the converted-home variety; everyone has a private entrance and bath. Breakfast is served buffet-style in a center courtyard, but you can take it to your room or up to the rooftop garden and savor a panoramic view of the Pacific. ~ 142 Chesterfield Avenue, Cardiff; 760-944-6474, fax 760-944-6841; www.cardifflodge.com, e-mail innkeeper@cardifflodge.com. DELUXE TO ULTRA-DELUXE.

Located on a lofty knoll above the Pacific, **Best Western Encinitas Inn and Suites** is built on three levels and looks like a condominium. With a pool and jacuzzi, it has many of the same features. The 90 rooms include private balconies overlooking the ocean. Deluxe continental breakfast is served at the poolside cabaña. ~ 85 Encinitas Boulevard, Encinitas; 760-942-7455, 866-362-8648, fax 760-632-9481; www.bwencinitas.com. DELUXE.

The best reasonably priced lodging near the beach in Encinitas is **Moonlight Beach Motel**. This three-story, 24-unit, family-run motel is tucked away in a residential neighborhood overlooking Moonlight Beach State Park. Guest rooms are modern as well as clean and contain everything you'll need, including full kitchens. Most of the accommodations command ocean views. ~ 233 2nd Street, Encinitas; 760-753-0623, 800-323-1259, fax 760-944-9827. MODERATE.

◄ HIDDEN

Carlsbad offers several nice oceanview facilities, including **Tamarack Beach Resort**, a contemporary Mediterranean-style hotel. Finished in peach and aqua hues, the Tamarack rents standard rooms as well as one- and two-bedroom suites. Most are smashingly decorated in upbeat tones and textures and incorporate such touches as potted plants and photographic prints.

Suites, though ultra-deluxe in price, may be the best value on the North Coast. They have kitchens and private balconies. Guests can make use of the oceanview restaurant, clubhouse, fitness center, jacuzzis, video library and activities program as well as enjoying the adjacent beach. Complimentary continental breakfast is included. ~ 3200 Carlsbad Boulevard, Carlsbad; 760-729-3500, 800-334-2199, fax 760-434-5942; www.tamarackresort.com, e-mail tamarack@pacbell.net. ULTRA-DELUXE.

Advertised as "a very special bed and breakfast," the **Pelican Cove Inn** is a lovely Cape Cod–style house with eight guest rooms. Each features a fireplace and is well-furnished with antique pieces, including feather beds; some rooms have spa tubs. Visitors share a sundeck and patio with gazebo. The inn is located just two blocks from the beach. ~ 320 Walnut Avenue, Carlsbad; 760-434-5995, 888-735-2683, fax 760-434-7649; www.pelican-cove.com, e-mail pelicancoveinn@pelican-cove.com. MODERATE TO ULTRA-DELUXE.

The **Best Western Beach Terrace Inn** is a 49-unit establishment with stucco facade and the feel of a motel. There's a pool and jacuzzi, plus a single feature that differentiates the Beach Terrace from most other places hereabouts—it is located right on the beach. A broad swath of white sand borders the property, making the price for a room with kitchen a worthwhile investment. ~ 2775 Ocean Street, Carlsbad; 760-729-5951, 800-433-5415, fax 760-729-1078; www.beachterraceinn.com. DELUXE TO ULTRA-DELUXE.

Sporting a fresh look, the fabled **La Costa Resort & Spa** can justly claim to be one of the world's great "total" resorts. This luxurious 400-acre complex boasts 474 guest rooms, two 18-hole championship golf courses, 21 tennis courts (hard, clay *and* grass), 10 shops, 2 restaurants and one of the country's largest and most respected spa and fitness centers. Simply put, the place is awesome. With rooms *starting* well up in the ethereal range, La Costa's appeal to the well-monied few is apparent. ~ 2100 Costa del Mar Road, Carlsbad; 760-438-9111, 800-854-5000, fax 760-438-3758; www.lacosta.com, e-mail info@lacosta.com. ULTRA-DELUXE.

The Mediterranean-style **Southern California Beach Club** is a 43-suite, time-share facility situated on the beach near Oceanside Pier. Each suite is graciously appointed with quality furnishings in contemporary hues of peach, heather and blue. Kitchens are standard; other extras include a mini-gym, a rooftop jacuzzi and laundry facilities. ~ 121 South Pacific Highway, Oceanside; 760-722-6666, fax 760-722-8950. DELUXE TO ULTRA-DELUXE.

San Luis Rey Downs is a casual little resort nestled northeast of Oceanside, along the San Luis Rey River. There are only 26 rooms, neat, clean and basic, in a two-story woodframe lodge overlooking the golf course. But this inviting hideaway also offers a restaurant, lounge, pool, jacuzzi and nearby tennis courts. ~ 31474 Golf Club Drive, Bonsall; 760-758-3762, 800-783-6967, fax 760-758-1597; www.slrd.com, e-mail reservations@slrd.com. MODERATE TO ULTRA-DELUXE.

DINING

Il Fornaio, an Italian restaurant/bakery, boasts magnificent ocean views, outside dining terraces, elegant Italian marble floors and bar, trompe l'oeil murals and an enormous exhibition kitchen. The place is packed with eager patrons ready to sample the pastas, pizzas, rotisserie, meats and *dolci* (desserts). There's also Sunday brunch. ~ 1555 Camino del Mar, Del Mar Plaza, Del Mar; 858-755-8876, fax 858-755-8906; www.ilfornaio.com. MODERATE TO DELUXE.

Since life is lived outdoors in Southern California, **Pacifica Del Mar**, part of a local restaurant mini-chain, features a terrace overlooking the ocean as well as a white-tablecloth dining room. The Pacific Rim accent here is on seafood, as in barbecued sugar-spiced salmon, Chinese five-spice ahi salad and miso-marinated sea bass. ~ 1555 Camino del Mar, Del Mar Plaza, Del Mar; 858-

AUTHOR FAVORITE

Whatever you do during your North County visit, don't pass up the chance to dine at **El Bizcocho**. Tucked away in the upscale Rancho Bernardo Inn, an early California-style resort, this award-winning restaurant rates among greater San Diego's best. The traditional French haute cuisine menu includes a nice balance of beef, veal, fish and fowl dishes. Try the roast duckling for two or indulge in the creamy lobster bisque. Dinner only. Closed Sunday. ~ 17550 Bernardo Oaks Drive, Rancho Bernardo; 858-675-8550, fax 858-675-8443; www.jcresorts.com. ULTRA-DELUXE.

792-0476, fax 858-792-0848; www.pacificadelmar.com, e-mail kipp@pacificadelmar.com. DELUXE TO ULTRA-DELUXE.

The place is mobbed all summer long, but **The Fish Market** remains one of my favorite Del Mar restaurants. I like the noise, the nautical atmosphere, the oyster bar, the on-the-run service and the dozen or so fresh fish items. Among the best dishes are the sea bass, yellowtail, orange roughy and salmon, either sautéed or mesquite charbroiled. ~ 640 Via de la Valle, Del Mar; 858-755-2277, fax 858-755-3912; www.thefishmarket.com. MODERATE TO ULTRA-DELUXE.

Scalini, housed in a classy contemporary-style building with arched windows overlooking a polo field, is strictly star-quality northern Italian fare. The place has been decorated in a mix of modern and antique furnishings and wrapped in all the latest Southern California colors. But the brightest star of all is the menu. The mesquite-broiled veal chops and osso buco are exceptional. There are many good homemade pasta dishes including lobster fettuccine, linguine and tortellini. Dinner only. ~ 3790 Via de la Valle, Del Mar; 858-259-9944, fax 858-259-2270; www.scalinisandiego.com. DELUXE TO ULTRA-DELUXE.

HIDDEN ▶ Mention the words "Mexican food" in Solana Beach and the reply is sure to be **Fidel's**. This favored spot has as many rooms and patios as a rambling hacienda. Given the good food and cheap prices, all of them are inevitably crowded. Fidel's serves the best *tostada suprema* anywhere and the burritos, enchiladas and *chimichangas* are always good. ~ 607 Valley Avenue, Solana Beach; 858-755-5292, fax 858-755-2392. MODERATE.

CRÈME DE LA CRÈME

Mille Fleurs tops everyone's list as San Diego's best French restaurant. The à la carte menu, which changes daily, provides exquisite appetizers, soup and such entrées as rack of lamb with black-olive crust, grilled Alaskan halibut with saffron sauce and loin of antelope. A sophisticated interior features fireside dining, Portuguese tiles and stunning trompe l'oeil paintings. There is also a Spanish courtyard for dining, as well as a piano bar. No lunch on the weekend. ~ 6009 Paseo Delicias, Rancho Santa Fe; 858-756-3085; www.millefleurs.com, e-mail milfleurs@aol.com. ULTRA-DELUXE.

Delicias, a comfortable and spacious restaurant with an adjoining bar, is decorated in a mixture of antiques and wicker, accented by woven tapestries and flowers. The chefs in the openview kitchen whip up contemporary California cuisine. Delicious food, personable service. No lunch. ~ 6106 Paseo Delicias, Rancho Santa Fe; 858-756-8000, fax 858-759-1739. MODERATE TO ULTRA-DELUXE.

Best of the beachfront dining spots in Cardiff is **Charlie's by the Sea**, where the surf rolls right up to the glass. Here you can choose from an innovative selection of fresh seafood items or an all-American menu of grilled chicken, steak and prime rib. Charlie's has a smartly decorated contemporary setting with a full bar, but still creates an easy, informal atmosphere. Sunday brunch. ~ 2526 South Coast Highway, Cardiff; 760-942-1300, fax 760-942-1228; www.charliesbythesea.com, e-mail charliesby thesea@sbcglobal.net. MODERATE TO DELUXE.

Pasta lovers should be sure to try the penne or fusilli in vodka-tomato sauce at **When In Rome**. The art-filled Roman decor provides the proper atmosphere, and the Italian owners certainly know their trade. All the breads and pastas are made fresh daily. Entrées include a variety of veal and seafood items. Dinner only. ~ 1108 South Coast Highway, Encinitas; 760-944-1771, fax 760-944-3849; www.wheninrome.signonsandiego. com. MODERATE TO ULTRA-DELUXE.

Most visitors to Encinitas never lay eyes on the **Potato Shack**   ◄ HIDDEN
Café, hidden away on a side street. But locals start packing its pine-paneled walls at dawn to tackle North County's best and biggest breakfast for the buck. There are three-egg omelettes and manhole-size pancakes, but best of all are the home-style taters and the old-fashioned biscuits and gravy. Lunch is also served, but the Potato Shack is really a breakfast institution, and as such serves breakfast until 2 p.m. ('til 2:30 p.m. on weekends). No dinner. ~ 120 West I Street, Encinitas; phone/fax 760-436-1282. BUDGET.

Another popular feeding spot is **Sakura Bana Sushi Bar**. The sushi here is heavenly, especially the *sakura* roll, crafted by Japanese masters from shrimp, crab, scallop, smelt, egg and avocado. The bar serves only sushi and sashimi, but table service will bring you such treats as teriyaki, tempura and shrimp *shumai*.

No lunch Saturday or Sunday; closed Monday. ~ 1031 South Coast Highway, Encinitas; 760-942-6414. MODERATE.

Encinitas' contribution to the Thai food craze is an intimate café called **Siamese Basil**, set along the town's main drag. At lunch and dinner this whitewashed eatery serves up about six dozen dishes. You can start with the spicy shrimp soup and satay, then graduate to an entrée menu that includes noodle, curry, seafood and vegetable selections. House specialties include roast duck with soy bean and ginger sauce, honey-marinated spare ribs and barbecued chicken. ~ 527 South Coast Highway, Encinitas; 760-753-3940. BUDGET TO MODERATE.

For a harbor view and daily entertainment, cast an eye toward Monterey Bay Canners. ~ 1325 Harbor Drive North, Oceanside; 760-722-3474.

Legends California Bistro at La Costa Resort & Spa bills its food as "Consciousness-in-cooking." This translates to incorporating Ayurveda guidelines from the Chopra Center. Breakfast offerings may include a power smoothie, apple walnut crêpes or a tofu scramble. Lunch is a variety of health-conscious bites such as ahi tuna tartare, crisp salads, sandwiches and veggie stir-fries. Dinner is a more upscale affair, with seafood, lamb and steak dishes. Sunday champagne and jazz brunch is served. ~ 2100 Costa del Mar Road, Carlsbad; 760-438-9111, 800-854-5000; www.lacosta.com, e-mail info@lacosta.com. DELUXE.

Neiman's, an eye-catching Victorian landmark, houses both a dining room and café/bar. My favorite for lunch or dinner is the café, where LeRoy Neiman lithographs hang on the walls and the menu includes trendy dishes such as coconut shrimp, chicken kabob and citrus-macadamia salmon. They also serve burgers, pasta and salads. The Sunday brunch in the sprawling early-1900s dining room is a definite "must," featuring a tremendous buffet assortment of breakfast and lunch items. ~ 300 Carlsbad Village Drive, Carlsbad; 760-729-4131, fax 760-729-6131; www.neimans.com, e-mail neimans1@hotmail.com. MODERATE TO DELUXE.

For light, inexpensive fare there's the **Daily News Café**. Breakfast features eggs, pancakes, French toast and their "world famous" sticky buns, while the heartier lunch fare includes an array of soups, salads, sandwiches and burgers. Breakfast and lunch only. ~ 3001-A Carlsbad Boulevard, Carlsbad; 760-729-1023. BUDGET.

The **Harbor House Café** is a great place for breakfast. Decorated with brightly colored murals, this eatery serves up innovative omelettes, buckwheat pancakes and delicious home fries. For lunch, try the mushroom burger with sautéed onions, mushrooms and jack cheese. Patio dining is also available. No dinner. ~ 714 North Coast Highway, Oceanside; 760-722-2254. BUDGET.

For a downright homey café, try **Robin's Nest**, a country-style establishment with good eats and a gregarious chef. The menu features omelettes, soups and burgers. With a decor of soft blues and artwork by local artists, this place is quite popular with locals and has an outdoor patio that faces the harbor. Breakfast and lunch served daily; served from May through September. ~ 280-A Harbor Drive South, Oceanside; 760-722-7837, fax 949-492-2665; www.robinsnestcafe.com. MODERATE.

◄ HIDDEN

SHOPPING

A seacoast village atmosphere prevails along Del Mar's half-mile-long strip of shops. Tudor-style **Stratford Square**, the focal point, houses a number of shops in what is the area's first commercial building. **Earth Song Bookstore** offers traditional books as well as an eclectic selection of titles focusing on health, spirituality and psychology. ~ 1440 Camino del Mar, Del Mar; 858-755-4254.

Carolyn's is a consignment shop with designer fashions from the closets of the community's best-dressed women. Closed Sunday. ~ 1310 Camino Del Mar, Del Mar; 858-481-4133.

The stylized **Del Mar Plaza** is a welcome addition. Home to over 20 retail shops, this tri-level mall sells everything from fashion accessories to upscale home furnishings and has a host of eateries. ~ 1555 Camino del Mar, Del Mar; 858-792-1555; www.delmarplaza.com.

Flower Hill Mall, a rustic mall, has the usual fashion and specialty shops. But the real draw here is **Bookworks** (858-755-3735; www.book-works.com) and an adjoining coffeehouse called **Pannikin Coffee and Tea** (858-481-8007). Together they're perfect for a relaxed bit of book browsing and a spot of tea. ~ 2670 Via de la Valle, Del Mar; 858-481-7131.

If little else, Solana Beach harbors an enclave of good antique stores. One of the best is the **Antique Warehouse**, with its collection of 101 small shops. Closed Tuesday. ~ 212 South Cedros Avenue, Solana Beach; 858-755-5156; www.antique-warehouse.com.

Detouring, as every sophisticated shopper must, to Rancho Santa Fe, you'll find an assortment of chic shops and galleries along Paseo Delicias. One of my favorites is **Marilyn Mulloy Estate & Fine Jewelers**, with its collection of old and new pieces. Closed Sunday. ~ 6024 Paseo Delicias, Rancho Santa Fe; 858-756-4010.

There are lots of millionaires per acre here, but bargains can still be found: **Country Friends** is a charity-operated repository of antique furniture, silver, glass and china priced well below local antique shops. Closed Sunday. ~ 6030 El Tordo, Rancho Santa Fe; 858-756-1192.

Carlsbad has blossomed with a variety of trendy shops. You will see many beach-and-surf-type shops, as well as a variety of gift shops. Swing by the **Village Faire Shopping Centre**, a New England–style specialty mall that has Sunday afternoon concerts in July and August. ~ 300 Carlsbad Village Drive, Carlsbad; www.villagefaire.com.

Jewelry is a high art form at **The Collector Fine Jewelry**, where every piece is crafted by hand. The owners go right to the source for the best gems—Colombia for emeralds, Burma for rubies, Africa for diamonds. Closed Sunday. ~ 912 South Live Oak Park Road, Fallbrook; 760-728-9121, 800-854-1598; www.collectorfinejewelry.com.

NIGHTLIFE Tucked away in the Flower Hill Mall, **Pannikin Coffee and Tea** brings a true taste of culture in the form of live jazz, classical guitarists and poetry readings on Friday nights. ~ 2670 Via de la Valle, Del Mar; 858-481-8007.

Solana Beach's low-profile daytime image shifts gears in the evening when the-little-town-that-could spotlights one of North County's hottest clubs. The **Belly Up Tavern** is a converted quonset hut that now houses a concert club and often draws big-name rock, reggae, jazz and blues stars. Cover. ~ 143 South Cedros Avenue, Solana Beach; 858-481-9022, 858-481-8140 (box office); www.bellyup.com.

HIDDEN ► **First Street Bar** is a neighborhood bar with three pool tables. It is consistently on the Best Neighborhood Bar list, voted on by locals. ~ 656 South Coast Highway, Encinitas; 760-944-0233.

Fans of old-time movie theaters will love **Star Theatre**, with its neon marquee and 1950s Googie Space Age architectural style. When movie theaters moved to malls as multiplexes, the

Star Theatre managed to survive and since 2001 has been treating the community to live performances that range from classic musicals like *Fiddler on the Roof* and *42nd Street* to concerts by the Gay Men's Choir and individual musicians. ~ 402 North Coast Highway, Oceanside; 760-721-9983; www.startheatre.org, e-mail startheatrecompany@yahoo.com.

Aquaterra, a classy and contemporary watering hole at Pala Mesa Resort, attracts mainly golfers fresh from a round on the links. ~ 2001 South Route 395, Fallbrook; 760-728-5881.

DEL MAR BEACH Though rather narrow from Torrey Pines to about 15th Street, the beach widens farther north. The part around 15th Street is Action Central, with teens playing sand volleyball and frisbee while the elders read magazines beneath their umbrellas. Surfers congregate at the foot of 13th Street. Quintessential North County! There are picnic tables, a snack bar, restrooms, showers and lifeguards. Fishing is good, and there are regular grunion runs. There is typical beach surf, with smooth peaks year-round. ~ Easiest beach access is at street ends from 15th to 29th streets off Coast Boulevard, one block below South Route 101, Del Mar; 858-755-1556, fax 858-259-3264; www.delmar.ca.us, e-mail msafety@cosb.org.

BEACHES & PARKS

FLETCHER COVE Lined by cliffs and carpeted with sand, this is a popular spot for water sports. There's a natural break in the cliffs where the beach widens and the surf eases up to allow comfortable swimming. Surfers gather to the north and south of Plaza Street where the beach is narrow and the surf much bigger. Facilities include restrooms, outdoor showers, lifeguards and basketball courts. ~ Located at the end of Plaza Street, Solana Beach; 858-755-1560, fax 858-793-7734; e-mail msafety@cosb.org.

Fletcher Cove is a prime area for grunion runs, which take place at night from March through July.

CARDIFF STATE BEACH This strand begins where the cliffs of Solana Beach end and where the town's most intriguing feature, a network of tidepools, begins. Popular with surfers because of the interesting pitches off its reef break, this wide, sandy beach is part of a two-mile swath of state beaches. At the beach there are restrooms, cold showers and lifeguards (summer only). Fishing, swimming and surfing are popular ac-

tivities here. Day-use fee, $6. ~ Off South Route 101 directly
west of San Elijo Lagoon, Cardiff; 760-753-5091.

SAN ELIJO STATE BEACH 🏃 🏊 ⛵ 🎣 🤿 ⚓ 🚣 ⛵
Although the beach is wide and sandy, low tide reveals a mantle
of rocks just offshore and there are reefs, too, making this another of North County's most popular surf fishing and skindiving spots. Surfers brave big breakers at "Turtles" and "Pipes"
reefs at the north end of the beach. Lifeguards are stationed here
during summer. There is a campground atop the bluff overlooking the beach. Most amenities are located at the campground and
include restrooms, showers, beach rentals and groceries. Day-use
fee, $4. ~ Off South Route 101 north of Chesterfield Drive,
Cardiff; 760-753-5091; e-mail sanelijo@ixpres.com.

▲ There are 171 tent/RV sites (some hookups), $21 to $39
per night. Reservations: 800-444-7275.

SWAMI'S PARK 🏊 ⛵ 🎣 🤿 ⚓ 🚣 North County's most
famous surfing beach derives its name from an Indian guru who
founded the Self-Realization Fellowship Temple here in the
1920s. The gold-domed compound is located on the cliff top just
to the north of the park. A small, grassy picnic area gives way to
stairs leading to a narrow, rocky beach favored almost exclusively by surfers, though divers and anglers like the spot as well.
The reef point break here makes for spectacular waves. The
stretch between this beach and D Street is a marine refuge, so
don't get any ideas about taking an invertebrate home with you.
Facilities include restrooms, picnic areas, lifeguards and a funky
outdoor shower. ~ 1298 South Route 101 about one mile south
of Encinitas Boulevard, Encinitas; 760-633-2740, fax 760-633-
2626; www.ci.encinitas.ca.us.

MOONLIGHT STATE BEACH 🏊 ⛵ 🎣 🤿 ⚓ 🚣 ⛵ A
very popular beach, Moonlight boasts a big sandy cove flanked
by sandstone bluffs. Surf is relatively tame at the center, enter-
taining swimmers and bodysurfers. Volleyball courts, a playground and fire circles are added attractions. Surfers like the
wave action to the south, particularly at the foot of D Street.
There are picnic areas, firepits, restrooms, showers, lifeguards, a
snack bar, equipment (surfboards, boogieboards, beach gear)
rentals and places to fish. ~ 400 B Street, Encinitas; 760-633-
2740, fax 760-633-2626; www.ci.encinitas.ca.us.

STONE STEPS BEACH 🏊 🏄 🚣 Locals come here to hide   ◀ HIDDEN
away from the tourists. It is indeed stony, and narrow to boot,
but secluded and hard to find. Much like Moonlight to the south,
its surf conditions are good for several types of water sports.
There are no facilities; a lifeguard is stationed here in summer. ~
The staircase to the beach is located at South El Portal Street, off
Neptune Avenue, Leucadia.

BEACON'S BEACH 🏊 🎣 🏄 🚣 A broad sand corri-
dor backdropped by coastal bluffs, this beach has appeal, though
it's certainly not North County's finest. The strand is widest at
the north end, but the breakers are bigger at the south end, a favorite with local surfers. Swimming, surfing and skindiving are
good. ~ There is a trail off the parking lot at Leucadia Boulevard
and Neptune Avenue, Encinitas; 760-633-2740, fax 760-633-
2626; www.ci.encinitas.ca.us.

SOUTH CARLSBAD STATE BEACH 🏊 🎣 🏄 🚣 This
is a big, bustling beachfront rimmed by bluffs. The pebbles
strewn everywhere put towel space at a premium, but the water
is gentle and super for swimming. The beach has restrooms, lifeguards, showers, groceries and beach rentals. Swimming, fishing,
surfing and skindiving are popular activities. ~ Located west of
Carlsbad Boulevard south of Palomar Airport Road, Carlsbad;
760-438-3143, fax 760-438-2762.

▲ There are 196 blufftop tent/RV sites (no hookups), $21 to
$31 per night. Reservations: 800-444-7275.

CARLSBAD STATE BEACH 🏊 🎣 🏄 🚣 Conditions
here are about the same as at South Carlsbad (see below), a sand
and rock beach bordered by bluffs. Rock and
surf fishing are quite good at this beach and even
better at the adjoining Encinas Fishing Area (at the
San Diego Gas and Electric power plant), where
Agua Hedionda Lagoon opens to the sea. The beach
extends another mile or so to the mouth of the Buena
Vista Lagoon. Facilities include restrooms and lifeguards.
The beach offers swimming, surfing and skindiving. ~ The
park entrance is at Tamarack Avenue, west of Carlsbad
Boulevard, Carlsbad; 760-438-3675, fax 760-438-2762.

> It is more than a rumor
> that some discreet
> nude sunbathing takes
> place at the end of
> beach path #6 at
> San Onofre.

OCEANSIDE BEACHES 🚲 🏊 🏄 🤿 🚣 🚤 ⛵ Over
three miles of clean, rock-free beaches front North County's

largest city, stretching from Buena Vista Lagoon in the south to Oceanside Harbor in the north. Along the entire length, the water can get rough in the summer and fall, and it's important to be wary of riptides here. Lots of Marines from nearby Camp Pendleton favor this beach. The nicest section of all is around Oceanside Pier, a 1900-foot-long fishing pier. Nearby, palm trees line a grassy promenade dotted with picnickers; the sand is as clean as a whistle. Added to the attractions is **Buena Vista Lagoon**, a bird sanctuary and nature reserve. Facilities include picnic areas, restrooms, lifeguards and basketball and volleyball courts. There are kayak rentals at the harbor; the only boat ramp for miles around is located here. Restaurants are at the end of the pier and harbor. Try fishing from the pier, the rocks or the beach. Swimming is good and surfing is reliable year-round. Day-use fee, up to $5. ~ Located along The Strand in Oceanside; 760-435-4018, fax 760-435-4022; www.ci.oceanside.ca.us.

▲ Limited to a few RV sites in a parking lot (no hookups); $15 per night.

SAN ONOFRE STATE BEACH 🏃 🚲 🐟 🏄 ⛵ San Diego County's northernmost beach is about 16 miles north of Oceanside, uneasily sandwiched between Camp Pendleton and the San Onofre nuclear power plant. It's well worth a visit, if you're not put off by the nearby presence of atomic energy. San Onofre has a number of sections separated by the power plant and connected via a public walkway along the seawall. On the north side of the power plant, off Cristianitos Road, is San Mateo Campground, with developed sites. Eroded bluffs rumple down to the beach, creating a variety of sandy coves and pockets. South of Bluffs and not far from famous Trestles Beach is Surf Beach, a favorite with surfers and kayakers. The southern side of the plant is Bluffs Campground, a superb campground with trailer spaces and primitive tent sites, the only primitive campsite anywhere on San Diego County beaches. Gentle surf, which picks up considerably to the north, makes this a good swimming and bodysurfing spot. You'll find restrooms, lifeguards and trails. Parking fee, $12. ~ From Route 5, take Basilone Road exit and follow the signs to the beach; 949-492-0802, fax 949-492-8412.

▲ There are 221 tent/RV sites (no hookups) at Bluffs Campground (949-492-4872), $21 per night; and 157 tent/RV sites

HIDDEN ►

(hookups and showers) at San Mateo Campground, $21 to $30 per night. Reservations: 800-444-7275.

Inland San Diego

Inland San Diego is an eclectic area, with plenty of open spaces, a rich history and some surprises. This is where you can attend mass at an 1816 mission, try your hand at panning for gold, or get up close and personal with a pack of wolves. Escondido is not only the largest town in the area, but one of the fastest growing places in California. In 1886, the Escondido Land and Title Company acquired the original Spanish land grant to the valley, laid out the town site and divided the rest of the area into small farms for growing grapes and citrus. Even today, agriculture is important to the area, which is home to 40 percent of the state's 59,000 acres of avocados and a growing number of vineyards, which

Julian

One of the nicest things about Julian's historic district is that it's not just a bunch of tarted-up early California buildings—strictly for show. It's a real working downtown, though, admittedly, many of the businesses are geared to tourists. In downtown Julian you can still sleep, eat or shop in buildings that have been around for a century or more.

JULIAN TOWN HALL   Before starting a stroll around town, stop in at the nearly 100-year-old Julian Town Hall on the corner of Main and Washington streets. Besides housing the Chamber of Commerce, where you can pick up a walking tour map, the Town Hall displays historic photos, and town meetings are still held here.

MAIN STREET   Map in hand, head down Main Street and pass by the **F.A. DeLuca Store**, now Jack's Market, and **A.P. Frary Jr. Residence**, currently occupied by a real estate company. Turn right on C Street and head for the **Julian Jail**. Built in 1914, this two-celler served mostly as a place for the town drunks to cool off and sober up. At one time it contained the only indoor toilet in town.

OLD-TIME BUSINESSES   Turn back up C Street and turn left on Main, passing by several more historic residences on the way to the **Hotel Robinson**. This restored Victorian hostelry is still an operating hotel, though it's now called The Julian Gold Rush Hotel Bed & Breakfast. In the next block, in front of the **Wilcox Building**, now Sprague Realty, is a plaque commemorating the **Wheelbarrow Odometer Survey**

climb the hillsides north and east of town. Though certainly not indigenous to the area, a remarkable number of exotic animals can be viewed at San Diego Zoo's Wild Animal Park, where they roam free within the 1800-acre park. In the historic town of Julian, the area's gold-mining past is remembered, though today it's better known for its apple crop than its gold nuggets.

SIGHTS   True to its grape-growing past, Escondido, inland from coastal Route 5 on Route 78, boasts a number of vineyards. You can chat with the folks at **Ferrara Winery** and stroll around the vineyards. A small family enterprise, the winery has been producing vintages for three generations. Wine tasting is free. ~ 1120 West 15th Avenue, Escondido; 760-745-7632, fax 760-743-2675.

of 1894, when civil engineer Porter P. Wheaton measured 2328 miles of country roads for a surveyor's map of San Diego County. Just next door is a building that was undoubtedly the scene of some riotous evenings when it was the **Swycaffer Saloon**, in the pioneer days. Down the street, in an 1886 building on the corner of Main and Washington, more benign libations are served at Miner's Diner's authentic 1930s soda fountain. In the same building, once the **Levi-Marks Store** is the Julian Drug Store.

JULIAN PIONEER MUSEUM   Turn left on Washington and walk the two blocks to the Julian Pioneer Museum (see also page 146). The museum building started out as a brewery in the mid-1880s, was converted into a blacksmith shop, which was operating until the 1930s, and opened as a museum in the early 1950s. Besides boasting the finest lace collection in California, it displays an eclectic mix of everything from an original Julian City buggy to indigenous-to-the-area birds mounted.

BAILY-KING HOUSE   Walk back up Washington to 3rd Street and turn right: on the left is the Baily-King House. Built in 1898 for successful gold miner Clarence King, today the house is occupied by Julian Tea and Cottage Arts, a lovely place to go for a proper afternoon tea in oh-so-appropriate surroundings.

JULIAN PIONEER CEMETERY   Head back to Main Street and turn right— it will become Farmer Road—and a short walk brings you to the last stop on the tour, also the last stop for many of Julian's early settlers, the Julian Pioneer Cemetery.

The **Deer Park Winery and Auto Museum** offers tastings of wines from its Napa and Escondido vineyards and displays a fine collection of vintage automobiles. Closed Tuesday and Wednesday. Admission. ~ 29013 Champagne Boulevard, Escondido; 760-749-1666, fax 760-751-1666; www.deerparkwinery.com.

The **Welk Resort**, an elaborate complex, contains a museum in its theater lobby that features the famous "one-ana-two" entertainer's (Lawrence, that is) memorabilia. High camp at its most bizarre. Closed during theater performances; call ahead. ~ 8860 Lawrence Welk Drive, Escondido; 760-749-3000; www. welkresort.com.

Heritage Walk Museum, located in the downtown area, is a collection of historic buildings, which include the town's first library, the city's Santa Fe Railroad depot, a Victorian home and an outhouse. Blacksmithing classes are taught in the working blacksmith shop, making this the only museum in Southern California where you can learn to shoe horses, amongst other things. ~ Grape Day Park, 321 North Broadway, Escondido; 760-743-8207, fax 760-743-8267; www.escondidohistoricalsociety.com.

Sister location to the museum in Balboa Park, **Mingei International Museum, North County Satellite** has the same focus. Displays of "arts of the people" from around the world encourage a new appreciation for the beauty of everyday objects. Besides 5000 feet of exhibition space, North County Satellite has a multimedia education center, offers hands-on activities and hosts artist demonstrations. ~ 155 West Grand Avenue, Escondido; 760-735-3355.

There's no finer wildlife sanctuary in the country than the remarkable **San Diego Zoo's Wild Animal Park.** This 1800-acre spread, skillfully landscaped to resemble Asian and African habitats, houses over 3500 animals. Among them are several endangered species not found in zoos elsewhere. Many of the animals roam free while you view them from a monorail. After visiting the fearsome lions and gorillas, you can follow that line of children to the "Petting Kraal," where the kids can fluff up a variety of exotic deer. For a really up-close and personal experience, a Photo Caravan Safari in special covered safari trucks gets you nose-to-nose with wildlife, where you can hand-feed the rhinoceroses and giraffes. To really feel like you're in the bush, consider participating in a Snore and Roar overnight camping trip, available April through October. Admission. ~ 15500 San Pasqual Valley Road, Escondido; 619-234-6541; www.wildanimalpark.org.

Two miles east of the animal park is **San Pasqual Battlefield State Historic Park,** where an interpretive center tells the story of a strange and little-known battle. It seems that during the Mexican War in 1846 about 100 U.S. Dragoons, including the famous scout Kit Carson, suffered an embarrassing defeat at the hands of the California Mexicans. Today, a small monument here marks the battle site. Closed Monday through Friday. ~ 15808 San Pasqual Valley Road, Escondido; 760-737-2201.

Orfila Vineyards and Winery, a producer of chardonnay, merlot, viognier and syrah, is open daily for tastings and tours. ~ 13455 San Pasqual Road, about six miles southeast of Escon-

dido; 760-738-6500, 800-868-9463, fax 760-745-3773; www.
orfila.com.

Also southeast of Escondido, **Bernardo Winery** is the oldest
operating winery in the county. You can take a self-guided tour
any day and taste wine for free. ~ 13330 Paseo del Verano Norte,
San Diego; 858-487-1866, fax 858-673-5376; www.bernardo
winery.com.

Continuing inland via Route 78 to its junction with Route
79, you'll come to the tiny town of Santa Ysabel. **Mission Santa
Ysabel**, where a 20th-century church stands on the site of an
1818 branch chapel, lacks the appeal of its sister missions. It
does, however, feature Indian burial grounds and a museum. ~
23013 Route 79, Santa Ysabel; 760-765-0810, fax 760-765-3494.

Most of the pilgrims in these parts are bound not for the
chapel but for **Dudley's Bakery**, where dozens of kinds of bread,
including a delicious jalapeño loaf, come steaming from the
oven. Closed Monday and Tuesday. ~ 30218 Route 78 at Route
79, Santa Ysabel; 760-765-0488, 800-225-3348, fax 760-765-
1565; www.dudleysbakery.com, e-mail dudleysbakery@dudleys
bakery.com.

Down the road in **Julian,** deemed a state historic site, you will   ◄ HIDDEN
come upon the belle of Southern California mountain mining
towns. During the 1890s, the local mines employed 2000 miners,
who hauled up $15 million in gold ore. Today, the region pro-
duces red apples rather than gold nuggets, and Julian, with its
dusty aura of the Old West, has become a major tourist attraction.

Some of the falsefront stores located along **Main Street** are
19th-century originals. Have a look, for instance, at the 1897

FOLLOWING THE SUNRISE

Near Lake Cuyamaca, just south of Julian, Route S1 (Sunrise Highway) leads
southeast to **Mount Laguna**, a region rich in recreational areas and desert
views. You can continue your backcountry adventure by following the highway (which becomes Buckman Springs Road) south toward the Mexican
border. This is rough, arid, scrub country, but you'll find an oasis at **Lake
Morena**, where an oak-shaded park borders a fishing lake. Farther
south lies the high desert outpost of **Campo**, with its sun-baked
streets and 19th-century ruins. From here you can head south across
the border or west toward the seaside metropolis of San Diego.

Julian Hotel, and don't miss the **Julian Drug Store**, an old-style soda fountain serving sparkling sarsaparilla and conjuring images of boys in buckskin and girls in bonnets. The white clapboard **Town Hall** still stands.

Over at the **Julian Pioneer Museum**, the townsfolk have turned an old blacksmith's shop into a charming hodgepodge of local collectibles. Closed Monday from April through November; open weekends only from December through March. Admission. ~ 2811 Washington Street, Julian; 760-765-0227.

See the "Walking Tour" for more information about Julian's old-time attractions.

Although the tunnels of the **Washington Mine** (the first hardrock mine in Julian) have long since collapsed, the Julian Historical Society displays mining memorabilia depicting the mining era. ~ At the end of C Street, Julian.

Operations closed in 1942, but the **Eagle Mining Company** still offer tours of the tunnels of the Eagle and High Peak mines, and an opportunity to pan for gold. What seems certain to be a "tourist trap" is actually an interesting and educational experience. Open daily, weather permitting. Admission. ~ At the end of C Street, Julian; 760-765-0036.

But remember, these days apples are actually the main business in Julian and dozens of orchards drape the hillsides below town. The countryside all around is quilted with pear and peach orchards as well, and there are Appaloosa ranches and roadside stands selling fruits and jams.

Also in the hills outside of town is the **California Wolf Center**, a site that is dedicated to studying, what else, wolves. Their main focus is on the conservation of the gray wolf, both the North American and Alaskan varieties. Through the packs of captive wolves living at the center, conservationists hope to find out more about wolves in the wild and educate the public. The center offers special reservations-only programs Saturdays at 2 p.m. ~ P.O. Box 1389, Julian, CA 92036; 619-234-9653, 760-765-0030; www.californiawolfcenter.org.

Route 79 points south from Julian along the ridge of the Laguna Mountains to the charred remains of **Cuyamaca Rancho State Park**. Isolated Indian country that was turned into a Spanish rancho in the 19th century, this former alpine sanctuary suffered a huge fire in October 2003 and is closed until further

notice. For further information, call 760-767-5311; www.cuya
maca.statepark.org.

Heading back north on Route 79, you'll course through
backcountry. Continuing your drive on Route 76, you'll reach a
spiraling road that will lead to that great silver dome in the sky,
Palomar Observatory. With a clear shot heavenward from its
6100-foot-high perch, one of the world's largest reflecting tele-
scopes scans the night skies for celestial secrets. Staffed by scien-
tists and astronomers from the California
Institute of Technology, this is an active research
facility and, only reluctantly, a tourist attraction.
You can glimpse the 200-inch Hale Telescope from
the visitor's gallery, view a movie on how research is
conducted and look at photos in the museum, but
there's little else to see or do. Unless of course you have
the time and the legs to hike around the mountain (see the
"Hiking" section at the end of Chapter One). ~ On Mount Palomar at the end of Route S6 off Country Road 76; 760-742-2119.

Located on the Pala Indian
Reservation, the Mission
San Antonio de Pala is
the only mission pri-
marily serving
American Indians.

From here you have two options. Driving west on Route 76
will take you through Pauma Valley to the town of Pala. **Mission
San Antonio de Pala** has been conducting mass since it was built
in 1816. The original chapel and bell tower have been faithfully
restored, and the long, low walls of the church interior are still
decorated with primitive Indian frescoes. Closed Monday and
Tuesday. Admission. ~ Pala Mission Road, Pala; 760-742-3317,
fax 760-742-3040.

Continuing west on Route 76 from Pala will bring you back
to Oceanside and coastal Route 5. Taking scenic Route S6 south
from Palomar Observatory will carry you from the pine-rimmed
high country of Cleveland National Forest to a verdant region of
citrus groves. Route S6 south eventually brings you back to the
town of Escondido.

LODGING

Palm Tree Lodge is clearly the nicest of the reasonably priced
motels in Escondido. Family-owned and -operated, it is sparkling
clean and well maintained. Some of the 38 rooms have kitchens
and fireplaces. You'll also find a restaurant, pool and sundeck on
the premises. Pets are welcome. ~ 425 West Mission Avenue, Escondido; 760-745-7613, 800-745-1062, fax 760-745-3377; www.
palmtreelodge.com, e-mail joy@palmtreelodge.com. MODERATE.

The **Ramona Valley Inn** is a 39-room roadside motel, clean and comfortable, located halfway between Escondido and Julian. There's a pool; some rooms have kitchenettes. ~ 416 Main Street, Ramona; 760-789-6433, 800-648-4618, fax 760-789-2889. MODERATE.

HIDDEN ► One of Southern California's oldest hostelries, the 1897 **Julian Hotel Bed and Breakfast** is a Victorian charmer. The place is often full, particularly on weekends, so reserve in advance. Two charming cottages and 18 rooms are done in period fashion, with plenty of brass, lace, porcelain and mahogany; all feature a private bath. In addition to a historic building, guests share a lovely sitting room. ~ Main and B streets, Julian; 760-765-0201, 800-734-5854, fax 760-765-0327; www.julianhotel.com, e-mail b&b@julianhotel.com. MODERATE TO ULTRA-DELUXE.

Located on three acres in the heart of Julian's historic district, **Orchard Hill Country Inn** is a winsome getaway. The two-story lodge houses ten guest rooms done in American country decor, while four Craftsman-style bungalows feature 12 suites complete with fireplace, whirlpool tub and wraparound porch. Stroll through the gardens of native plants and fruit trees or head for the hammock for a little cat nap. A full breakfast and afternoon hors d'oeuvres are included in the tab. ~ 2502 Washington Street, Julian; 760-765-1700, 800-716-7242, fax 760-765-0290; www.orchardhill.com, e-mail information@orchardhill.com. ULTRA-DELUXE.

HIDDEN ► **Shadow Mountain Ranch Bed and Breakfast**, a large, attractive country house near Julian, provides the area's most unusual lodging in its "enchanted cottage," complete with pot-bellied stove, the "gnome home," with a stone waterfall shower and "grandma's attic cottage," containing all of granny's antiques.

AUTHOR FAVORITE

The 23-room **Julian Lodge**, designed after a 19th-century hotel, is a wood-frame structure that nicely recaptures the original. The rooms are small but well decorated with country Victorian furnishings. The breakfast parlor, where an expanded continental breakfast is served, is also quite homey, with oak tables and an inviting fireplace. ~ 2720 C Street, Julian; 760-765-1420, 800-542-1420, fax 760-765-2752; www.julianlodge.com. MODERATE TO DELUXE.

For the adventurous, they even have a tiny treehouse with built-in toilet. There are more conventional rooms and cottages available as well. Full breakfast is included in the price. Reservations strongly recommended. Two-night minimum stay required on weekends. ~ 2771 Frisius Road, Pine Hills; phone/fax 760-765-0323; e-mail jcketch@julianweb.com. MODERATE TO DELUXE.

Also consider **Pine Hills Lodge**, a wonderfully rustic complex with a lodge and cabins that date back to 1912. Surrounded by pines and cedars, this cozy retreat features six European-style rooms (with shared bath) in the lodge. The ten cozy, deluxe-priced cabins are woodframe structures complete with clawfoot tubs. Located at 4500 feet elevation, Pine Hills is a miniresort featuring a restaurant, bar and dinner theater. ~ 2960 La Posada Way, Pine Hills; 760-765-1100, fax 760-765-1121; www.pine hillslodge.com, e-mail info@pinehillslodge.com. MODERATE TO DELUXE.

Overnighting in the Mount Palomar area is limited to camping, except for the **Lazy H Ranch**. When the proprietor said the place "dates back to the '40s," I wondered which '40s—it has the look and feel of an early California homestead. The 11 rooms include only the amenities you'd expect from a budget-priced establishment—and no TVs or phones. But here you can adjourn to the Spanish-style patio, stroll through a garden with lemon trees or take a dip in the pool. ~ 18767 Route 76, Pauma Valley; 760-742-3669, fax 760-742-3305. BUDGET.

DINING

There are a couple of well-established ethnic Escondido restaurants that are worth a try. **El Nopal Restaurant** has been dishing up Mexican food in the downtown area for more than 30 years. It's a friendly place with a loyal following. Vegetarians can enjoy chili corn chowder or guacamole tacos, while carnivores wolf down carnitas and chili verde. Its proximity to the California Center for the Arts makes it a great place for dinner before the show. Closed Sunday. ~ 126 South Kalmia Street, Escondido; 760-741-8723, fax 760-741-8844; www.elnopal.signonsan diego.com. BUDGET.

◄ *HIDDEN*

What makes **China Bistro**, in business since 1979, stand out is its variety of sauces. Chicken, meat, seafood and vegetarian dishes are prepared in sauces that range from an apple, melon and pineapple fruit sauce to a black pepper steak sauce. For those who like their Chinese food with a little heat, there are honey and garlic sauces that can be made just as hot as you can stand. Closed Sunday. ~ 1330 East Valley Parkway, Suite M, Escondido; 760-741-0330. BUDGET TO MODERATE.

The **Julian Grill,** situated in a 1920-vintage house, is cozy and folksy, especially around the living room fireplace. The menu emphasizes such hearty fare as steaks, prime rib, seafood, scampi and chicken breast. They also feature sophisticated chef's specials like Chicken Jerusalem. There's patio dining and a full bar. Champagne brunch is served on Sunday. No dinner on Monday. ~ 2224 Main Street, Julian; 760-765-0173; www.juliangrill.com. MODERATE TO DELUXE.

HIDDEN ▶︎   At **Romano's Dodge House** you will feel like a family guest. This intimate Italian restaurant, with its homespun ambience, dishes out delicious chicken cacciatore, lasagna and authentic homemade sausage. With its reasonable prices, Romano's is hard to beat. Closed Tuesday. ~ 2718 B Street, Julian; 760-765-1003, fax 760-765-3435; www.romanosjulian.com, e-mail panda@ thegrid.net. MODERATE.

HIDDEN ▶︎   For buffalo burgers and local gossip, the townsfolk all head over to **Buffalo Bill's.** This friendly café, with its all-American cuisine and early American decor, serves up a standard-fare breakfast and lunch menu. No dinner. ~ 2603 B Street, Julian; 760-765-1560. BUDGET.

Hikers will appreciate **Palomar Mountain General Store,** whose adjacent vegetarian café serves hearty soups, salads, sandwiches and hot entrées at lunch and dinner. The store is open daily; the café is closed Tuesday and Wednesday from Labor Day to Memorial Day. ~ Routes S6 and S7, Palomar Mountain; store 760-742-3496, café 760-742-4233, fax 760-742-2220. BUDGET.

JUST LIKE MOM USED TO MAKE . . .

At least a dozen places in Julian prepare the local specialty, apple pie. But buyer beware: all pies are not created equal: Some are definitely better than others. The pies at the **Julian Pie Company,** for instance, always have flaky crusts and just the right mix of apples, cinnamon and sugar. ~ 2225 Main Street, Julian; 760-765-2449; www.julianpie.com, e-mail julian piecompany@aol.com. BUDGET.

El Rey is a favorite among smart locals and savvy travelers. The tasty Mexican-American fare includes huge servings of enchiladas, tostadas, tacos and quesadillas. On the gringo side of the menu, there are steak, chicken and seafood dishes. The rustic interior is paneled with pine. Closed Monday. ~ 16220 Route 76, Pauma Valley; 760-742-3343. BUDGET TO MODERATE.

The **Lazy H Ranch** serves up steaks, prime rib, chicken and fish dishes in a family-style dining room set in the leafy environs of a four-acre orchard. Closed Monday. ~ Route 76, Pauma Valley; 760-742-3669. MODERATE TO DELUXE.

◄ HIDDEN

Mega-malls are popping up all around San Diego these days, but few match Escondido's **Westfield Shoppingtown North County**. This 87-acre complex has a half-dozen major department stores and a host of independent shops. ~ 272 East Via Rancho Parkway and Route 15, Escondido; 760-489-2332; www.westfield. com.

Even if you're not in the market for nuts, dried fruit or candy, a visit to **Bates Nut Farm** is mandatory. Name the nut and they have it—walnuts, cashews, pistachios, pecans, almonds and peanuts—attractively displayed with an equally amazing variety of dried and glazed fruits, jellies, honey and candy. ~ 15954 Woods Valley Road, Valley Center; 760-749-3333; www.batesnut farm.biz.

Main Street in Julian is lined with dozens of antique, gift, clothing and curio shops. Among the more intriguing ones are the **Antique Boutique**, with an especially nice selection of furniture and collectibles. ~ 2626 Main Street, Julian; 760-765-0541. **Julian's Toy Chest** features unusual educational toys and children's books. ~ 2116 Main Street, Julian; 760-765-2262. Located in the same building, **Quinn Knives** is where you can buy anything from a sword to a Swiss Army knife. ~ 2116 Main Street, Julian; 760-765-2230. Nearby is the **Old Julian Book House**, specializing in used and out-of-print antiquarian volumes. Call for hours. ~ 2230 Main Street, Julian; 760-765-1989.

SHOPPING

California Center for the Arts is a multifaceted facility located on a 12-acre campus right in the heart of downtown. This happening place has a 1500-seat concert hall, a 400-seat theater, a visual arts museum, art and dance studios, and a conference cen-

NIGHTLIFE

ter, all of which work to achieve the center's goal, which is to both educate and entertain. ~ 340 North Escondido Boulevard, Escondido; 760-839-4100, 619-220-8497, 800-988-4253; www. artcenter.org.

Built in 1926 as a training camp for Jack Dempsey, **Pine Hills Lodge & Dinner Theatre** uses the champ's old ring as a dinner theater stage. And it looks as though they've scored a knockout. Nationwide, professional companies perform year-round. Admission. ~ 2960 La Posada Way, Pine Hills; 760-765-1100; www.pinehillslodge.com.

PARKS **PALOMAR MOUNTAIN STATE PARK** 🚶🚴‍♂️🛶 Thick forests of pine, fir and cedar combine with rambling mountain meadows to create a Sierra Nevada–like atmosphere. The average elevation here on the side of Mount Palomar is 5500 feet, so the evenings are cool and heavy snow is common in the winter. Doane Pond is stocked with trout. Biking is permitted on paved roads. Facilities include picnic areas, barbecues, restrooms and showers. Day-use fee, $6. ~ Route S7 on top of Mount Palomar; 760-742-3462.

CLEVELAND NATIONAL FOREST 🚶🚴‍♂️🏇🚣 A major mountain preserve, this sprawling retreat is divided into three districts, two of which encompass more than 400,000 acres in San Diego County. Northernmost is the Palomar District, covering 189,000 acres around the famous observatory and stretching south beyond Lake Henshaw. Its main feature is the rugged Agua Tibia Wilderness Area, with several excellent trails. Horseback riding is permitted on trails designated for equestrian use. Farther south, the 216,000-acre Descanso District adjoins Cuyamaca Rancho State Park. Here, the Laguna Mountain Recreation Area offers camping, picnicking and hiking. There are picnic areas and restrooms. Day-use fee, $5. ~ Access to the Palomar District is via Routes 79, S6 and S7; the Descanso District and the Laguna Mountain Recreation Area are located on Route S1 (Sunrise Highway) a few miles north of Route 8; 619-445-6235, fax 619-445-1753; www.r5.fs.fed.us/cleveland.

▲ There are five campgrounds in the Palomar District, three of which accommodate RVs (no hookups); $12 to $15 per night. There are six campgrounds in the Descanso District, all of which accommodate both tents and RVs (no hookups); $10 to $14 a night. Reservations: 877-444-6777.

WILLIAM HEISE PARK 🚶🐎 Beautifully situated in a forest of ◄HIDDEN
pines and oaks, this preserve rests at a 4200-foot elevation near
the Laguna Mountains and Julian. The park is largely undeveloped and provides more than 1000 acres of hiking and riding
trails (although only 200 trails are open for use ••••••••••••••••••••••••
after the 2003 wildfires). Picnic areas, restrooms,   William Heise Park is
a playground and showers are available. Parking   one of the few county
fee, $2. ~ From Route 79 (one mile west of Julian)   parks where the
go south on Pine Hills Road for two miles, then east   snowfall is sufficient
on Frisius Road for two more miles; 858-565-3600, fax   for winter recre-
858-495-5840; www.co.san-diego.ca.us/parks.   ation.

▲ There are 100 tent/RV sites (no hookups), $14 to
$16 per night; and 4 cabins equipped with heat and electricity,
$35 per night.

ANZA-BORREGO DESERT STATE PARK Comprising more than
600,000 acres, Anza-Borrego is the largest state park in
California and encompasses rugged mountains as well as desert
terrain. Lucky visitors may also get a glimpse of the area's most
famous inhabitant, the desert bighorn sheep. You'll find picnic
areas, restrooms and showers. Day-use fee, $5. ~ Route 78 leads
into the park from the west; 760-767-5311, fax 760-767-3427;
www.anzaborrego.statepark.org.

LAKE MORENA PARK 🚶🐎🚣🛶⛵🎣 As its name suggests,
the highlight of this hideaway is a 1000-acre lake renowned for
its bass, crappie, bluegill and catfish. Located near the Mexican
border, the park covers a total of 3250 acres, which range from
flat terrain to low hills covered with oak and scrub. There are
picnic areas, restrooms and showers. Fishing facilities and boat
rentals are available. Parking fee, $2. ~ Off Route 8 (Buckman
Springs Road) in the southeast corner of San Diego County; 858-
565-3600, fax 858-495-5840; www.scparks.org.

▲ There are 80 tent/RV sites; 50 have hookups; $12 to $16
per night. Ten wilderness cabins are also available; $25 per night.

LOS PEÑASQUITOS CANYON PRESERVE 🚶🐎 This 3000-acre
parcel, a canyonland wilderness several miles from the coast, features narrow rock gorges, mesa plateaus and streamside wood-
lands. There are hiking trails as well as historic adobe houses to
explore. Restrooms are available. Parking fee, $2. ~ Located off
Black Mountain Road near Mira Mesa.

SIX

South Bay & Northern Baja

Several cities straddle Route 5, the freeway that links downtown with the Mexican border city of Tijuana, 20 miles south. But most visitors tend to overlook the South Bay as they jet toward their favorite San Diego daytrip destination. Imperial Beach has perhaps the most tourist appeal, thanks to its oceanfront location and white-sand beach. Chula Vista, National City and San Ysidro are basically thriving manufacturing, commercial and residential communities.

Coils of razor wire top the 150-mile-long chain-link steel fence, nicknamed the Tortilla Curtain, that stretches from the Pacific Ocean to the Colorado River delta, separating the state of California from the state of Baja California. Most of Baja's population lives within seven kilometers of the border, enticed from all over Mexico by the promise of steady factory jobs in the *maquiladoras*, the dream of crossing the border for better pay in southern California or, in some cases, the fast-money gamble of smuggling drugs or guns. Rich with opportunity, wracked with poverty and desperation, the California–Baja border forms a sociological fault line between two lands that are utterly unlike one another.

One of Baja California's largest cities, Tijuana is a city of paradoxes: one of the wealthiest cities in Mexico, brimming with free-trade economic opportunities—yet sobered by the suffering of hundreds of thousands of people living in desperate poverty. All Spanish-speaking "undocumented workers" found in California, Nevada, Oregon and Washington are deported to Tijuana, regardless of their state or country of origin. According to unofficial estimates, as many as half a million Tijuana residents either are on their way to the United States or have recently been expelled from there.

Ensenada, the third-largest city in Baja, accommodates cruise ships with the biggest, busiest tourist-oriented shopping district between Tijuana and Los Cabos.

A cool morning fog drifts in off the ocean to shroud the hills behind this port city. The Pacific coast around Rosarito and Ensenada is the setting for numerous luxury beach resorts, and an elbow-to-elbow party atmosphere characterizes the weekend beach scene around both cities.

Although the area south of downtown leans toward residential communities and commercial ventures that sustain it (car dealerships, strip malls, shopping centers), there are several sites of interest to passing travelers.

South Bay

SIGHTS

The **Chula Vista Nature Center** is located in the Sweetwater National Wildlife Refuge on San Diego Bay and, through interactive exhibits especially appealing to children, offers a close-up look at the history and geology of Southern California wetlands. There is a shark and ray tank, birds of prey exhibits, and a composting garden. Closed Monday. Admission. ~ 1000 Gunpowder Point Drive, Chula Vista; 619-409-5900, fax 619-409-5910; www.chulavistanaturecenter.org, e-mail barbara@chulavistana turecenter.org.

Visitors to Chula Vista also have an opportunity to glimpse Olympic athletes in training at the **U.S. Olympic Training Center**. Guided tours are conducted from the visitors center hourly, Monday through Saturday, from 10 a.m. to 3 p.m., and on Sunday, from 11 a.m. to 3 p.m. ~ 2800 Olympic Parkway, Chula Vista; 619-656-1500, fax 619-482-6200; www.usolympic team.com.

Anyone looking for watery thrills won't want to miss **Soak City Water Park**. Older kids with plenty of nerve can try rides such as Cyclone or Riptide, while toddlers can get their waterpark training wheels in the Tykes Trough. Closed October through April. ~ 2052 Entertainment Circle, Chula Vista; 619-661-7373; www.knotts.com/soakcity/sd.

Imperial Beach's proud surfing history is celebrated by **Surfhenge**, the 16x20-foot-high abstract surfboard arches at the refurbished Imperial Beach Pier Plaza. In addition to the brightly colored acrylic sculpture are benches resembling different surfboard styles, each with bronze plaques commemorating surfing legends who hung ten in the waters off Imperial Beach. ~ Imperial Beach Pier Plaza.

Along this southern coastline is the **Tijuana River National Estuarine Research Reserve**, which comprises the county's largest and most pristine estuarine sanctuary (Tijuana Slough National Wildlife Refuge) and a three-mile stretch of sandy beach (Border Field State Park). For nature lovers, this haven of salt marsh and sand dunes is a must-see diversion: more than 370 species of birds are found there. The visitors center features exhibits and a library. Trails lead to the beach and wildlife refuge at this fascinating wetland (see "Hiking" in Chapter One for more information). ~ Visitors center: 301 Caspian Way, Imperial Beach; see "Beaches & Parks" below for directions to the state park; 619-575-3613, fax 619-575-6913; www.tijuanaestuary.com, e-mail trnerr@ixpress.com.

The town of **San Ysidro** is best known for being one of the world's busiest border crossings. More than 60 million people cross here each year—pedestrians and bus riders as well as motorists in 33 million private vehicles. The town itself is full of discount shopping outlets and chain motels and eateries.

LODGING   Among all those identical motels grouped around the freeway exits in Chula Vista, **The Traveler Inn & Suites** is perhaps your best bet. Conveniently located just a block from the highway, this family-owned 85-unit motel is early Holiday Inn throughout, but its rates hark back to 1960s. Not that you would really expect them, but extras include two pools, a spa, laundry facilities, and cable TV. Continental breakfast is served. ~ 235 Woodlawn Avenue, Chula Vista; 619-427-9170, 800-748-6998, fax 619-427-5247; thetravelerinn.com. MODERATE.

Situated on a main commercial street just a few blocks from the trolley station and the freeway, the **Chula Vista Travel Inn** has 77 clean and tidy rooms and suites overlooking a pool and hot tub. The palm trees and stucco-and-tile exterior exude a Mediterranean air; accommodations are standard motel style with phone, cable TV, and coffee makers, and some rooms have spas. There are laundry facilities and an adjacent greasy-spoon diner. Continental breakfast is included. ~ 394 Broadway, Chula Vista; 619-420-6600, 800-447-0416, phone/fax 619-420-5556; www.travelinnsandiego.com, e-mail travelinn7@aol.com. BUDGET TO DELUXE.

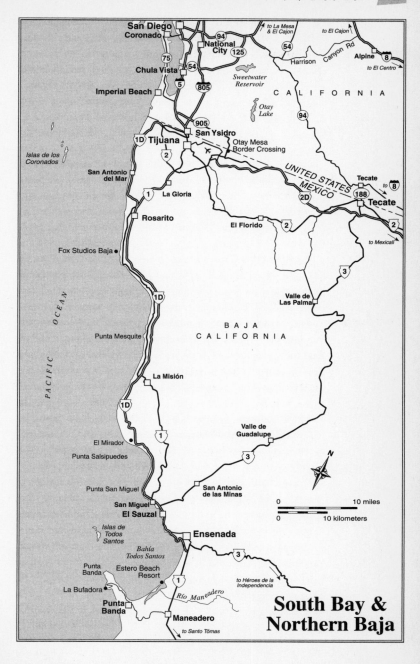

San Diego
Coronado
National City
Chula Vista
Imperial Beach
to La Mesa & El Cajon
to El Cajon
Harrison
Canyon Rd
Alpine
to El Centro
CALIFORNIA
Sweetwater Reservoir
Otay Lake
San Ysidro
Tijuana
Otay Mesa Border Crossing
UNITED STATES
MEXICO
Tecate
to 8
Tecate
San Antonio del Mar
Islas de los Coronados
La Gloria
El Florido
to Mexicali
Rosarito
Fox Studios Baja
Valle de Las Palma
PACIFIC OCEAN
Punta Mesquite
BAJA CALIFORNIA
La Misión
Valle de Guadalupe
El Mirador
Punta Salsipuedes
N
Punta San Miguel
San Antonio de las Minas
0   10 miles
0   10 kilometers
San Miguel
El Sauzal
Islas de Todos Santos
Bahía Todos Santos
Ensenada
Punta Banda
Estero Beach Resort
La Bufadora
to Héroes de la Independencia
Punta Banda
Río Maneadero

South Bay & Northern Baja

Maneadero
to Santo Tómas

The **Seacoast Inn of Imperial Beach** is the only hostelry located directly on the sands of Imperial Beach. Decked out with a heated outdoor pool and hot tub, this 38-room complex looks good inside and out. Beachside units are especially nice and have full kitchens. It helps to make summer reservations well in advance. ~ 800 Seacoast Drive, Imperial Beach; 619-424-5183, 800-732-2627, fax 619-424-3090; www.theseacoastinn.com. DELUXE.

DINING

There's no shortage of fast-food joints along Broadway. **Roberto's Taco Shop** has been serving up cheap and tasty Mexican fare since the early 1980s. Rolled tacos, burritos bursting with juicy shredded beef, savory chicken fajitas—it's hard to go wrong here. Open 24 hours. ~ 444 Broadway, Chula Vista; 619-425-0444. BUDGET.

La Bella Pizza Garden is like an annex to Chula Vista's town hall, and owner Kitty Raso is known as the "Mayor of Third Avenue." But the food will interest you far more than the latest political gossip. Besides pizza, there's great lasagna, rigatoni, and ravioli. La Bella features tender veal dishes, too, from a menu that amazingly rarely strays beyond BUDGET prices. Best Italian food for the money in San Diego, and it's open from 7 a.m. to 1 a.m. every day. ~ 373 3rd Avenue, Chula Vista; 619-426-8820, fax 619-426-1302; www.labellapizza.com. BUDGET.

SHOPPING

The pastel-colored, open-air **Chula Vista Center** is anchored by Macy's, Mervyn's, and Sears, and comprises over 60 chain stores as well as unique boutiques. Kids love the carousel. ~ 555 Broadway, Chula Vista; 619-427-6700; www.chulavista.com.

For something more unique, you might peruse the eclectic offerings on 3rd Avenue between E and G streets. This historic strip harbors shops bearing antiques, religious curios and books, and kitschy knickknacks.

Just west of the border is a sprawling consumer paradise: **The Shops at Las Americas.** The Spanish colonial–style structures here house a bevy of factory outlets for brand names such as Tommy Hilfiger, Nike, Guess and Levi's. Bargain hunters may have a field day. ~ 4211 Camino de la Plaza, San Ysidro; 619-934-8400.

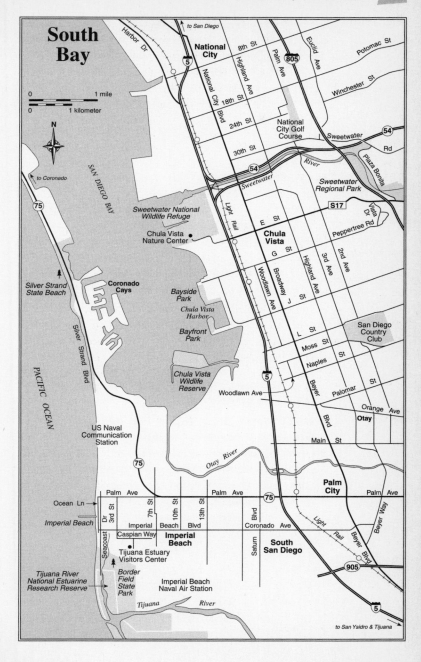

South Bay

to San Diego

National
City

Harbor Dr

8th St

Euclid Ave

Potomac St

Palm Ave

805

Winchester St

National City Blvd

Highland Ave

18th St

24th St

30th St

National
City Golf
Course

Sweetwater

54

Rd

Plaza Bonita

54

Sweetwater

River

SAN DIEGO BAY

to Coronado

75

Sweetwater National
Wildlife Refuge

Chula Vista
Nature Center

Silver Strand
State Beach

Coronado
Cays

Silver Strand Blvd

PACIFIC OCEAN

Bayside
Park

Chula Vista
Harbor

Bayfront
Park

Chula Vista
Wildlife
Reserve

Light Rail

E St

Chula
Vista

G St

J St

Woodlawn Ave

Broadway

Highland Ave

3rd Ave

2nd Ave

L St

Moss St

Naples St

Sweetwater
Regional Park

S17

Vista Dr

Peppertree Rd

San Diego
Country
Club

St

St

Beyer

Blvd

Palomar

St

Orange Ave

Woodlawn Ave

5

Otay

US Naval
Communication
Station

75

Otay River

Main St

Palm
City

Palm Ave

75

Palm Ave

Ocean Ln

Imperial Beach

Palm Ave

Dr St

3rd St

7th St

10th St

13th St

Imperial Beach Blvd

Caspian Way

Imperial
Beach

Tijuana Estuary
Visitors Center

Tijuana River
National Estuarine
Research Reserve

Border
Field
State
Park

Imperial Beach
Naval Air Station

Tijuana

River

Coronado Ave

Saturn

Blvd

South
San Diego

Light Rail

Beyer Way

Beyer Blvd

905

5

to San Ysidro & Tijuana

0 ___ 1 mile
0 ___ 1 kilometer

N

NIGHTLIFE   If you're looking for nighttime entertainment in these areas, you'll probably want to consider a trip downtown or to Tijuana (see "Tijuana" below). Otherwise, be content with scattered restaurant bars and local pubs.

The one exception is **OnStage Playhouse**, Chula Vista's only live community theater. Sharing space with the Chula Vista Art Guild, this award-winning theater group produces at least six plays a year. ~ 291 3rd Avenue, Chula Vista; 619-422-7787; www.onstageplayhouse.org.

BEACHES & PARKS   **SILVER STRAND STATE BEACH** ⚓ This one-mile strip of fluffy white sand fronts a narrow isthmus separating the Pacific Ocean and San Diego Bay. It was named for tiny silver sea shells found in abundance along the shore. The water here is shallow and fairly calm on the ocean side, making it a good swimming beach. Things are even calmer and the water much warmer on the bay shore. Silver Strand State Beach is also popular for shell hunting. Facilities include picnic areas, restrooms, lifeguards (summer only), showers, and food concessions (summer only). Parking fee, $6. ~ Located on Route 75 and Coronado Cays Boulevard between Imperial Beach and Coronado; 619-435-5184.

Each July Imperial Beach hosts the annual U.S. Open Sandcastle Competition, attracting huge crowds.

▲ There are 137 sites for self-contained RVs and trailers (no hookups); $24 per night.

IMPERIAL BEACH ⚓ 🏊 🏄 🎣 A wide, sandy beach, popular at the south end with surfers; boogie-boarders and swimmers ply the waters between the two jetties farther north, just past the renovated fishing pier. The crowd is mostly young with many military personnel. There are restrooms and lifeguards. There is also a deli nearby. Surfing is very popular on both sides of the pier and rock jetties. ~ Take Palm Avenue exit west off Route 5 all the way to the water; 619-686-6200, fax 619-686-6200.

BORDER FIELD STATE PARK 🚶 🚴 🐎 True to its name, this oceanfront park within the Tijuana River National Estuarine Research Reserve actually borders on Mexico. It features a three-mile-long stretch of sandy beach, backed by dunes and salt marshes studded with daisies and chaparral. Equestrian and hiking trails crisscross this unsullied wetlands area which adjoins a federal wildlife refuge at the mouth of the Tijuana River. Sounds idyllic except for the constant racket from Border Patrol helicopters and the ever-present threat of untreated sewage drifting north from Mexico. Picnic areas and restrooms are available, and a visitors center houses exhibits and a library. Fishing and swimming are not recommended because of pollution. ~ Take the Dairy Mart Road exit off Route 5 and go west. The name changes to Monument Road about a mile before reaching the park entrance. The visitors center is at 301 Caspian Way, Imperial Beach; 619-575-3613, fax 619-575-6913; www. tijuana estuary.com, e-mail trnerr@ixpress.net.

Tijuana

Tijuana got its start in 1889 as a customs house on the edge of a large cattle ranch called Rancho Tía Juana, meaning "Aunt Jane." The "Aunt Jane" after whom the Tía Juana River and Tijuana were named established the first travelers' inn in the area in 1769. The outpost was of little importance until the 1920s, when Prohibition sent hordes of Californians across the border for liquor, as well as horse races, casino gambling and sleazy nightclubs featuring stage shows whose depravity has passed into legend. In the early thirties, Prohibition was repealed in the United States, and casino gambling was banned in Mexico. Tijuana's fortunes floundered.

President Lázaro Cárdenas sought to rescue the city's economy by declaring Baja a free-trade zone, a move designed to stimulate retail sales of imported goods to southern California shoppers at tax-exempt discount prices. The plan initially met with only limited success, as the Great Depression strangled the flow of free-spending shoppers across the border. When economic salvation finally arrived, it came in the form of World War II, bringing a huge U.S. naval force to San Diego, just 18 miles north of Tijuana. A hectic red-light district flowered overnight as hookers and street hustlers from all over Mexico were drawn to Tijuana like pelicans to a fishing fleet.

Tijuana earned its reputation as the quintessential badass border town, and it has yet to live down that reputation. Half a century later, many Americans' mental picture of Tijuana is a city brimming with dark-alley easy, slightly slimy, sticky-fingered guilty pleasures. The fact is, today you can find more lowlife and scary cops in Los Angeles than in Tijuana.

CROSSING THE BORDER

Crossing into Tijuana from San Ysidro is easy. If you're not venturing any farther than Tijuana and don't anticipate making huge purchases, consider parking on the U.S. side and walking across the border—far easier and less time-consuming than driving. From there, you can catch a taxi or bus into town. There are numerous huge lots around the border you can park at for a fee. For a less-hectic experience, you can also park for free at various trolley points near the border (in Chula Vista or Imperial Beach, for example) and take the trolley from there.

If you're driving, Route 5 from San Diego takes you directly to the border, where Mexican officials normally wave cars with U.S. plates right through. Keep to the center lanes as the freeway takes you over the Río Tijuana, a deep concrete ditch that flows northward into the United States, on the rare occasions when it flows at all. Right on the other side of the river, you'll find yourself in a dizzying three-level freeway interchange. Follow the signs to "Downtown/Centro" to reach the downtown tourist zone, "Paseo de los Héroes" to reach the cultural center and public market, and "Mex 1-D Cuota" to get onto the toll highway south to Ensenada.

Reentering the United States is a different story. Border security has been tight in the wake of the 9-11 terrorist attacks. Every car must come to a complete stop, and all drivers and passengers must be prepared to present ID and citizenship documents; this obstructs the traffic flow enough so that you can expect to wait in line before reaching the gates. And wait, and wait . . . it often takes four to six hours to get across the border. Make sure you fill up your gas tank before getting in the traffic line. Sundays and U.S. holidays should be avoided, when you can sometimes wait all day. Lines are shortest on weekdays before 10 a.m. and after 10 p.m.

Here's a secret for those who simply must brave the border at rush hour: The U.S. inspection area has 24 gates, of which 16 are open at any given time. They are evenly divided between the east and west sides of a center median filled with street vendors' stalls. The west lanes come from Highway 1, downtown and Paseo de los Héroes—all the places gringo tourists go. The east lanes are fed by Via Oriente, Paseo de Tijuana and Avenida Padre Kino, the main thoroughfares on the northeast side of the river.

Rarely used by visitors from the U.S., these lanes typically take half as long as the west lanes. To reach them, cross the river on Avenida Independencia, which runs between the Centro Cultural and the Palacio Municipal, and turn left on any of the three main streets. For more transportation options, see "Getting to Baja" on page 164.

SIGHTS

Visitors who cross the border into Tijuana on foot can walk directly from the customs and immigration area through **Viva Tijuana**, a mall full of curio shops and restaurants, then over a pedestrian bridge that spans the Tijuana River, and be in the downtown tourist zone in a matter of minutes.

Avenida Revolución, the heart of the tourist zone, runs south from the border for 11 blocks. Visitors crossing the pedestrian bridge get there by walking two blocks along Calle 1, encountering many street vendors along the way. Motorists cross the river a few blocks to the east and immediately find themselves in an amazing multilevel traffic whirl. The Calle 2 and Calle 3 exits lead to Avenida Revolución, where parking lots are plentiful if not cheap. Curio shops, boutiques and galleries share the avenue with nightclubs, sports betting parlors, hotels and restaurants, all packed with Americans. Along Avenida Revolución, the sleazy character of old-time Tijuana has been transformed for better or worse by international chains; within a couple of blocks are a Jack in the Box, a KFC, a Burger King and a Hard Rock Café. Older buildings converted to mini-malls house hundreds of small shops side-by-side with chic international designer outlets, all vying to assist tourists with their duty-free shopping needs.

> For more information before you visit, contact Comité de Turismo y Convenciones de Tijuana. ~ 664-684-0537, or 800-252-5363 in the U.S.

Running diagonally away from the border crossing along the west bank of the Tijuana River, the **Zona Río** represents contemporary Tijuana in sharp contrast to the traditional tourist zone. Interspersed among financial institutions, upscale hotels and stylish retail stores line the broad Paseo de los Héroes. Even though a 30-foot-tall bronze statue of U.S. President Abraham Lincoln presides over the paseo from a traffic circle, local government has been largely unsuccessful in its strategy of enticing American tourists to this flashy urban redevelopment area.

Text continued on page 166.

Getting
to Baja

Regardless of whether you're hopping across the border for a quick cultural exchange or a longer getaway, there are several ways to make the trip, and a number of ways to get around once you're at your destination.

BY CAR

Tijuana's San Ysidro Border Crossing is at the end of U.S. **Interstate 5** south from San Diego. The Otay Border Crossing is reached via the last exit from U.S. **Interstate 805** before it merges into I-5 at the border.

Route 1, the Carretera Transpeninsular or Baja Highway, runs from Tijuana to Ensenada, a distance of 190 kilometers. On this segment of the route, you have two choices—the *carretera libre* (free highway), which makes its slow way through the busiest part of Rosarito, or the fast, four-lane *carretera cuota* (toll highway), which covers the distance in no time.

BY BUS

The **San Diego Trolley** shuttles passengers from downtown San Diego to and from the San Ysidro Border Crossing, within walking distance of downtown Tijuana, every 15 minutes from 5 a.m. to midnight.

Greyhound operates bus service across the border from San Diego to Tijuana. ~ www.greyhound.com.

Autotransportes de Baja California (ABC) and **Tres Estrellas de Oro** operate frequent first-class bus service up and down the

Baja peninsula, stopping in Ensenada at the bus terminal at Calle 1 and Avenida Riveroll; 646-178-6680.

BY PUBLIC TRANSIT

Tijuana's colorful, modern buses run to all parts of the city and make it easy to reach Zona Río and Agua Caliente district attractions from Avenida Revolución.

Several private companies provide inexpensive bus service along main avenues in Ensenada.

BY TAXI

In Tijuana, call **Yellow Taxis** (664-682-4617) or **Taxi Dispatch of Tijuana** (664-683-1801). Look for independent taxis around the border crossings and the major hotels. Cab rates are regulated and authorized fare cards are supposed to be posted. Price gouging is common on border pickups, though, so it is a good idea to ask first what the fare will be. Some taxi drivers like to drive tourists across the border to U.S. Customs—where Mexican price controls do not apply—and then ask for an outrageous amount.

Besides private taxis, Tijuana has *combis* (also called *taxis de ruta*), shuttle vans that travel specific routes and cost more than a bus ride but less than a taxi cab.

Ensenada has many independent taxis. It is not customary to hail taxis when they are moving; instead, you board them at any of the many taxi stands, called *sitios*, all along Avenida López Mateos and Avenida Benito Juárez, as well as elsewhere around the downtown area and in front of the larger hotels.

The main attraction of the Zona Río is the **Centro Cultural Tijuana,** the hub of the city's performing-arts scene, nicknamed "La Bola" because of its shape, which resembles the world's largest golf ball. The symphony orchestra, the ballet folklórico, repertory companies and lecturers use the center's 1000-seat theater. Also in the cultural center are an art exhibition gallery that presents changing shows by local artists, an astronomy room, and the big, round Omnimax theater that gives the center its distinctive shape; it shows wraparound movies in English and Spanish. The highlight for many visitors is the **Museo de las Californias,** which traces the history of Baja from prehistoric times to the present with wax figures, miniature dioramas, artifacts and reproductions of ancient Indian cave paintings. Admission to museums. ~ Avenida Paseo de los Héroes at Calle Mina; 664-487-9600.

If you drive south from the tourist zone, Avenida Revolución curves around to the east to become **Boulevard Agua Caliente,** lined with big, modern hotels and shiny new restaurants. The **Toreo de Tijuana** (see "Seda, Sangre y Sol" in this chapter), the older of the city's two bullrings, marks the beginning of the hotel strip. Route 1 *libre*, the free highway to Ensenada, turns off to the south at the bullring.

At the east end of the hotel zone is **Caliente Race Track.** Formerly called the Hipódromo de Agua Caliente, the famous race track for which the boulevard was named ended live horse racing in 1993. Greyhounds race there nightly as well as Saturday and Sunday afternoons. There is also betting on closed-circuit horse race broadcasts from California, viewed on television monitors in the track's sports club. ~ Boulevard Agua Caliente at Avenida Salinas; 664-686-3958.

LODGING   The **Hotel Caesar** is an atmospheric old-timer from Prohibition days. Though its glory days are long past, the 42 clean, comfortable, air-conditioned rooms have the kind of character that comes with age, and the halls are decorated with framed photos and posters of bullfights. ~ Avenida Revolución 827; 664-688-1666. BUDGET.

If you're in need of rock-bottom budget accommodations in Tijuana, the safest can be found outside the downtown area near the beach at **Hostel Barnes.** ~ Seccion Dorado 1230, Playas de

Tijuana; 664-630-1126, fax 664-680-4870; e-mail multicopias@ mail.com. BUDGET.

Most upscale hotels in Tijuana are found along Boulevard Agua Caliente. The largest and finest, the **Grand Hotel Tijuana** has 422 light, spacious rooms splashed with fiesta-color accents in twin 25-story towers that are Tijuana's tallest buildings. In-room amenities range from cable TV to computer data ports. The hotel has a heated pool, tennis courts and a jacuzzi. The higher the room, the better the view and the steeper the rate. ~ Boulevard Agua Caliente 4500; 664-681-7000, fax 664-681-7016, or 866-472-6385 in the U.S.; www.grandhoteltj.com.mx, e-mail reser vaciones@grandhoteltj.com.mx. DELUXE.

Downtown Tijuana

CALIFORNIA

U.S. Customs

N

Calle Michoacán

Calle Baja California

ZONA NORTE

Calle Coahuila

Calle 1

Calle Commercio

Pedestrian Bridge

Río Tijuana

Av Padre Kino

Paseo de Tijuana

Via Oriente

Pedestrian Bridge

Calle 2

Calle 3

Calle 4

Calle 5

Av Martínez

Av Niños Héroes

Av Constitución

Av Revolución

0   .2 mile
0   .2 kilometer

Calle 6

Calle 7

Av Madero

Av Negrete

Av Ocampo

ZONA RÍO

Paseo de los Héroes

Boulevard

Av Pío Pico

Av Quintana Roo

Sanchez

Av Independencia

Calle 8

Calle 9

Calle 10

Calle 11

Taboada

POINTS OF INTEREST
- **A** Centro Cultural Tijuana
- **B** Mercado de Artisanías
- **C** Mercado Hidalgo
- **D** Mexitlán
- **E** Plaza Fiesta
- **F** Plaza Río Tijuana
- **G** Pueblo Amigo
- **H** Viva Tijuana

Secluded in a canyon between the highway and the ocean, with picturesque views of the Coronado Islands offshore, the **Real del Mar Marriott Residence Inn** offers golf enthusiasts an international playground just 11 miles south of the border. In low Mediterranean-style buildings scattered around the resort grounds, the 76 brightly appointed guest suites range from spacious to palatial. Besides 18 holes of golf, the resort has tennis courts, spa facilities and horseback riding. ~ Route 1-D Km. 18; 664-631-3671, 664-631-3677, or 800-662-6180 in the U.S.; www.marriott.com. ULTRA-DELUXE.

DINING

Along Avenida Revolución are dozens of budget-priced places for lunch—many of them hauntingly familiar. For something completely different from the international burger franchises, try **La Especial,** a busy taco-and-enchilada eatery that still feels like a typical Mexican *comedor*. ~ Avenida Revolución 718; 664-685-6654. BUDGET.

One of the longest-established and best-known restaurants in the tourist zone, **TiaJuana Tillies** is packed with noisy gringos morning, noon and night. There's a good reason. Tillies serves big portions of some of the best Mexican food on the border—not only familiar dishes but also more exotic ones from distant parts of Mexico—*cochinita pibil* (pork barbecued in a Seville orange marinade), *pollo en mole* (chicken in chile-and-chocolate sauce) and enchiladas *suizas* (chicken enchiladas in a tangy sauce with ranch cheese melted over them). ~ Avenida Revolución at Calle 7; 664-685-9015. MODERATE.

The Caesar salad was invented at **Caesar's**. As atmospheric now as in Prohibition days, the restaurant still serves salads made according to the original recipe (though not by the same chef). Dinner only. ~ Avenida Revolución 827; 664-688-2794. MODERATE.

For some of the freshest, most unusual seafood dishes in the city, go to **Los Arcos**, a bright, family-style restaurant near the bull ring. You'll find a selection of dishes like marlin tacos and *caldo pescado* (fish stew), as well as the house specialty, *zarandeado*, a large whole fish scored and broiled with heaps of chiles and onions. ~ Boulevard Salinas 1000; 664-686-4757. MODERATE.

The dozens of fast-food stalls at **Mercado Hidalgo**, the city's main public market near the Zona Río, offer a varied choice of

Seda, Sangre y Sol

The poetic turn of speech "silk, blood and sun" is often used to refer to bullfighting, a spectacle that is popular throughout Mexico, and nowhere more so than along the Baja California border. Latinos who live across the border in California and Arizona, where bullfights are illegal, flock to the *corridas de toros* in Tijuana and Mexicali on Sundays. Mexicans and Mexican Americans believe that gringos misunderstand the nature of bullfights, unable to see beyond the horror and cruelty of hacking livestock to death with barbed darts, spears and swords.

Though the rules and trappings of the spectacle originated in 18th-century Spain and came to Mexico in the last years of colonial rule, bullfighting also mirrors the ritual public sacrifices of the Aztecs and Toltecs in earlier times. Mexicans see each bullfight as display of courage—not a sport like boxing or riding in *charreadas* (rodeos), but a ritual that links them to heritage and primal instinct. Several mounted *picadores* and *banderilleros* on foot participate in the first half-hour of a fight, but the *matador* (literally, "killer") is the star of the show, so icy of nerve that he—or she—can not only stand within inches of a charging thousand-pound behemoth with horns that can rip a horse apart or toss a man in the air, but at the same time execute customary cape passes with the precision and grace of a ballet dancer. The bull too is judged on its courage. Though it is hand-selected at an early age for belligerence and trained in the art of fighting on a special ranch for four years, there is no predicting how a bull, bloodied and tormented, will face the certainty of death.

Any gringo who wishes to understand the Mexican people on their own terms must attend at least one *corrida de toros*. A word of caution, though: Take care not to give voice to feelings of horror or disgust unless a human is gored. Mexican spectators take offense at negative reactions by gringos at bullfights, and they may bring various nasty substances to throw at disgraced *matadores*—or rude tourists.

Six bulls are fought in an afternoon's *corrida*, which lasts about six hours. Tijuana has two bullrings—the older **Toreo de Tijuana** (Boulevard Agua Caliente 100; 664-686-1510) and the larger **Plaza Monumental** (Route 1-D; 664-680-1808). Bullfights are held every Sunday from May through September at one ring or the other—in August at both. Mexicali's bullfights are held every other week from October through May at the **Plaza Calafia** (Calle Calafia; 664-657-0681). Admission at all three bullrings is around $15 for seats in the sun and $25 in the shade.

inexpensive dishes from all over Mexico. For a dollar or two, you can buy a fistful of fish tacos or pineapple tamales, a grilled pork sandwich, a steaming bowl of *posole* stew or a plastic plate of beans and rice with an egg on top, and eat it at a picnic table at a little distance from the market fray. ~ Avenida Independencia at Boulevard Sanchez Taboada. BUDGET.

In the Zona Río, **Victor's** has been a local favorite for more than four decades. The restaurant is divided into an elegant, clublike dining room and a casual café under an atrium. While the dining room menu features a larger choice of pricey entrées—mostly thick slabs of beef—most items are available in both dining room and café, including the house specialty, *carne adovada* (beef strips marinated in a red chile sauce and grilled). ~ Boulevard Sanchez Taboada at Calle Joaquín Clausell; 664-634-3355. BUDGET TO MODERATE.

HIDDEN ►

When it comes to beef, Argentinians are the experts. A glance at the menu in **Restaurante Argentino de Tony** may lead you to believe that's all they eat in South America. A colonial-style ambience of dark wood, beamed ceilings, potted plants and spotless white linen sets the stage for huge servings of sizzling red meat. Try the mixed grille, an artery-clogging meal big enough for two that includes some surprise ingredients you wouldn't likely find north of the border. This local favorite rarely sees tourists. ~ Pueblo Amigo Shopping Center; 664-682-8111. MODERATE.

The penetrating stare of a huge portrait of Salvador Dali sets the stage for the artsy atmosphere of **Gypsys**. (Check out the life-size nude figures in the restrooms.) This long, narrow restaurant specializes in Spanish-style *tapas* and also serves full meals, such as Spanish *tortillas*—an omeletlike egg-and-potato dish, no relation to the Mexican tortilla—and vegetarian paella. The restaurant is in a shopping center just half a mile from the San Ysidro

AUTHOR FAVORITE

I thought I'd tasted just about everything in Mexico—until I dined at **Cien Años**, Tijuana's trendy pre-Columbian restaurant where the bill of fare includes such delicacies as ant eggs in garlic sauce, washed down with more kinds of tequila than one can sample without falling over. See page 171 for more information.

border crossing. Closed Monday. ~ Pueblo Amigo Shopping Center; 664-683-6006. MODERATE.

Reputed to be the best restaurant in Baja, or at least the trendiest, is **Cien Años**, the Pacific coast's premier example of the new wave in Mexican restaurants—resurrecting Aztec and other pre-Columbian ingredients and recipes, prepared with careful attention to authenticity and served with gourmet flair. Yet to appear in the United States, this cuisine includes items bizarre enough to challenge the most adventurous palate—fried cactus worms, ant eggs in garlic sauce, crêpes *de huitlacoche* (corn fungus), manta ray burritos and *medula con sesos* (spine marrow soup) to mention a few. Though nothing on the menu is likely to be familiar, there are also plenty of choices for the gastronomically timid, such as squash blossom soup, filet mignon *en salsa borracha de pulque* (marinated in Mexican Indian corn liquor) and *mixote* (an Aztec dish made with shrimp and thin-sliced nopal cactus leaves). There's also a separate menu listing 38 brands of tequila. Reservations are essential. ~ Calle José María Velazco 1407; 664-634-3039. MODERATE TO DELUXE.

Two blocks south of the intersection of Cuauhtémoc and Agua Caliente, **La Fonda de Roberto** is part of the new gourmet trend in Mexican restaurants. The friendly, contemporary upstairs dining room is best known for its specialty, *chiles en nogada*, poblano chiles stuffed with meat and fruit and smothered in walnut sauce topped with pomegranate and cilantro, a favorite Mexican dish that is traditionally eaten on Día de la Independencia because its colors—red, white and green—are the same as those of the national flag. The "menu," which features a choice of five entrées and changes daily, isn't really a menu at all; instead, the waiter brings out actual plates of food as examples, and you can order simply by pointing. Closed Monday. ~ Boulevard Cuauhtémoc 2800; 664-686-4687. DELUXE.

GROCERIES

You'll find an abundance of fresh produce, along with meat stalls that may convert the squeamish to vegetarianism, at the big, busy **Mercado Hidalgo**, the city's main public market, located a block from the Centro Cultural Tijuana. Especially tempting to travelers are the stands selling exotic tropical fruits such as mamay, zapote, cherimoya, tunas (candied cactus fruit) and giant papayas. This is also a good place to shop for "real" souvenirs such as fresh spices, uniquely Mexican kitchen utensils and curiosities like mango-flavored bubble gum. ~ Avenida Independencia at Boulevard Sanchez Taboada.

The major supermarket chain in Tijuana and all of Baja California is **Calimax**. There are branches on Avenida Constitución between Calles 1 and 2; on Avenida Revolución between Calles 9 and 10 on Paseo de los Héroes at Avenida Cuauhtémoc and on Boulevard Agua Caliente across from the Caliente race track. All are open 24 hours a day. ~ 664-688-0894.

Look for Mexican and imported gourmet foodstuffs at **Ley**, located in the Pueblo Amigo. ~ Via Oriente 9211; 664-684-2771.

SHOPPING   It doesn't get much more touristy than Tijuana's **Mercado de Artisanías**, located where visitors step off the pedestrian bridge from the border over the Tijuana River. Here, vendors display Mexican "arts and crafts"—mostly factory-made curios and gift items—along with a fair selection of Guatemalan clothing. The main purpose in establishing this open market was to keep street vendors from clogging the sidewalks of Avenida Revolución. ~ Calle 2 between Avenidas Ocampo and Negrete.

When visiting Mercado Hidalgo, don't miss photographing the vendors' shrine to the Virgin of Guadalupe, conveniently situated on the roof of the cleanest restrooms in Tijuana.

Apple, S.A. also offers a large selection of *artesanía* and leather goods, as well as duty-free imports ranging from Swiss watches to Asian electronics. ~ Avenida Revolución 812; 664-685-1609.

Avenida Revolución is so shopper-friendly that you'll find an array of possibilities for every taste and budget here. You may have to fend off youths whose job is to steer you into their families' stores, and you may have to dig through endless clutters of onyx elephants and huge, brocaded mariachi sombreros, but in the end you'll most likely find something that tugs at your pursestrings. Leather goods, from boots and belts to suitcases, are the best bargain in Tijuana, and there are plenty of others. A wooden dance mask from Michoacán? A delicately embroidered Oaxacan wedding dress? Guess jeans or Ralph Lauren sportswear? Avenida Revolución is the place to look.

Start your shopping spree at **Tolán**, reputedly Tijuana's finest Mexican folk art gallery. Prices here may be high, but the quality and selection of both museum-quality indigenous work and contemporary ethnic paintings, jewelry, sculpture, weaving and ceramics set the standard for comparison in Baja gift shopping. ~ Avenida Revolución between Calles 7 and 8; 664-688-3637.

A good one-stop shopping center for Mexican *artesanía* is the **Bazar de Mexico**, where 40 permanent vendors sell quality gift items from all parts of the country—Talvera pottery, rustic wood furniture, fountains large and small, Huichol Indian art, pre-Columbian reproductions, handmade leather goods, Oaxacan *albrijes* (wood carvings of animal dreams) and much more. ~ Avenida Revolución at Calle 7; 664-638-4737, fax 664-688-3526; www.bazardemexico.com, e-mail info@bazardemexico.com.

Nearby is **Sanborn's,** part of the nationwide department store chain that is the Mexican counterpart of Macy's. Sanborn's has responded to the invasion of international discount stores like Wal-Mart and Sam's Club by stocking higher-quality merchandise to attract a more upscale clientele. In Tijuana, with its free-trade status, this policy has translated into attempts to tantalize American tourists with quality imports, from Japanese consumer electronics to French perfume, at prices somewhat lower than you'd expect to find in San Diego or L.A. The restaurant and book-and-magazine department of Sanborn's are reputed to be among the most popular gay meeting places in the city. ~ Avenida Revolución at Calle 8; 664-688-1462.

Though you'd never know it if all you saw was ultra-touristy Avenida Revolución, Mexicans too come from far and wide to indulge in Tijuana shopping sprees. **Pueblo Amigo**—within easy walking distance of the border crossing—and **Plaza Río Tijuana** and **Plaza Fiesta**, farther along Paseo de los Héroes, are landmarks in the Zona Río. All three indoor shopping malls contain an improbably large number of stores selling silver jewelry from Taxco, the famous silversmithing center in the southern Mexico state of Guerrero. Across the street from the Plaza Río, vendors at **Plaza Zapato** sell shoes, bags, leather clothing, saddles and tack at a fraction of U.S. prices. There are also many stores featuring quality European and Asian imports—as well as imports from the United States, aimed at Tijuana's growing young urban professional market.

◄ *HIDDEN*

From the sleazy to the ultrachic, nightlife is one of the main attractions that lures visitors over the border to Tijuana. Many never get farther than Avenida Revolución, which becomes a

NIGHTLIFE

bright, loud, touristy dance club scene after dark. Street barkers will try persistently to lure into their clubs any gringo male who looks like he has money to spend. You know you're not drunk enough yet if you find yourself trying to figure out why you went to another country just to hang out in a **Hard Rock Café**. ~ Avenida Revolución 520; 664-685-0206.

For something a little more un-American, check out **Red Square,** with its vaguely Kremlinesque facade and its rooftop bar overlooking the main street. ~ Avenida Revolución at Calle 6; 664-688-2782.

The last of the old-timers, **Bar San Marcos** dates back to World War II and entertains its patrons with lavish mariachi productions. ~ Avenida Revolución at Calle 5; 664-688-2794. **Disco Salsa** blares high-energy Latino dance music until dawn. ~ Avenida Revolución between Calles 1 and 2; 664-634-8615. Bars and discos along Revolución typically stay open until 3 a.m. on weekdays, 5 a.m. on weekends.

Just off Avenida Reforma are a number of "hidden" places that you don't have to be a tourist to go to. You'll find Latino dance rhythms, cheap tequila and plenty of usually amiable Mexican rowdiness at **La Estrella**. Cover for men. ~ Calle 6 east of Avenida Revolución; 664-688-1349.

Another side of Tijuana nightlife can be found in the **Zona Río**, the redeveloped commercial district around Paseo de los Héroes and Calle Diego Rivera, east of the traditional downtown tourist zone. Discos here tend to be sleek and trendy, catering to upper-class Mexicans as much as to gringos. Many have dress codes and are selective about who they allow in. **Baby Rock**, part of a chain of chic Mexican rock-and-roll clubs found mostly in beach resort towns, is frequented by the city's young, moneyed and fashionable. Cover. ~ Boulevard Paseo de los Héroes at Avenida Río Tijuana; 664-634-2404. **Jala la Jarra**, next to the Guadalajara Grill, is another popular disco, always packed on weekends. Cover. ~ Calle Diego Rivera at Paseo de los Héroes; 664-634-3065.

The three-level **Rodeo Santa Fe** in the Pueblo Amigo Shopping Center has live *norteño* dance music downstairs and a contemporary disco upstairs, as well as a *quebradita* (mechanical bull) and, nightly at midnight, a live indoor rodeo. Cover. ~ Avenida Paseo Tijuana; 664-682-4967.

The hot dance club in downtown Tijuana is **El Lugar de Nopal,** where live salsa or rock music is featured most nights. Cover. ~ Cinco de Mayo 1328; 664-685-2413.

Tijuana has a lively gay scene. Things get started late. **Mike's Disco,** a prominent club in the heart of the tourist zone, draws mostly male crowds with its nightly Mexican female impersonator stage shows. They start at midnight and continue until nearly dawn. ~ Avenida Revolución 1220; 664-685-3534. For more information on the city's constantly changing GLBT world, call or visit the **Tijuana Gay and Lesbian Center.** ~ Calle 1 no. 7648; 664-685-9163.

Tijuana's red-light district is the **Zona Norte,** between Calle Comercio (Calle 1) and the Tijuana River, within walking distance of the pedestrian bridge from the border crossing. The district centers on Calle Coahuila between Avenida Martinez and Avenida Niños Héroes, which run one-way in opposite directions for convenient cruising. No-nonsense gay bars, strip joints and sordid little establishments of every description pack this self-consciously seedy district where for a price you can get anything you want and (if you're not careful) more. Assume that everyone you meet here, regardless of gender or putative sexual preference, is a trained professional.

If gambling is your preferred vice, there are ten branches of **Caliente Race & Sports Books** around the city, including the big Centro Caliente on Revolución, where you can bet on televised sporting events daily until midnight. ~ Avenida Revolución at Calle 4; 664-686-3958. Another option is jai alai, a fast-as-a-horserace game played by teams hurling a hard rubber ball at

AUTHOR FAVORITE

I have no qualms about venturing into the desert or the depths of the ocean, but I have to admit, the back streets of Tijuana make me nervous after dark. To get away from the laser discos of Avenida Revolución without leaving the relative safety of the tourist zone, I head down the pedestrian alleyway that starts by the tourist information office at Revolución and Calle 1 and runs diagonally to Avenida Constitución. It's lined with no-name, hole-in-the-wall bars showcasing mariachis and marimba groups in a ceaseless battle of the bands.

speeds up to 160 miles an hour according to rules guaranteed to bewilder the ignorant. You can watch it, and place parimutuel bets, at the **Palacio Frontón**, an entertainment complex that also houses three restaurants and a disco. Closed Wednesday. Cover. ~ Avenida Revolución at Calle 8; 664-686-3958. There's video horse racing and live greyhound racing nightly and on weekend afternoons at the **Caliente Race Track**, an 11-kilometer drive or bus trip south of downtown. You can't miss its grandiose Moorish-style entrance, which dates back to 1916. ~ Boulevard Agua Caliente; 664-686-3958.

BEACHES & PARKS

PLAYAS DE TIJUANA 🏃 This string of narrow beaches, where Route 1-D, the toll highway south to Ensenada, reaches the Pacific coast and turns south, is fronted by Tijuana's nicest residential area. The concrete and chain-link border fence runs across the north end of the beach. Although the beaches are open to the public, neighborhood security and border patrols make sunbathing uncomfortable and camping unthinkable. Most visitors pass by Playas de Tijuana in favor of the developed resort area of Rosarito, ten minutes' drive farther on (see "Ensenada Area," below). Still, you can often spot dolphins frolicking just offshore here. ~ Paseo Playas de Tijuana, off Route 1-D less than a kilometer north of the tool booths.

ISLAS LOS CORONADOS 🦀 🛥️ ⚓ Seven miles off the coast of Playas de Tijuana lies a chain of four tiny desert islands, occupied by the ruins of a Prohibition-era resort hotel and a small Mexican Navy detachment that enforces the law prohibiting humans from setting foot on the islands. Boaters can circle around and between them, though, for fishing, diving and wildlife watching. Los Coronados host one of the largest pelican rookeries on the Baja coast, along with a large sea lion colony and smaller groups of elephant and harbor seals. ~ Accessible by fishing *panga* from San Antonio, south of Playas de Tijuana on the toll highway.

▼▼▼▼▼▼▼▼▼▼▼▼

Ensenada Area

Steep hills on the landward side and a ten-mile-long peninsula on the ocean side protect the Bahía de Todos Santos from storms, making it the best location for a shipping port on the entire Pacific coast of Baja. The exclusive gringo neighborhoods that blanket the hillsides swell the port's population to a quarter of a million full-time residents; it is Baja's largest city that is not on the border.

Spanish ships first dropped anchor in the bay in 1542, and over the centuries it sheltered both the Spanish Empire's treasure galleons from Manila and the pirate ships that preyed on them. In the 1700s, Todos Santos became a favorite hunting area for whalers. The one obstacle to settlement was the absence of fresh water.

Relying on rain catchments and intermittent streams from the eastern mountains, ranches sprang up during the early 1800s, but it was not until 1872, when gold was discovered in the Sierra de Juárez, that a port settlement began to flourish. Ten years later, Ensenada was declared the capital of the Territory of Baja California. But in time, the mines played out and Ensenada faded into oblivion. In 1915, the territorial capital was relocated to

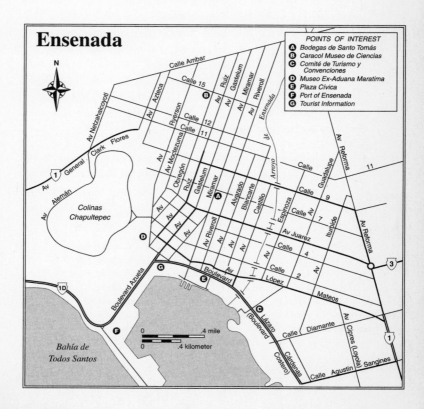

Mexicali, leaving Ensenada as nothing more than an obscure fishing village.

Prosperity returned in the 1920s, as Prohibition in the United States drove Hollywood's party set south of the border. The Playa Ensenada Hotel and Casino opened as the most lavish resort in Baja, but this playground of the rich and famous lasted less than a decade before the Mexican government outlawed casino gambling and closed it down. Ensenada's dependence on tourism and foreign money, however, has continued to the present day.

Today, the city's shipping port hosts several cruise ships from Los Angeles each week, spilling stampedes of daytrippers into the curio shops that line Avenida López Mateos. Thousands of gringo retirees and expatriates have swelled the city's permanent population to a quarter of a million. This is not a place where people retire to live cheaply; the property prices and overall character of the *norteamericano* Chapultepec Hills district are not much different from comparable neighborhoods in San Diego or Orange County. A major reason gringos move here, rather than someplace farther down the peninsula, is that Ensenada has the best medical facilities in Baja, including the only hospital that accepts U.S. medical insurance instead of requiring patients to pay cash and file for insurance reimbursement on their own. Mexicans from all parts of the peninsula also travel to Ensenada for health care.

SIGHTS

The **Carretera Escénica**, or scenic route, from Tijuana to Ensenada covers 190 kilometers, hugging the coastline the whole way. Two roads follow the same route—the *cuota*, or toll high-

sights

AUTHOR FAVORITE

The best view of the city is from the **Colinas Chapultepec**, which enclose the downtown area on the west. The Spanish name sounds more poetic than its English translation—"Grasshopper Hills." Irregardless, the panorama is a sight to behold and I enjoy doing so while cruising slowly through this exclusively gringo hillside suburb. To get there, follow Calle 2 west from downtown; it immediately starts climbing into the hills. There is an overlook where the street joins Avenida Alemán, which loops all the way around the hills before returning you to the same overlook.

way, which speeds you from the border to Ensenada in less than an hour and costs around $6, and the traffic-clogged *libre*, or free highway, which serves the coastal resorts and takes three times as long.

Between **San Antonio del Mar**, on the southern outskirts of Tijuana, and **San Miguel**, just over the hill from Ensenada, once-upon-a-time fishing villages now merge in an unbroken strip of beachfront hotels, restaurants and condominium complexes. The epicenter of all this beach fun is the string of towering ocean-view condos at the south end of **Rosarito**. The Hotel California is located directly across the highway from Rock'n'Roll Taco in this whitewashed, red-tile-roofed strip town of 50,000 sand-wiched between the beach and the Route 1 *cuota*. Rosarito has signs not only in English but also in Spanish. This is because re-sorts in the area enjoy a modest summer season of visitors from mainland Mexico. In the winter, Rosarito is overrun by hordes of rich gringos every weekend, laid-back and mainly Mexican during the week.

Twentieth Century Fox built **Fox Studios Baja** on the south-ern outskirts of Rosarito in 1996 for the filming of *Titanic*. Although Fox has not shot another movie there since then, it has rented the facility out to several other Hollywood studios for such films as *Pearl Harbor* and the James Bond thriller *Tomorrow Never Dies*. One-hour tours of this starkly industrial site, offered on Sundays only, include a look at the 20-million-gallon water tank sound stage where Leonardo DiCaprio's char-acter sunk into the icy depths, as well as an opportunity to ex-plore remnants of the giant *Titanic* cruise ship set. A "Making of *Titanic*" video and footage from the original film let visitors compare illusion with reality. Another exhibit focuses on the Mexican film industry. The "Foxploration" tour takes visitors behind the scenes to view production work and see the sound stages. Admission. ~ Route 1 Km. 32.8; 646-614-9000, fax 646-614-0184; www.foxbaja.com, e-mail info@foxbaja.com.

El Mirador, high on a rocky promontory north of Bahía de Todos Santos, is the most scenic rest area between Rosarito and Ensenada. Whale watchers throng to this place during migra-tions, and at any time of year the sunset view is as magnificent as any on the Pacific coast.

Entering the city on Route 1, motorists find the **Comité de Turismo y Convenciones** tourist information office at the crowded intersection near the port entrance gate. ~ Boulevard Costero 540; 646-178-2411. Road access to the **Port of Ensenada**, on a spit of land that juts into the bay parallel to the waterfront, is restricted. Passengers from the cruise ships that dock at the port's wharf take a shuttle to the downtown shopping district.

Located two blocks west of the tourist information office, a 19th-century Mexican customs house has been resurrected as the **Museo Ex-Aduana Maratima**. The museum does not have much in the way of permanent displays of artifacts from the local area. Instead, it provides space for touring exhibits from the Instituto Nacional de Antropología y Historia, which has jurisdiction over all of Mexico's historical districts and ancient ruins. If you stop here on your way south, you may find an exhibit on the colonial missions of Baja California, for instance, and then discover on your northbound return trip that it has been replaced by Mayan sculptures or Empress Carlotta's furniture. Exhibits are captioned in Spanish only. Closed Monday. ~ Avenida Reyerson 99; 646-178-2531.

Three blocks south of the tourist information office on Boulevard Costero is the **Plaza Cívica**, nicknamed Tres Cabezas ("three heads") because the broad paved square contains 12-foot-tall busts of three revered Mexican historical figures: priest-turned-rebel-leader Miguel Hidalgo, organizer of the 1810 rebellion that would lead to Mexico's independence from Spain; President Benito Juárez, who led the fight to drive the French imperialist government of Emperor Maximillian out of the country in 1867; and President Venustiano Carranza, who reigned over the constitutional convention that created modern Mexico in 1917. ~ Boulevard Costero at Avenida Alvarado.

HIDDEN ▶

From downtown, museum buffs can follow Avenida Obregón north (away from the waterfront) for 14 blocks to visit the **Caracol Museo de Ciencias**. Situated in a two-story house, the science museum emphasizes astronomy, paleontology, oceanography and marine biology. Its educational displays on environmental protection and endangered species are aimed more at school classes than tourists. This museum is one of the best places to learn about the California gray whale and its migrations—if you can read the Spanish-only explanations.

Admission. ~ Avenida Obregón 1463; 646-178-7192; www.astro
sen.unam.mx/~museo-en/mus-0.html.

The big edifice that houses the **Museo de História** was originally built in 1930 as the Playa Ensenada Hotel and Casino, the
most elegant hotel in Baja for a few years, and it's worth a visit
as much to see the building itself as for the museum's exhibits on
Baja's indigenous people, early European explorers and missionaries. Managed by retired prizefighter Jack Dempsey, reputedly
with financial backing from Al Capone, the resort played host to
Hollywood's beautiful people until 1938, when the government
outlawed casino gaming. Visitors can stroll through the
Moorish-style lobby with its striking murals, the ballroom with
its dazzling wrought-iron chandelier, the chapel where eloping
movie stars used to tie the knot, and the old casino, which has
repeatedly inspired Ensenada residents to petition the Mexican
federal government to legalize gambling again in the Baja free
trade zone as an economic stimulus. Although, until recently, the
government showed no inclination to consider the idea,
President Vicente Fox has begun voicing support for legalized
casino gambling in Mexican tourist areas. Admission. ~ Boulevard Lázaro Cárdenas at Avenida Riviera; 646-176-4310, 646-
177-2584.

Baja history buffs may also want to visit the **Museo Histórico
Regional**, featuring a permanent exhibit on the people and cultures of Mesoamerica, which occupies a 19th-century military
headquarters that served as the city jail until 1996. ~ Avenida
Gastelum at Calle 1; 646-178-2351; www.inah.gob/mx/muse2/
htme/mure0201a.html.

Ensenada's best-known sight is **La Bufadora**, a sea geyser at
a rocky point across the bay from the city. Its name comes from
bufa, Spanish for "snort" and colloquial Mexican for bison; La

SPOTTING SPOUTS

Peninsula Punta Banda is one of the best whale-watching spots in Baja
California Norte. Gray whales are bottom feeders, so they travel close to
shore. Many of them veer into the bay and must swim the length of the
Peninsula Punta Banda to find their way back to the open ocean.
Whales can be spotted from December to mid-February.

Bufadora is commonly translated as "the buffalo snort." This waterspout is created by the entrance to a long, narrow cavern just above sea level, between steep cliffs that narrow to a "V." When a wave rolls in, water crashes over the cavern's mouth, compressing the air inside. As the surf subsides, the air trapped in the cave blasts the water back out with amazing force, beginning with a low rumble and climaxing with a plume of sea spray that can reach almost 100 feet. The phenomenon is at its most spectacular with a high tide and big waves. La Bufadora becomes quite crowded on weekends. Parking fee. ~ Carretera Punta Banda.

La Bufadora is at the end of the long, narrow **Peninsula Punta Banda**, which shelters the Bahía de Todos Santos from the open ocean. It's a 40-kilometer trip from Ensenada. The well-marked road to La Bufadora turns off Route 1 south of the city and runs along a ridge high above the bay. Several parking areas along the road provide fantastic views—especially during the southward whale migration, December to mid-February.

HIDDEN ►

Just outside the mouth of the bay are the **Islas de Todos Santos**. The smaller northern island contains a Mexican Navy base and is off-limits to civilians, but you can visit the larger southern island by tour boat or sea kayak. Pelicans, ospreys and many other bird species nest there, and sea caves and grottos dot the island's south end. Surfers say the Todos Santos waves reach 30 feet in height. Local legend holds that the islands inspired the setting for *Treasure Island*, which Robert Lewis Stevenson is said to have written while living at the north end of the bay. Most historians agree that in fact Stevenson never set foot in Baja, though his widow lived farther south on Isla Cedro for a while after his death.

LODGING

Beachfront hotels from Rosarito to Ensenada fill up on Friday and Saturday nights, so reservations are advised. Except during the mid-July to mid-September peak season, there is no problem finding vacancies on weeknights, when room rates drop as much as 30 percent. *Note*: Kilometer markers on Route 1 north of town indicate the distance from Tijuana, while south of town they show the distance from Ensenada.

The **Rosarito Beach Hotel and Spa** is one of the few remnants from the days when Rosarito was a tiny, hard-to-reach fishing village on a great beach where silent-movie stars went to hide

The Lost Treasure of Rosarito

You don't have to travel far south of the border to discover the kind of remote, rugged wilderness that adventurous travelers expect of Baja. Look inland (left) from Route 1-D as you drive south from Tijuana to Rosarito and you'll see a jagged volcanic peak rise in the distance from the flat coastal plain. Its name is El Coronel, after a mysterious hermit who lived more than a century ago in the caves you can see with binoculars high on the almost sheer mountain slopes.

In the 1870s a U.S. Army colonel absconded with an undisclosed amount of army gold and paper currency and fled south down the old Camino Real, which ran near the base of the mountain. He made his home on the mountain, an ideal defensive position commanding a view of the entire coastal plain, and moved from cave to cave over the years. Artifacts of his occupation remain to this day. That much is documented by the Rosarito Historical Society.

The rest of the story is a mystery. What became of the colonel, whose remains have never been found? Although several locals have found small caches of gold and old U.S. dollars on the mountain, none of them approximate the fortune that legend says the colonel stole. Does the rest of the treasure still lie hidden somewhere on El Coronel? Or did it ever exist at all? What of the gringo ghost who, many say, roams the mountains guarding the gold? And what would the colonel have thought if he could look out over modern Rosarito—an array of condos, beach resorts and even an oceanic movie studio, all served by a fast four-lane superhighway—and realize that his hideout more than a century ago is as hidden as ever.

Although the mountain and its caves are easy to spot, getting there is another matter. There's no established trail; the approach is hot, dry and covered in dense brush, leading to a climb that traverses slippery rock slopes and edges along treacherous cliffs. Visitors can reach the caves and the hidden lake that kept the colonel supplied with fresh water and wild game on a long day's horseback ride with a guide from the stables south of town on old Route 1. To attempt the trip on foot, head south from Rosarito on old Route 1 and turn left between kilometer markers 39 and 40 at the sign for "Ciudad de Misericordia," which leads to an old mine in the foothills. This road will take you within day-hike distance of El Coronel. From there, you're on your own as you scramble your way up the slope without a trail.

from the outside world. Built in 1926, this elegant hotel originally had only 12 rooms; it was the only hotel in town with running water. Expanding with each road improvement and corresponding tourist influx, the hotel has grown to 275 rooms. The exterior of today's big, white Mediterranean-style hotel is typical of the beach resort complexes toward the south end of Rosarito; inside, the restored lobby, dining rooms and ballroom ooze Roaring Twenties ostentation. The mix of old and new buildings offers a full range of room choices, from older, very affordable and relatively plain rooms (some without air conditioning) facing away from the ocean to spacious luxury suites with private balconies overlooking the beach at triple the cheap rooms' price. All guests have the use of facilities that include two heated swimming pools, tennis and racquetball courts, jacuzzis and a steam room. The hotel offers a special "half-your-age" discount. If you're 30 years old, for instance, you get 15 percent off the regular room rate; if you're 50, you get 25 percent off. Availability of these discounted rooms is limited, and reservations must be made in advance to qualify for the discount. ~ Boulevard Benito Juárez 31, Rosarito; 661-612-0144, 661-612-1111, fax 661-612-1125, or 800-343-8582 in the U.S.; www.rosaritohtl.com. MODERATE TO ULTRA-DELUXE.

A peculiar blend of surprisingly affordable resort ambience and theme park–style contrivance, the **Hotel Calafia** proclaims itself a "historic and cultural center" because it is built around a cluster of white facades replicating the various colonial missions of Baja California. There's also an ecological park with tidepools and a conference center where talks on Baja history are sometimes presented. The 72 guest rooms and suites have ocean views, and the open-air dining terrace is perched above surf crashing on

AUTHOR FAVORITE

Topping my list of Ensenada-area hideaways is **Estero Beach Resort**, thanks to its peaceful out-of-town setting with abundant bird life and an occasional whale cruising past just offshore, plus affordable lodging and all kinds of sports-gear rentals. Sure, it's far enough away so you have to drive into town; but then again, if you stayed in town, you'd have to drive to get here. Estero Beach is better. See page 185 for more information.

the rocks. ~ Route 1 Km. 35.5, Rosarito; 661-612-1581, fax 661-612-0296; e-mail calafia1@telnor.net. MODERATE.

You'll find the best youth hostel in Baja California Norte six miles north of Ensenada. The **Hostel Sauzal** offers male, female ◀ *HIDDEN* and co-ed dormitory accommodations in four-bed rooms, each with a writing desk, and a wide porch with a hammock and an ocean view. There are hot showers, laundry facilities, a kitchen and barbecue, picnic facilities and a library of Baja books and maps—all for $15 per person per night. ~ 344 Avenida L, Sauzal; 646-174-6381; hostelsauzal.tripod.com. BUDGET.

Queen of Ensenada's casually elegant small resort hotels is **Las Rosas**, magnificently located on a bluff overlooking the beach at the north end of Bahía de Todos Santos. Downtown is a two-mile drive away. All of the two-story hotel's 31 spacious, pastel-hued rooms and suites have balconies with ocean and pool views, and many have jacuzzis and fireplaces. There is a two-night minimum stay. ~ Route 1, Km. 105; phone/fax 646-174-4595, or 619-654-7166 in the U.S. DELUXE.

Centrally located between the main shopping and restaurant street and the Centro Artesanal next to Tres Cabezas Plaza, the 12-story **Hotel Villa Marina** is within easy walking distance of everything downtown, and there's no problem finding your way back—it's the tallest highrise in town. The upper floors on the ocean side offer great views of the port and bay, though on weekend nights the din from the nightclub on the top floor can make guests wish they'd settled for a lower angle of view. Other rooms overlook Avenida López Mateos and the heart of the downtown tourist zone. The 130 cozy, cool and contemporary guest rooms are decorated in shades of blue, and most have narrow private balconies. ~ Avenida López Mateos at Avenida Blancarte; 646-178-3351. MODERATE.

The **Estero Beach Resort** fronts on a secluded stretch of sand at the south end of Bahía de Todos Santos, far from the pandemonium of downtown Ensenada. This beautifully landscaped complex has 106 light, modern guest rooms, ranging from small, bungalow-style units and spacious one- and two-bedroom units with balconies overlooking the ocean to large suites, equipped with kitchens, that can sleep four adults. There are no phones in the rooms. Outdoor sports are the best reason to pick this resort (the resort is the site of the world's biggest international beach volleyball tournament). There are tennis courts and a boat ramp, and you'll find saddle horses, fishing equipment, Wave Runners, kayaks, canoes and bicycles for rent. The resort sits at the edge of an estuary that attracts abundant pelicans, cormorants, egrets and hawks. It's quite a ways into town, but the resort has a restaurant and nightclub. ~ Route 1, Km. 10.5; 646-176-6225, fax 646-176-6925, or 800-762-2494 in the U.S.; www.hotelestero beach.com. MODERATE.

DINING   The place to go for elegant dining in Rosarito is **Chabert's Restaurant**. Located at the Rosarito Beach Hotel and Spa, in the mansion of the hotel's founder, the restaurant evinces nostalgia for the opulence of the 1920s. The French and Continental cuisine may be the best in the Baja. ~ Boulevard Benito Juárez, Rosarito; 661-612-0144. DELUXE.

For more casual fare, **Ortega's Place** in Rosarito offers $1.99 breakfasts and an all-you-can-eat soup-and-salad bar. The specialty in this upstairs restaurant is *langosto estilo Puerto Nuevo*—lobster sliced in half lengthwise, fried in a pot of boiling oil and served with butter, lime and salsa. The Ortega family also operates several lobster restaurants under the same name in Puerto Nuevo. ~ Boulevard Benito Juárez 200, Rosarito; 661-612-0222. BUDGET TO MODERATE.

El Patio in Rosarito's Festival Plaza Hotel serves gourmet "Aztec-style" Mexican food—the kind you won't find north of the border. The shopping-mall atmosphere of this place does little to distract from the savor of such delicacies as *crepas xochimilco* (crêpes stuffed with shrimp and smothered in *mole pepián*, a spicy sauce made from poblano chiles and crushed pumpkin seeds). Other intriguing entrées include *huachinango estilo guayabitos* (red snapper in a sweet coconut-mango sauce) and Chihuahua-style quail in tangy *rielera* sauce. ~ Boulevard Benito Juárez, Rosarito; 661-612-2950. MODERATE TO DELUXE.

Adventuresome souls who prefer to seek out the catch of the day in an authentically ramshackle fishing village with nary a T-shirt shop or curio hawker in sight will find it in **Popotla**. This little town just south of Rosarito seems determined to avoid the notoriety that has brought tourists to neighboring Puerto Nuevo in overwhelming numbers. In fact, the fishermen's wives who run the 30 or so nameless seafood stands along the waterfront often outnumber the gringo visitors. Stroll among them and take your pick of huge chocolate clams, conch, oysters, octopus cocktails, sea urchins, deep-fried barracuda, crabs, lobsters and whatever else the morning's fishing brought in—all lovingly prepared before your eyes. To get there, follow Rosarito's main street for four miles south of town, watch for a concrete archway near kilometer marker 33, turn right and drive under the arch. Continue down the rough, unpaved road for half a kilometer to the parking lot at the edge of the village. Visit early; having no electricity, Popotla is an early-to-bed, early-to-rise kind of town. ~ Route 1, Km. 33. BUDGET TO MODERATE.

As you approach Ensenada from the north, watch for **Enrique's Restaurant** on the ocean side of the highway. Long a local institution, this hole-in-the-wall place got its start as a roadside fried-shrimp stand. Over the decades, it has expanded into a romantic restaurant with a great view of the port. The menu has expanded, too, highlighting exotic Continental dishes like frog legs and glazed quail, but it's still the shrimp that justify the restaurant's reputation. ~ Route 1, Km. 101; 646-178-2461. MODERATE.

Ensenada's **Mercado de Mariscos**, at the north end of the waterfront near the tourist information office and sport-fishing docks, is surrounded by open-air stands selling fish tacos—sticks of fresh fish battered, deep-fried and wrapped in a corn tortilla. Condiments range from guacamole to sliced radishes. ~ North end of Boulevard Costero. BUDGET.

The downtown tourist zone is packed with overpriced Mexican restaurants with menus so unimaginative that you might as well be back home at a Taco Bell. Locals who work downtown join the tourist throngs in **El Charro**, which offers some of the

AUTHOR FAVORITE

There's nothing like seafood right off the boat. That's why I make a point of stopping at **Popotla**, a small fishing village south of Rosarito, where fishermen's wives grill fresh fish, lobsters and other *mariscos* at open-air stands along the beach. It's the "hidden" counterpart to the more famous lobster village of Puerto Nuevo nearby. See page 186 for more information.

best prices around on enchiladas, burritos and *chiles rellenos*. The specialty is *pollo asado*—whole chickens roasted on spits in the restaurant's front window. ~ Avenida López Mateos 475; 646-178-3881. BUDGET.

One of the longest-established restaurants in Ensenada, **El Cid** (located in the hotel of the same name) serves a full range of less familiar Mexican specialties, such as *pescado veracruzano* (fish in a tangy salsa) and *chiles Gertrudis* (a special kind of stuffed chile), as well as international gourmet dishes like quail in rosé sauce and the restaurant's award-winning "Oscaritos"— baby squid stuffed with clams. The atmosphere is shadowy, candlelit and Spanish. ~ Avenida López Mateos 993; 646-178-2401. MODERATE.

El Rey Sol has been serving authentic French cuisine in Ensenada since 1947, when the restaurant was opened by a Frenchman and his Mexican wife; they met while working as chefs in Paris. Under their family's management ever since, El Rey Sol maintains the highest standards in food and service. Stained glass and heavy, dark furniture set the mood. The menu is built around fish and seafood selections, including such exotica as filet of manta ray. Besides using freshly caught fish, the chef uses produce from the owners' farm in Santo Tomás. Bread and pastries are baked on the premises. ~ Avenida López Mateos 1000; 646-178-1733. DELUXE.

The exterior of **Bronco's Steak House** proclaims *"¡la nueva costumbre mexicana—de comer steaks!"* ("The new Mexican custom—of eating steaks!") In fact, many local Mexican families who would never set foot in a downtown tourist restaurant come to Bronco's to celebrate birthdays and other holidays. The interior is wood-paneled and decorated with ranch memorabilia, and the food contains a good selection of traditional Mexican dishes such as *carne asada* (beef strips marinated in red chile sauce and barbecued) as well as steaks cut thick and grilled over mesquite coals and south-of-the-border specialties like *boca del río*, a strip steak that is split and stuffed with chiles and spices. The all-you-can-eat luncheon buffet and Sunday brunch mix Mexican and gringo food. ~ Calle 1 at Avenida Guadalupe; 646-176-4900; e-mail broncos@telnar.net. MODERATE.

While Ensenada boasts more than its share of fine dining, most Mexican food in restaurants is Americanized for the gringo

Mexico's
Finest Wineries

The most enduring legacy of the Spanish missionaries who first colonized Baja is vineyards. Just as Alta California is regarded as having the United States' best wineries, so northern Baja has a well-deserved reputation for producing Mexico's finest wines.

Situated in the northern part of Ensenada, **Bodegas de Santo Tomás** makes wine from some of the oldest vines in California. The vineyards themselves are down in the Valle de Santo Tomás, 51 kilometers south of the city on Route 1, where Dominican brothers founded a mission in 1791. There they planted cuttings from grape vines that had originally been brought to the Baja peninsula by Jesuits more than a century earlier. Underground springs and coastal fog helped create an exceptionally good environment, and the vineyards flourished until 1840, when the Mexican government seized all agricultural land owned by the church, and the grapevines were abandoned. Spanish immigrants bought the the old vineyards and revived them in 1888, and Russian immigrants later brought new strains of grapes.

The winery was moved to Ensenada in 1937 to make shipping easier. Today, Bodegas de Santo Tomás produces fine Pinot Noir, Cabernet Sauvignon and Chardonnay varietal wines, which are exported to Europe as well as to the Mexican mainland but are not sold in the United States. Guided tours of the winery, including tastings, are offered several times daily. Admission. ~ Avenida Miramar at Calle 7; 646-178-2905, 646-178-3333; www.santotomas.com.mx, e-mail info@sdro.com.

Wine, whether red (*tinta*) or white (*blanco*), is properly called *vino de uva* (grape wine). The more generic *vino* is used to refer to all types of alcoholic beverages, and low-quality tequila is sometimes called *vino blanco*.

palate. To try authentic local food, stop at one of the roadside **tamal stands** that line Route 1 south of town on the way to the La Bufadora turnoff. Tamales—cakes of corn meal mush that are stuffed, wrapped in corn husks and steamed—come not only in the meat-stuffed variety familiar in the United States but also with an assortment of other fillings ranging from diced shrimp to pineapple. Some vendors may stare dumbfounded when you order, because of the widely held belief that gringos can't eat real Mexican food without getting sick. My experience with roadside stands in Ensenada and most other parts of Baja suggests that this fear is unfounded. ~ Route 1 south. BUDGET.

You can enjoy a spectacular view along with your dinner of fresh seafood, pasta or gourmet Mexican food at **Restaurante Costa Azul**, a four-story open-air restaurant overlooking the bay at La Bufadora. Local fishermen deliver their catch fresh daily, and the international team of cooks prepares it in styles that range from Puerto Nuevo to Cajun and Pacific Northwestern. ~ La Bufadora; 646-154-2540. MODERATE.

GROCERIES **Supermercado Gigante** carries most of the same food items you'd expect to find in a supermarket in the United States. ~ Avenida Gastelum 672; 646-178-2644. The waterfront **Mercado de Mariscos**—a genuine public fish market, not just another tourist trap—is the place to go for fresh-caught fish, shrimp, squid, octopus, clams and lobsters. ~ North end of Boulevard Costero. For natural foods, organic produce and herbal remedies, try **La Milpa**. ~ Calle 4 1329; 646-176-1005.

SHOPPING Ensenada is the best gift-shopping town north of Los Cabos, thanks to the large numbers of free-spending cruise ship passen-

THE SIGN OF SILVER

Many street vendors in the tourist zone offer jewelry that they insist is made of sterling silver. Mexican law requires manufacturers to stamp a number—".925" (the percentage of silver in sterling), ".950" or ".999" (pure silver)—into each piece of jewelry, along with a mark showing who made it. If the number and the mark aren't there or are illegible, chances are it's *alpaca*. Sometimes called German silver, alpaca is an alloy of copper, nickel and zinc and actually contains no silver.

gers who stroll the sidewalks of Avenida López Mateos. There's a wide selection of merchandise in all price ranges, and although you won't find Third World prices in Ensenada—or anywhere in Baja—there are bargains to be found in items such as leather goods, silver jewelry, Mexican designer fashions and ceramics. Bartering is inappropriate in stores here, although street vendors are willing to negotiate prices, as are merchants at La Bufadora's flea market and Mercado Los Globos.

Silver prices in retail shops are highly competitive and significantly lower than in U.S. jewelry stores. One reliable shop is **Los Castillo**, a family-owned jewelry chain that started in Ensenada in 1969 and has expanded to resort areas throughout Mexico. The Castillos represent many of the finest designers in Taxco, Mexico's premier silversmithing center, with jewelry in both .925 (sterling silver) and .950 purities. They also carry pewter and ceramic items and handcarved furniture. ~ Avenida López Mateos 815, 646-176-1187; second location at Avenida López Mateos 656.

The best feature of the **Santa Paula Bazar**, a crowded curio mini-mall in the heart of the tourist zone, is the stained glass and handblown glass of Armando Ozuna, who practices his craft daily in the front display window to the fascination of onlookers. ~ Avenida López Mateos 537.

There are bargains to be found in Mexican leather goods, including leather jackets, hats, huaraches, handbags, daypacks, belts, boots and even saddles. Many small shops in the cruise-ship shopping zone along Avenida López Mateos carry similar selections at similar prices. You'll find a wider choice of leather clothing and accessories at **Nuevo México Lindo Talabarteria**, a shop known for its handmade saddles. ~ Calle 1 688; 646-178-1381.

Look for authentic Paipai and Kumai Indian arts and crafts at **Taller de Artesanos Indigenes** in the Bodega de Santo Tomas shopping complex. ~ Avenida Miramar at Calle 6; 646-178-8780. Another good source for Indian arts from both Baja and the northern Mexico mainland is **Galería de Perez Meillon** in the Centro Artesanal. ~ Boulevard Costero 1094-39; 646-174-0394.

Many tourist zone shops specialize in contraband—especially Cuban cigars, firecrackers and switchblade knives. All are illegal in the U.S.; that's the only reason they're sold here. As a practical matter, the risk of being caught at the border with any of these items is low enough to put this kind of casual smuggling in the cheap-thrills category. Mexican vendors mock U.S. laws that let Americans buy all the firearms they want but outlaw cherry bombs.

HIDDEN ▶

Ensenada does have a swap meet–style flea market, **Mercado Los Globos**. On the east side of town in an area rarely frequented by tourists, the vast eight-block market operates every day but has the most vendors, as well as the biggest crowds, on Saturdays and Sundays. Browsers can spot occasional Mexican collectibles and curiosities scattered among the produce stalls and piles of cheap plastic housewares. ~ Calle 9 east of Avenida Reforma.

You'll find original paintings, sculptures and handcrafts by Baja artists at the **Galería Los Arcos**, located on the road to La Bufadora. ~ Ejido Esteban Cantú; 646-614-2066.

At La Bufadora, the street that leads to the geyser overlook is lined with curio shops for blocks. The merchandise is similar to that found in many stores downtown, with an emphasis on leather goods; asking prices start higher than downtown but are negotiable. This tourist shopping area has been dubbed the **flea market** by tour guides, and if you ask a taxi driver to take you to the flea market, this is where you'll wind up. ~ Carretera Punta Banda.

South of Ensenada, olive orchards cover thousands of acres. At **roadside stands** along Route 1, farmers' daughters sell olive oil and several varieties of olives in glass jars.

NIGHTLIFE   Rosarito's **Papas and Beer** (papas means "potatoes," or in this case, french fries) is not so much a nightclub as a huge nonstop beach party. With a big dancefloor, live music, food, drink and volleyball courts, all that's missing is Frankie Avalon and Annette Funicello . . . or maybe they're just lost in the crowd that packs this place on weekends. Papas and Beer claims the dubious distinction of being the largest bar in Baja. ~ Playa Rosarito, one block north of the Rosarito Beach Hotel; 661-612-2140.

If you plan to make the bar scene in Ensenada, the one place you must not miss is **Hussong's Cantina**, Baja's oldest saloon. It hasn't changed much inside or out, they say, since it opened in 1892, when it catered to Ensenada's then mostly-non-Mexican population of gold miners, gamblers and adventurers. Especially on weekends, loud and rowdy doesn't begin to describe this place—sort of like a historic landmark on perpetual spring break. ~ Avenida Ruiz 113; 646-178-3210.

There are a half a dozen or so other big discos downtown. Designed for crowd management during spring break, these places can seem cavernous on many nights. Check out **Bananas,** if only for the disco's spectacular lightshow. ~ Boulevard Costero 277; 646-178-2004.

For a less rowdy crowd and a panoramic view, visit **El Navigante,** the nightclub on the top floor of the Hotel Villa Marina, the tallest building in the city. There's live music Thursday through Saturday nights and disco during the week. Cover. ~ Avenida López Mateos at Avenida Ruiz; 646-178-3351.

Ensenada's only gay bar is the low-profile **Coyote Club.** Cover. ~ Avenida Costero 1000.

> People live in luxury condos along Playa Rosarito and commute to work in San Diego.

The Pacific Ocean beaches of Baja California Norte are most attractive in the summer and early fall, when they present a less crowded alternative to San Diego and L.A. beaches. The water is too cold for comfort in winter and spring, and it is often windy.

BEACHES & PARKS

PLAYA ROSARITO This is the closest great Mexican beach to the U.S. border, so it is full of funseekers on most weekends. If peace and quiet is what you want, Rosarito isn't the place to look for it. Surfers say the waves here are awesome. ~ Located 24 kilometers south of Tijuana on Route 1.

▲ **Chuy's Trailer Park** has 26 RV campsites on the beach with full hookups, hot showers and a restaurant; $25 per night. 661-612-1608.

PLAYA CANTAMAR Calmer than Rosarito, this pretty three-mile beach is separated from the highway by a broad field of sand dunes—a favorite weekend playground for noisy ATVers. There are resort hotels but no camping. ~ Located 47 kilometers south of Tijuana on Route 1.

PLAYA MAL PASO This wide, soft beach runs for almost three miles and is largely undeveloped. It is known for its grunion runs, which draw a small crowd of fishwatchers and curiosity seekers every full-moon and new moon night in spring and summer. Silvery, seven-inch adult fish lay their eggs in the beach sand, somehow timing it so that ten days later they will hatch during a peak high tide. When they do hatch, the surf boils with thousands of baby fish, as locals scurry around catching them in buckets. ~ You can reach this beach through the Mal Paso RV Park, 71 kilometers south of Tijuana on Route 1, or Outdoor Resorts of Baja, one kilometer farther south.

▲ Despite its name, the **Mal Paso RV Park** is rustic enough to suit tent campers better than RVers. Sites are undefined; beach camping is permitted. No hookups, though there are restrooms and cold showers. Sites cost just $4 per night. ~ Route 1 Km. 71, La Misión. In contrast, **Outdoor Resorts of Baja,** a kilometer down the highway on the same beach, has it all: hot showers, a laundry room, a sauna, a swimming pool, a hot tub, a game room, lighted tennis courts and even a miniature golf course. The 137 sites are on concrete pads and have full hookups, including cable TV. Sites cost $24 to $35 per night, with an extra charge for pets. Reservations are accepted. ~ Route 1 Km. 72; reservations: 1177 Broadway, Suite 2, Chula Vista, CA 91911; 619-942-2264, 800-356-2252.

BAHÍA DE TODOS SANTOS 🏃 🐎 🚤 🚣 🏊 �ⅽ 🚁 ⏚ All the way around the rim of the bay, beaches arc north and south from the Port of Ensenada. The northern reaches, around Las Rosas Resort, are the most attractive segment of the beach, and the southern part around Estero Beach Resort is also good. Closer to the port, the beach is less appealing, its waters clouded and discolored by oil films and muck stirred up from the bay's shallow bottom by ship propellers. Even in its urban sections, though, the beach makes for an interesting walk. ~ Route 1 from Punta San Miguel north of Ensenada to Ejido Chapultepec south of the city.

▲ Ensenada's most centrally located beach campground is **Campo Playa RV Park,** just over the bridge south of downtown on the east side of Boulevard Lázaro Cárdenas; you must walk across this bridge to reach the beach. There are 90 sites, all with concrete pads and hookups, and hot showers. Fees are $16 per night. ~ Boulevard Las Dunas at Calle Diamante; 646-176-2918. For about the same price you could camp at the **Estero Beach Resort,** toward the south end of the bay, and enjoy the resort's facilities, including snorkeling, horse, bicycle, sailboard and jet ski rentals and tennis courts. There are 60 sites, all with concrete

pads and hookups, and hot showers. Fees are $18 per night. ~
Route 1, Km. 10.5; 646-176-6225, fax 646-176-6925.

PLAYA PUNTA BANDA 🏃 🚴 🏊 ⛵ 🛶 🛥 ⛴ A long,
straight, sandy beach runs along the north side of Punta Banda,
the narrow peninsula that encloses the Bahía de Todos Santos.
Like the peninsula itself, the beach is largely undeveloped. Surf
fishing here is said to be the best in the area. ~ Turn west off
Route 1, 18 kilometers south of Ensenada.

▲ **La Jolla Beach Camp** is a modest resort for RVers and ten-
ters, with hot showers, a restaurant, a boat ramp and horse
rentals. Campsites are on the beach and undefined; $6 per night.
No hookups. ~ Carretera Punta Banda Km. 12.5. Several ejido
camping areas are located on the Punta Banda road between Km.
2 and Km. 8, offering primitive camping without such niceties as
hookups, flush toilets or water. The steep dirt-road descent from
the main road to the beach in this area makes these campgrounds
all but inaccessible to motor homes but pleasantly secluded for
tent and pickup campers. The fee is $1 per night.

Index

Air travel, 31
Amtrak, 32
Anza–Borrego Desert State Park, 153
Avenida Revolución (Tijuana), 163;
   dining, 168; lodging, 166; nightlife,
   173–74; shopping, 172–73

Bahia de Todos Santos, 194–95
Baily-King House, 143
Baja California. *See* Northern Baja
Balboa Park, 51–59; dining, 57–58;
   lodging, 56–57; map, 53; nightlife,
   58–59; shopping, 58; sights, 52–56;
   visitor information, 52
Ballooning, 20
Bazaar del Mundo, 72; dining, 75;
   shopping, 76
Beacon's Beach, 139
Bed and breakfasts. *See* Lodging
Belmont Park, 98
Bernardo Winery, 145
Biking, 28–29
Birch Aquarium at Scripps (UCSD),
   108–109
Bird Rock, 119
Black's Beach, 109, 117–18
Boating, 24–25; permits, 20
Bodegas de Santo Tomás (winery), 189
Bonita Cove, 103
Bonsall: lodging, 131
Border crossings, 162–63
Border Field State Park, 160–61
Botanical Building (Balboa Park), 52–53
Boulevard Agua Caliente (Tijuana), 166;
   groceries, 172; lodging, 167–68;
   nightlife, 176
Broadway Flying Horses Carousel, 88
Buena Vista Lagoon, 140
Bullfighting, 169
Bus travel, 31–32

Cabrillo National Monument, 91
Calendar of events, 9–12
Caliente Race Track, 166, 176
California Surf Museum, 125–26
California Tower, 54
California Wolf Center, 146
Camping, 19; permits, 20. *See also*
   Camping *in area and town entries*
Campo: sights, 145

Car rentals, 32
Car travel, 31
Caracol Museo de Ciencias, 180–81
Cardiff: dining, 133; lodging, 129
Cardiff State Beach, 137–38
Carlsbad: dining, 134; lodging, 128,
   129–30; shopping, 136; sights, 124–25
Carlsbad State Beach, 139
Carretera Escenica, 178–79
Casa de Balboa, 52
Casa de Bandini, 72; dining, 75
Casa de Estudillo, 72
Central San Diego, 34–78; map, 37. *See
   also* Balboa Park; Hillcrest & Uptown
   neighborhoods; Inland neighborhoods;
   San Diego downtown; San Diego Old
   Town area
Centro Cultural Tijuana, 166
Children, traveling with, 14–15
Children's Discovery Museum of North
   County, 124
Children's Pool Beach, 118
Chinese Benevolent Society, 41
Chula Vista: dining, 158; lodging, 156;
   nightlife, 160; shopping, 158; sights,
   155
Chula Vista Nature Center, 155
City Heights neighborhood, 67
Cleveland National Forest, 152
Clothing to pack, 13
Coast Boulevard Park, 119
Colinas Chapultepec (Ensenada), 178
Commerce Row, 41
Coronado, 79–86; beaches & parks, 86;
   dining, 83–84; lodging, 80, 82–83;
   map, 83; nightlife, 85–86; shopping,
   84–85; sights, 79–80; walking tours, 33
Coronado City Beach, 86
Coronado Museum of History and Art, 80
Coronado Shores Beach, 86
Crown Point Shores, 103
Crystal Pier, 98; lodging, 99
Cuyamaca Rancho State Park, 146–47

Dana Landing, 103
De Anza Cove, 103
Deer Park Winery and Auto Museum, 143
Del Mar: dining, 131–32; lodging,
   127–28; nightlife, 136; shopping, 135;
   sights, 122, 126

Del Mar Beach, 137
Del Mar Race Track and Fairgrounds, 126
Dining (overview), 14. *See also* Dining *in area and town entries; see also Dining Index*
Disabled travelers, 17
Diving, 22–23
Downtown San Diego. *See* San Diego downtown
Dudley's Bakery, 145

Eagle Mining Company mine tours, 146
East Shore, 103
East Village, 35–36; nightlife, 50, 51
El Carmel Point, 103–104
El Mirador (view point), 179
Ellen Browning Scripps Park, 118
Embarcadero (San Diego), 87
Embarcadero Marina Parks, 90–91
Encinitas: dining, 133–34; lodging, 129; nightlife, 136; sights, 123, 124; visitor information, 122
Ensenada area, 176–95; beaches & parks, 193–95; camping, 193, 194–95; dining, 186–88, 190; groceries, 190; lodging, 182, 184–86; map, 177; nightlife, 192–93; shopping, 190–92; sights, 178–82; visitor information, 180
Escondido area: dining, 149–50; lodging, 147; nightlife, 151–52; shopping, 151; sights, 142–45
Events, 9–12

Fairbanks Ranch, 122
Fallbrook: nightlife, 137; shopping, 136
Ferrara Winery, 142
Fiesta Island, 103
Fifth Avenue area, 40–41
Fishing, 20–22
Fletcher Cove, 137
Footbridges, 64
Foreign travelers, 17–19
Fort Rosecrans National Cemetery, 91
Fox Studios Baja, 179

Gaslamp Quarter (San Diego), 35, 40–41; dining, 43–45; lodging, 39–42; nightlife, 49; shopping, 48; walking tours, 33, 40–41
Gay-friendly travel, 16; nightlife, 50, 175, 193. *See also* Hillcrest & Uptown neighborhoods
Girard Avenue (La Jolla), 106; dining, 113, 114; nightlife, 117; shopping, 115–16
Glorietta Bay Inn, 80; lodging, 82
Golden Hill neighborhood, 66; dining, 68, nightlife, 70

Golf, 25–26
Guajome County Park, 126–27

Hall of Champions Sports Museum, 54–55
Hang gliding, 25
Harbor Island, 97
Heritage Park, 74
Heritage Walk Museum, 143–44
Hermosa Terrace Park, 119
Hiking, 29–31
Hillcrest & Uptown neighborhoods, 59–66; dining, 60–63; lodging, 60; map, 61; nightlife, 64–66; shopping, 63–64
Horseback riding, 27–28
Horton Plaza, 34–35; dining, 43; shopping, 48
Hostels, 39–41, 92, 94, 100, 166–67, 185
Hot-air ballooning, 20
Hotel del Coronado, 80; dining, 83–84; lodging, 82; nightlife, 85; shopping, 85
Hotels. *See* Lodging

Imperial Beach (town): lodging, 158
Imperial Beach, 155, 160
Inland neighborhoods, 66–71; dining, 68–69; lodging, 68; map, 67; nightlife, 70–71; shopping, 69–70; sights, 66–68
Inland San Diego, 141–53; camping, 152, 153; dining, 149–51; lodging, 147–49; maps, 123, 141; nightlife, 151–52; parks, 152–53; shopping, 151; sights, 142–47
International travelers, 17–19
Islas de Todos Santos, 182
Islas Los Coronados, 176

Japanese Friendship Garden, 54; dining, 57
Julian: dining, 150; lodging, 148; shopping, 151; sights, 142–43, 145–46; walking tour, 142–43
Julian Drug Store, 146
Julian Hotel, 145–46
Julian Pioneer Cemetery, 143
Julian Pioneer Museum, 143, 146
Julian Town Hall, 142
Junipero Serra Museum, 73

Kayaking, 22
Kellogg Park, 118
Kensington neighborhood, 68; dining, 69; nightlife, 71; shopping, 70

La Bufadora, 181–82; dining, 190; shopping, 192

La Jolla, 105–20; beaches & parks, 117–20; dining, 112–14; lodging, 110–12; map, 107; nightlife, 116–17; shopping, 115–16; sights, 106, 109
La Jolla Cove, 118
La Jolla Ecological Reserve, 118
La Jolla Shores Beach, 118
La Valencia Hotel, 106, 108; lodging, 110
Lake Morena, 145
Lake Morena Park, 153
LEGOLAND, 124
Lesbian travelers. See Gay-friendly travel
Lily Pond, 52
Lindbergh Field (San Diego International Airport), 31
Little Italy (San Diego), 38; dining, 47; lodging, 42, 43; shopping, 48; nightlife, 50
Lodging (overview), 13–14. See also Lodging in area and town entries; see also Lodging Index
Los Peñasquitos Canyon Preserve, 153–54

Magee House Museum, 124–25
Mandeville Special Collections Library (UCSD), 109
Marine Street Beach, 119
Mariner's Point, 103
Maritime Museum of San Diego, 87–88
Marston House, 55
Mexico, 161–95; border crossings, 162–63; map, 157; transportation, 164–65; visitor information, 163. See also Ensenada area; Tijuana
Midtown neighborhood, 38; dining, 47
Military reviews (San Diego), 88
Mingei International Museum, 54; North County Satellite, 144
Mission Bay Park, 103–104; shopping, 101
Mission Bay Park area, 97–104; beaches & parks, 103–104; camping, 104; dining, 100–101; lodging, 99–100; map, 81; nightlife, 102–103; shopping, 101–102; sights, 97–98
Mission Beach (town): dining, 100; lodging, 99; nightlife, 102; shopping, 102; sights, 98
Mission Beach Park, 104
Mission Hills: dining, 77; sights, 77
Mission San Antonio de Pala, 147
Mission San Diego de Alcalá, 73
Mission San Luis Rey, 126
Mission Santa Ysabel, 145
Missions, 73, 126, 145, 147
Moonlight State Beach, 138
Mount Laguna, 145

Mount Palomar, 147
Mount Soledad, 106
Mukilteo Lighthouse, 88
Museo de História, 181
Museo de las Californias, 166
Museo Ex-Aduana Maratima, 180
Museo Histórico Regional, 181
Museum of Contemporary Art, 36, 38
Museum of Contemporary Art San Diego (La Jolla/San Diego), 106
Museum of Making Music, 124
Museum of Photographic Arts, 52

Normal Heights neighborhood, 67; dining, 69; nightlife, 70, 71; shopping, 70
North County, 121–41; beaches & parks, 137–41; camping, 138, 139, 140–41; dining, 131–35; lodging, 127–31; maps, 123, 125; nightlife, 136–37; shopping, 135–36; sights, 122–27
North Park neighborhood, 67; dining, 68, 69; lodging, 68; map, 157; nightlife, 70–71; shopping, 70
Northern Baja, 161–95; border crossings, 162–63; map, 157; transportation, 164–65; visitor information, 163. See also Ensenada area; Tijuana

Ocean Beach (town): dining, 94–95; lodging, 92, 94; nightlife, 95–96; shopping, 95; sights, 91–92
Ocean Beach, 96
Oceanside: dining, 135; lodging, 130–31; nightlife, 136–37; sights, 125–27
Oceanside beaches, 139–40
Oceanside Museum of Art, 126
Old Globe Theatre, 55; nightlife, 58
Old Point Loma Lighthouse, 91
Old Town (San Diego). See San Diego Old Town area
Old Town San Diego State Historic Park, 71–72; walking tours, 71–72
Older travelers, 16–17
Olympic Training Center, 155
Orfila Vineyards and Winery, 144–45
Outdoor adventures, 19–31

Pacific Beach (town): dining, 100–101; lodging, 99–100; nightlife, 102–103; shopping, 102; sights, 98
Pacific Beach, 98
Pacific Beach Park, 104
Packing, 13
Pala: sights, 147
Palomar Mountain area: dining, 150; sights, 147
Palomar Mountain State Park, 152
Palomar Observatory, 147

Pauma Valley (town): dining, 151; lodging, 149

Peninsula Punta Banda, 182

Permits, 20

PETCO Park, 36

Pine Hills: lodging, 148–49; nightlife, 152

Playa Cantamar, 193

Playa Mal Paso, 193–94

Playa Punta Banda, 195

Playa Rosarito, 193

Playas de Tijuana, 176

Plaza Calafia (Mexicali bullring), 169

Plaza Cívica (Ensenada), 180

Plaza Monumental (Tijuana bullring), 169

Point Loma area, 91–97; beaches & parks, 96–97; dining, 94–95; lodging, 92, 94; map, 93; nightlife, 95–96; shopping, 95; sights, 91–92

Popotla: dining, 186–87

Port of Ensenada, 180

Price ranges used in book: dining, 14; lodging, 13–14

Prospect Street (La Jolla), 106, 108; dining, 113; lodging, 110; nightlife, 116; shopping, 115, 116

Public transit, 32–33

Quail Botanical Gardens, 122

Quivira Basin, 103

Ramona: lodging, 148

Rancho Bernardo: dining, 131; lodging, 129

Rancho Guajome Adobe, 126–27

Rancho Santa Fe: dining, 132, 133; lodging, 128; shopping, 136; sights, 122

Restaurants. See Dining

Reuben H. Fleet Science Center, 52

Riding stables, 27–28

Riviera Shores, 103

Rosarito area: dining, 186; lodging, 182, 184–85; nightlife, 192; sights, 179, 183

Royal Pie Bakery, 40

Sail Bay, 103

Sailing, 24–25

Salk Institute, 109

San Diego (overview), 1–33; areas, 6–8; dining, 14; events, 9–12; itinerary, suggested, 4–5; lodging, 13–14; map, 3; outdoor adventures, 19–31; transportation, 31–33; visitor information, 12–13; weather, 8–9. See also specific areas and towns

San Diego Aerospace Museum, 54

San Diego Aircraft Carrier Museum, 88

San Diego Bay Ferry, 80

San Diego central area, 34–78; map, 37. See also Balboa Park; Hillcrest & Uptown neighborhoods; Inland neighborhoods; San Diego downtown; San Diego Old Town area

San Diego Chinese Historical Museum, 35

San Diego Convention Center, 88–89

San Diego downtown, 34–51; dining, 43–47; lodging, 38–43; map, 39; nightlife, 48–51; shopping, 48; sights, 34–38; walking tour, 40–41

San Diego Harbor, 87–91; beaches & parks, 90–91; dining, 89; map, 87; nightlife, 90; shopping, 89–90; sights, 86–89

San Diego Harbor Excursion, 86–87

San Diego Historical Society, 52

San Diego International Airport, 31

San Diego Model Railroad Museum, 52

San Diego Mormon Temple, 109

San Diego Museum of Man, 54

San Diego Museum of Art, 53–54

San Diego Natural History Museum, 52

San Diego Old Town area, 71–78; dining, 75–76; lodging, 74–75; map, 73; nightlife, 78; shopping, 76, 78; sights, 71–73; walking tours, 33

San Diego Old Town Plaza, 72

San Diego Sheriff's Museum, 72

San Diego State Historic Park, 71–72; walking tours, 71–72

San Diego Union building, 72

San Diego waterfront, 79–104; map, 81. See also Coronado; Mission Bay Park area; Point Loma area; San Diego Harbor

San Diego Zoo, 55–56; dining, 57

San Diego Zoo's Wild Animal Park, 144

San Elijo State Beach, 138

San Onofre nuclear power plant, 127

San Onofre State Beach, 127, 140

San Pasqual Battlefield State Historic Park, 144

San Ysidro: shopping, 158; sights, 156

Santa Clara Point, 103–104

Santa Fe Depot, 38

Santa Ysabel: sights, 145

Sauzal: lodging, 185

Scripps Beach, 118

Scripps Institution of Oceanography (UCSD), 108–109

Sea kayaking, 22

Seaport Village, 88; dining, 89; nightlife, 90; shopping, 89–90

SeaWorld San Diego, 97–98

Seeley Stables, 72

Self-Realization Fellowship Retreat, 122, 124

Senior travelers, 16–17
Shelter Island, 96
Silver marks, 190
Silver Strand State Beach, 160
Ski Beach, 103
Skindiving, 22–23
Soak City Water Park, 155
Solana Beach (town): dining, 132; nightlife, 136; shopping, 135
South Bay, 154–61; beaches & parks, 160–61; camping, 160; dining, 158, lodging, 156, 158; map, 157; nightlife, 160; shopping, 158; sights, 155–56
South Bay & Northern Baja area, 154–95; map, 157. *See also* Ensenada area; South Bay; Tijuana
South Bird Rock, 119
South Carlsbad State Beach, 139
South Park neighborhood, 66; dining, 68–69, shopping, 69–70
South San Diego County. *See* South Bay
South Shores, 103
Spanish Landing Park, 97
Sportfishing, 20–22
Sports, 19–31
Spreckels Organ Pavilion, 54
Stables, 27–28
Stone Steps Beach, 139
Stuart Collection of Sculpture (outdoor sculpture; UCSD), 108
Sunset Cliffs Park, 96
Sunset Park, 86
Surfhenge, 155
Surfing, 23–24
Swami's Park, 138

Taxis, 33
Tennis, 26–27
Tijuana (Mexico), 161–76; beaches & parks, 176; dining, 168, 170–71; groceries, 171–72; lodging, 166–68; map, 167; nightlife, 173–76; parks, 176; shopping, 172–73; sights, 163, 166; transportation, 164–65; visitor information, 163

Tijuana River National Estuarine Research Reserve, 156
Timken Museum of Art, 53
Toreo de Tijuana (Tijuana bullring), 166, 168
Torrey Pines Glider Port, 109
Torrey Pines State Reserve and Beach, 109, 117
Tourmaline Surfing Park, 120
Tours, 33
Trails, 29–31
Train travel, 32

U.S. Navy base (San Diego), 88
U.S. Olympic Training Center, 155
University Art Gallery (UCSD), 108
University of California–San Diego (UCSD), 108–109; nightlife, 117
Utility Art Box Project, 59

Vacation Isle, 103
Valley Center (town): shopping, 151
Ventura Cove, 103
Villa Montezuma–Jesse Shepard House, 36
Visitor information, 12–13. *See also* Visitor information *in area and town entries*
Viva Tijuana (mall), 163

Walking tours, 33
Washington Mine, 146
Weather, 6, 8–9
Welk Resort, 143
Whale Watch Lookout Point, 91
Whale watching, 22
Wilderness permits, 20
William Heath Davis House, 40
William Heise Park, 153
Windansea Beach, 119
Windsurfing, 23–24
Wineries, 142, 143, 144–45, 189
Women travelers, 15

Zona Rio, 163, 166; nightlife, 174

Lodging Index

Andrea Villa Inn, 111

Balboa Park Inn, 60
Beach Haven Inn, 99–100
Bed and Breakfast Inn at La Jolla, 111
Best Western Bayside Inn, 43
Best Western Beach Terrace Inn, 130
Best Western Encinitas Inn and Suites, 129
Bristol Hotel, 42

Cabrillo Garden Inn, 38
Cardiff-by-the-Sea Lodge, 129
Carole's B&B Inn, 68
Casa-Granada, 57
Chula Vista Travel Inn, 156
Comfort Inn, 56
Coronado Inn, 83
Coronado Victorian House, 82
Crystal Pier Hotel, 99

Days Inn–Hotel Circle, 75
Del Mar Motel on the Beach, 127
Dmitri's Guesthouse, 56

El Cordova Hotel, 80
Empress Hotel, 110–11
Estancia La Jolla Hotel & Spa, 112
Estero Beach Resort, 184, 185–86

Glorietta Bay Inn, 82
Grand Hotel Tijuana, 167
Grande Colonial, 110

Handlery Hotel Resort, 75
Hawthorn Suites San Diego, 75
Heritage Park Inn, 74
Hillcrest Inn, 60
Hilton La Jolla Torrey Pines, 112
Horton Grand Hotel, 42
Hotel Caesar, 166
Hotel Calafia, 184–85
Hotel Churchill, 38–39
Hotel del Coronado, 82
Hotel Villa Marina, 185
Humphrey's Half Moon Inn, 92

Inn at Rancho Santa Fe, 128
Inn at Sunset Cliffs, 92

Julian Hotel Bed and Breakfast, 148
Julian Lodge, 148

Keating House, 56

La Costa Resort & Spa, 130
La Jolla Travelodge, 112
La Pensione, 43
La Valencia, 110
Las Rosas, 185
L'Auberge Del Mar Resort and Spa, 128
Lazy H Ranch, 149
Les Artistes, 127
Little Italy Inn, 42

Moonlight Beach Motel, 129

Ocean Palms Beach Resort, 128
Old Town Inn, 74
Orchard Hill Country Inn, 148

Palm Tree Lodge, 147
Park Manor Suites Hotel, 56–57
Pelican Cove Inn, 130
Pine Hills Lodge, 149

Ramona Valley Inn, 148
Rancho Bernardo Inn, 129
Real del Mar Marriott Residence Inn, 168
Red Lion Hanalei Hotel, 74–75
Rosarito Beach Hotel and Spa, 182, 184

San Diego Paradise Point Resort & Spa, 99
San Luis Rey Downs, 131
Sands of La Jolla, 110
Sea Lodge on La Jolla Shores Beach, 111–12
Seacoast Inn of Imperial Beach, 158
Shadow Mountain Ranch Bed and Breakfast, 148–49
Southern California Beach Club, 130–31
Super 8 Bayview, 41–42

Tamarack Beach Resort, 129–30
Town and Country Hotel, 75
Traveler Inn & Suites, 156

U.S. Grant Hotel, 42–43

Ventanas al Mar, 99

HOSTELS
Banana Bungalow, 100
Hostel Barnes, 166–67

Hostel Sauzal, 185
Hostelling International—San Diego
    Downtown, 40–41
Hostelling International—San Diego
    Point Loma, 92
OB International Hostel, 92, 94
USA Hostels San Diego, 39–40

Dining Index

A La Francaise, 77
Albert's Restaurant, 57
Anthony's Fish Grotto, 89
Asti Ristorante, 44

Bai Yook, 60
Bay Beach Cafe, 84
Berta's, 75–76
Big Kitchen, 68–69
Bread & Cie, 62
Broken Yolk Café, 100–101
Bronco's Steak House, 188
Bronx Pizza, 60–61
Buffalo Bill's, 150

Caesar's, 168
Cafe on Park, 61
Café Pacifica, 76
California Cuisine, 62–63
Casa de Bandini, 75
Casa de Pico, 75
Chabert's Restaurant, 186
The Chalkboard, 101
Charlie's by the Sea, 133
Château Orleans, 101
Chez Loma, 84
China Bistro, 149–50
Cien Años, 170, 171
City Delicatessen & Bakery, 62
Corvette Diner, 62
The Cottage, 114
Croce's Restaurants and Bars, 44
Crown-Coronet Room, 83–84

Daily News Café, 134
Dakota Grill & Spirits, 44
Delicias, 133

El Bizcocho, 131
El Charro, 187–88
El Cid, 188
El Indio, 76
El Nopal Restaurant, 149
El Patio, 186
El Rey, 151
El Rey Sol, 188
Enrique's Restaurant, 187

Fidel's, 132
Fifth and Hawthorn, 58

Fish Market, 132
Fresh, 114

Gaslamp Strip Club, 44–45
George's at the Cove, 112–13
Girard Gourmet, 114
Greek Islands Cafe, 89
Green Tomato Restaurant, 69
Gypsys, 170–71

Hamburger Mary's, 61–62
Harbor House Café, 135
Harry's Coffee Shop, 114
Hob Nob Hill, 47
The Huddle, 77
Humphrey's by the Bay, 94

Ida Bailey's Restaurant, 45
Il Fornaio, 131

Jimmy Carter's Mexican Cafe, 77
Jose's Court Room, 113
Julian Grill, 150
Julian Pie Company, 150
Just Fabulous Kensington, 69
Jyoti Bihanga, 69

Kansas City Barbeque, 89
Karl Strauss Brewing Company, 114
Krakatoa, 68

La Bella Pizza Garden, 158
La Especial, 168
La Fonda de Roberto, 171
La Vache, 63
Las Fajitas, 45
Laurel Restaurant & Bar, 58
Lazy H Ranch, 151
Legends California Bistro, 134
Liaison, 58
Lips, 62
Living Room, 113
Los Arcos, 168

Maison en Provence, 77
Manhattan, 113
Mercado de Mariscos, 187
Mercado Hidalgo, 168, 170
Miguel's Cocina Coronado, 84
Mille Fleurs, 132

Mission Cafe, 100
Mister Tiki Mai Tai Lounge, 45–46
Monsoon, 45

Neiman's, 134

O.B. People's Organic Foods Co-op, 94
Orbit Earth Cafe, 47
Ortega's Place, 186

Pacifica Del Mar, 131–32
Palomar Mountain General Store, 150
Panda Inn, 43
Parallel 33, 63
Pasta Expresso, 101
Peohe's, 84
Point Loma Seafoods, 94
Pokez Mexican Restaurant, 46–47
Popotla, 186–87
Portugalia, 94–95
Potato Shack Café, 133
Prado Restaurant, 57
Prince of Wales Room, 84

Ranchos Cocina, 69
Restaurante Argentino de Tony, 170
Restaurante Costa Azul, 190

Roberto's Taco Shop, 158
Robin's Nest, 135
Romano's Dodge House, 150

Sadaf, 46
Saffron Chicken, 76
Saffron Noodles, 76
Sakura Bana Sushi Bar, 133–34
San Diego Chicken Pie Shop, 68
Saska's Restaurant, 100
Scalini, 132
Sevilla, 46
Siamese Basil, 134
South Beach Bar & Grille, 94
Spice & Rice Thai Kitchen, 113
Star of the Sea, 89

Tea Pavilion, 57
TiaJuana Tillies, 168
Tin Fish, 46
Turf Supper Club, 68

Victor's, 170
Vincenzo Ristorante, 47

When In Rome, 133

Yummy Maki Yummy Box, 113

HIDDEN GUIDES

Adventure travel or a relaxing vacation?—"Hidden" guidebooks are the only travel books in the business to provide detailed information on both. Aimed at environmentally aware travelers, our motto is "Where Vacations Meet Adventures." These books combine details on unique hotels, restaurants and sightseeing with information on camping, sports and hiking for the outdoor enthusiast.

PARADISE FAMILY GUIDES

Ideal for families traveling with kids of any age—toddlers to teenagers—Paradise Family Guides offer a blend of travel information unlike any other guides to the Hawaiian islands. With vacation ideas and tropical adventures that are sure to satisfy both action-hungry youngsters and relaxation-seeking parents, these guides meet the specific needs of each and every family member.

Ulysses Press books are available at bookstores everywhere. If any of the following titles are unavailable at your local bookstore, ask the bookseller to order them.

You can also order books directly from Ulysses Press
P.O. Box 3440, Berkeley, CA 94703
800-377-2542 or 510-601-8301
fax: 510-601-8307
www.ulyssespress.com
e-mail: ulysses@ulyssespress.com

HIDDEN GUIDEBOOKS

____ Hidden Arizona, $16.95
____ Hidden Bahamas, $14.95
____ Hidden Baja, $14.95
____ Hidden Belize, $15.95
____ Hidden Big Island of Hawaii, $13.95
____ Hidden Boston & Cape Cod, $14.95
____ Hidden British Columbia, $18.95
____ Hidden Cancún & the Yucatán, $16.95
____ Hidden Carolinas, $17.95
____ Hidden Coast of California, $18.95
____ Hidden Colorado, $15.95
____ Hidden Disneyland, $13.95
____ Hidden Florida, $18.95
____ Hidden Florida Keys & Everglades, $13.95
____ Hidden Georgia, $16.95
____ Hidden Guatemala, $16.95
____ Hidden Hawaii, $18.95
____ Hidden Idaho, $14.95
____ Hidden Kauai, $13.95
____ Hidden Los Angeles, $14.95
____ Hidden Maui, $13.95

____ Hidden Miami, $14.95
____ Hidden Montana, $15.95
____ Hidden New England, $18.95
____ Hidden New Mexico, $15.95
____ Hidden New Orleans, $14.95
____ Hidden Oahu, $13.95
____ Hidden Oregon, $15.95
____ Hidden Pacific Northwest, $18.95
____ Hidden San Diego, $14.95
____ Hidden Salt Lake City, $14.95
____ Hidden San Francisco & Northern California, $18.95
____ Hidden Seattle, $13.95
____ Hidden Southern California, $18.95
____ Hidden Southwest, $19.95
____ Hidden Tahiti, $17.95
____ Hidden Tennessee, $16.95
____ Hidden Utah, $16.95
____ Hidden Walt Disney World, $13.95
____ Hidden Washington, $15.95
____ Hidden Wine Country, $13.95
____ Hidden Wyoming, $15.95

PARADISE FAMILY GUIDES

____ Paradise Family Guides: Kaua'i, $16.95
____ Paradise Family Guides: Maui, $16.95

____ Paradise Family Guides: Big Island of Hawai'i, $16.95

Mark the book(s) you're ordering and enter the total cost here 🠖 [_____]

California residents add 8.25% sales tax here 🠖 [_____]

Shipping, check box for your preferred method and enter cost here 🠖 [_____]

❏ BOOK RATE   FREE! FREE! FREE!

❏ PRIORITY MAIL/UPS GROUND   cost of postage

❏ UPS OVERNIGHT OR 2-DAY AIR   cost of postage   [_____]

Billing, enter total amount due here and check method of payment 🠖

❏ CHECK   ❏ MONEY ORDER

❏ VISA/MASTERCARD _____EXP. DATE_____

NAME _____PHONE_____

ADDRESS _____

CITY_____ STATE _____ ZIP_____

MONEY-BACK GUARANTEE ON DIRECT ORDERS PLACED THROUGH ULYSSES PRESS.

ABOUT THE AUTHORS

ELLEN CLARK, an award-winning writer and photographer, is author of *Hidden Picture-Perfect Escapes Santa Barbara* and co-author of *Hidden Los Angeles*. A native Californian based in Los Angeles, her work has appeared in numerous newspapers and magazines, including the *Los Angeles Times*, *American Way* and *Outside* magazine.

RAY RIEGERT is the author of eight travel books, including *Hidden Southern California*. His most popular work, *Hidden Hawaii*, won the coveted Lowell Thomas Travel Journalism Award for Best Guidebook as well a similar award from the Hawaii Visitors Bureau. In addition to his role as publisher of Ulysses Press, he has written for the *Chicago Tribune*, *Saturday Evening Post*, *San Francisco Chronicle* and *Travel & Leisure*. A member of the Society of American Travel Writers, he lives in the San Francisco Bay area with his wife, co-publisher Leslie Henriques, and their son Keith and daughter Alice.